Microprocessor Principles
Level IV

Units in this series

Microprocessor Principles

Level IV

Glyn Martin

and

Nick Heap

Open University

TECHNICIAN EDUCATION COUNCIL
in association with
HUTCHINSON
London Melbourne Sydney Auckland Johannesburg

Hutchinson & Co. (Publishers) Ltd

An imprint of the Hutchinson Publishing Group

17-21 Conway Street, London W1P 6JD

Hutchinson Publishing Group (Australia) Pty Ltd
PO Box 496, 16-22 Church Street,
Hawthorne, Melbourne, Victoria 3122

Hutchinson Group (NZ) Ltd
32-34 View Road, PO Box 40-086, Glenfield, Auckland 10

Hutchinson Group (SA) (Pty) Ltd
PO Box 337, Bergvlei 2012, South Africa

First published 1982
Reprinted 1984

Set in Times

Printed and bound in Great Britain by
Anchor Brendon Ltd, Tiptree, Essex

British Library Cataloguing in Publication Data
Microprocessor principles Level IV
   1. Microcomputers
   2. Microprocessors
   I. Technician Education Council
   621.3819'58   TK7888.3

ISBN 0 09 149821 0

Contents

Preface

This book is one of a series on microelectronics/microprocessors published by Hutchinson on behalf of the Technician Education Council. The books in the series are designed for use with units associated with Technician Education Council programmes.

In June 1978 the United Kingdom Prime Minister expressed anxiety about the effect to be expected from the introduction of microprocessors on the pattern of employment in specific industries. From this stemmed an initiative through the Department of Industry and the National Enterprise Board to encourage the use and development of microprocessor technology.

An important aspect of such a development programme was seen as being the education and training of personnel for both the research, development and manufacture of microelectronics material and equipment, and the application of these in other industries. In 1979 a project was established by the Technician Education Council for the development of technician education programme units (a unit is a specification of the objectives to be attained by a student) and associated learning packages, this project being funded by the Department of Industry and managed on their behalf by the National Computing Centre Ltd.

TEC established a committee involving industry, both as producers and users of microeletrconics, and educationists. In addition widespread consultations took place. Programme units were developed for technicians and technician engineers concerned with the design, manufacture and servicing aspects incorporating microelectronic devices. Five units were produced:

Microelectronic Systems	Level I
Microelectronic Systems	Level II
Microelectronic Systems	Level III
Microprocessor-based Systems	Level IV
Microprocessor-based Systems	Level V

Units were also produced for those technicians who required a general understanding of the range of applications of microelectronic devices and their potential:

Microprocessor Appreciation	Level III
Microprocessor Principles	Level IV

This phase was then followed by the development of the learning packages, involving three writing teams, the key people in these teams being:

Microelectronic Systems I, II, III	— P. Cooke
Microprocessor-based Systems IV	— A. Potton
Microprocessor-based Systems V	— M. J. Morse
Microprocessor Appreciation III	— G. Martin
Microprocessor Principles IV	— G. Martin

The project director during the unit specification stage was N. Bonnett, assisted by R. Bertie. Mr Bonnett continued as consultant during the writing stage. The project manager was W. Bolton, assisted by K. Snape.

Self-learning

As an aid to self-learning, questions are included in every chapter. These appear at the end of the chapters with references in the margin of the chapter text (for example, Q1.2), indicating the most appropriate position for self-learning use. Answers to each question are given at the back of the book.

The books in this series have therefore been developed for use in either the classroom teaching situation or for self-learning.

Introduction

This book is intended for students whose main line of study is not in electronics. It seeks to take students with some appreciation of microprocessors one step further towards a working familiarity with a technology that is making more and more impact on non-electronics-based technologies. Indeed, this book follows on from *Microprocessor Appreciation* (TEC U79/639) and is written to the TEC objectives specified in TEC Unit U79/640.

It is not the aim of this book to convert a non-electronics student into an electronics student, but to allow students to feel confident in the electronics technology to the benefit of their main line of work.

Our teaching aims in this book are to:

1   Extend the student's ability to develop and use software.
2   Develop a student's comprehension of microelectronics devices.
3   Enable a student to appraise transducers and controllers.
4   Introduce a student to maintenance requirements.

It is our firm belief that these aims are best met with a mix of theoretical and practical work. We have, therefore, included practical exercises where relevant. The exercises are based on the Intel 8080/8085 type of microprocessor, but they could be readily adapted to other types.

Additional practical details are also included for those students able to use the Open University *Hektor* kit.

Included in the appendices are examples of manufacturers' product information. Our intention is that this information should only serve as an example of the literature and product comparisons that are available. *It should not be used as a primary source for your design information.* Owing to the rapid advance of microelectronics, more up-to-date information will probably be available by the time you read this book.

However, all the devices mentioned in this book will be around for many years and although the fine details of their specifications may change, the principles of their operation will not.

Acknowledgements

Our thanks go to Christine Martindale who organised the efficient typing of the manuscript. GM also thanks especially Sue, whose support made this book and a tidy garden possible.

GLYN MARTIN and NICK HEAP

Chapter 1 The structure of a microprocessor

Objectives of this chapter *When you have completed studying this chapter you should be able to:*

1 Draw a block diagram of a microprocessor showing its internal structure.

2 Describe the function of the following components of the microprocessor:

(a) ALU

(b) Instruction decoder

(c) Clock

(d) General registers

(e) Program counter

(f) Control section

(g) Program status register

3 Recognise the major differences between the more popular types of microprocessor.

4 Explain the need for clock signals and supply voltages.

1.1 Introduction

The aim of this chapter is to describe the internal features common to virtually all microprocessors and to point out the differences between some of the more important types of microprocessor. Of course, the 'structure' of a microprocessor can be described at many levels from the atomic structure of the material from which it is made to the physical construction of the package placed around the device. I intend to describe the device in sufficient detail to be able to explain the operation of a microprocessor system in terms of the operations within the processor and so as to be able to explain microprocessor programming.

1.2 The elements of a microcomputer (revision)

The diagram shown in Figure 1.1 should be quite familiar to you in that it shows the basic elements of a microcomputer system. It shows that a microcomputer system consists of not only the microprocessor but also contains memory devices used to store the computer's program (ROM) and data (RAM). In addition, in any microcomputer system there will be a variety of peripheral devices that enable the microprocessor to be interfaced to transducers, switches, VDUs, etc.

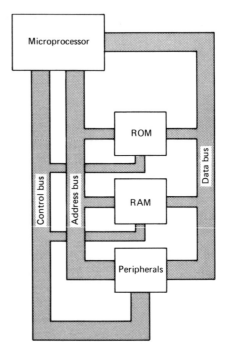

Figure 1.1   A microcomputer system

The various system elements are connected to the microprocessor via groups of wires called *buses*.

There are basically three buses used in a microprocessor system and these are:

1   *The data bus* – this bus is used to send data between the processor, memory, and the peripherals.
2   *The address bus* – this bus is used to transmit memory addresses to both the ROM and RAM memories so that the processor can have access to the program instructions and the data storage areas.
3   *The control bus* – this bus is used for control purposes such as informing the RAM whether data is being written to it or read from it. Also this bus contains wires which enable the use of interrupts.

The execution of a typical microprocessor instruction may well involve the use of all three of these buses. Firstly, the processor would obtain the instruction by placing its address on the address bus. This address, consisting of a binary pattern of voltages, is recognised by the corresponding memory location, which sends the required instruction to the processor via the data bus. If, for instance, this instruction required some data to be sent from the processor and stored in a memory location in RAM, the address bus would be used by the processor to indicate the required location, the data bus to send the data and the control bus to indicate that the processor is writing to the RAM.

All of this sequence is under the control of the microprocessor and to understand how it does this it is necessary to examine the structure of the processor in terms of its constituent parts.

1.3 The internal structure of microprocessor

Figure 1.2 shows a block diagram representing the typical internal structure of a microprocessor. This internal structure is often called the *architecture* of the microprocessor. It contains more detail than the register model introduced in *Microprocessor Appreciation: Level III* and reproduced in Figure 1.3, but many of the features of that model are retained here. Shown in the figure are the general-purpose registers used for temporary storage of data, the program counter, the stack pointer, the accumulator and the condition code register. The major addition to the new diagram is that the registers within the processor are shown to be connected by buses in much the same way as the components are connected outside the processor. The analogy can be taken further because the instruction and control block could

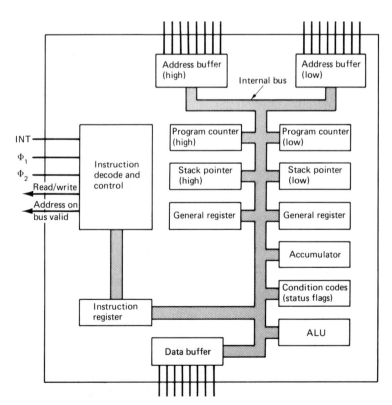

Figure 1.2 Typical internal structure of a microprocessor

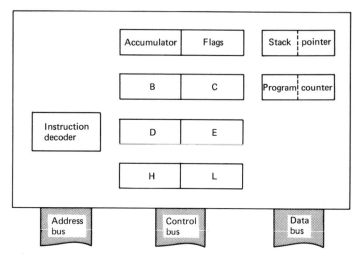

Figure 1.3 A simple register model for a microprocessor

be considered as a processor within the processor communicating to its memory (the registers) via these buses.

The instruction and control section therefore plays a very important function within the processor but before I describe its action in detail I want to revise the purpose of the various registers introduced previously, and describe the purpose of the new blocks in the figure.

The registers, which should be familiar, are:

1 *Program counter* – this is used by the processor to keep track of the memory location from which the next instruction or part instruction is to be fetched.
2 *Stack pointer* – this is used to keep track of the location of data sent to the stack area of memory during such operations as subroutine calls.
3 *Accumulator* – the purpose of this register is to store the results of arithmetical and logical operations performed by the processor.
4 *Condition code register* – this register shows the status of the register which may include amongst other things an indication that the result of an arithmetical operation was zero. This register is sometimes referred to as the status or flag register. Details of the status register of the Intel 8080/8085 processor are shown in Figure 1.4.

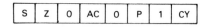

Figure 1.4 Status/flag register for an Intel 8080 processor

The new blocks in Figure 1.2 are the ALU, the address and data buffers, and the instruction register. The purpose of these is as follows.

Arithmetic logic unit

The ALU or *arithmetic logic unit* is the circuit which carries out the

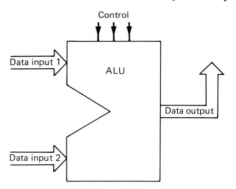

Figure 1.5 An arithmetic logic unit (ALU)

arithmetical and logcial operations within the processor. Typical operations would be the addition of two binary numbers or the ANDing of two binary numbers. The ALU is shown in block diagram form in Figure 1.5. It has two inputs for the two binary inputs and one output for the result plus control inputs which tell it which function to perform. It is important to remember therefore that the simple ALU block shown on the structure of Figure 1.2 is more complex than implied by the figure. However for our purposes Figure 1.2 is quite complex enough.

Where do the control signals to the ALU come from? They come, of course, from the instruction decoder and the control unit since it is the instruction that tells the processor what it is to do and the control unit's purpose is to implement the instruction.

The address and data buffers

These are circuits that have two functions. They amplify the electrical signals within the microprocessor so that they are capable of driving all of the various memories and peripheral devices connected to them. These buffers also capture data and addresses from the internal microprocessor buses and hold them steady until they have been accepted by the various devices on the external buses. Alternatively if the devices on the external buses are supplying the binary signals then these buffers may be necessary to capture and hold the information until such time as it can be passed to the internal microprocessor bus.

The instruction register

As you should already appreciate, an instruction describes the actions the processor must take. It is therefore important that the particular instruction being obeyed at any one time must be held within the microprocessor so that it can be interpreted. This is the function of the instruction register.

The instruction decode and control block

As you can see from the block diagram of Figure 1.2, this is the part of the processor that is concerned with the signals on the control bus. In addition, it is this block that controls the operations within the processor. It decodes the instruction that has been fetched from the program memory and manipulates data around the internal bus so that the instruction is obeyed. To do this it makes use of internal connections between it and the other blocks which are not shown on Figure 1.2 because they are so numerous that they would be confusing. It is with the aid of these connections that it can, for example, move the result of an addition in the ALU to the accumulator via the internal bus.

One of the most important functions of these control blocks is to automatically increment the program counter so as to keep track of the next instruction to be fetched.

A simple example will help to show the operation of this instruction and control block. Suppose this generalised microprocessor is to execute the instruction which places 40 (hex) in the accumulator. The instruction will be stored in the program memory area as shown in Figure 1.6. The first word stored in memory contains the binary pattern which represents the instruction 'store in the accumulator the following number'. The second word in the memory is the number.

In this example suppose that the program counter contains the address of the first memory location. The first action of the control block within the microprocessor is to move the address in the program counter to the address buffer via the internal data bus so that it may be applied to the address bus connected to the external memory. The control block may also send a signal on one of the control bus wires to indicate that a memory read is required. The memory location addressed places its contents on the data bus. In our examples these contents are the binary pattern corresponding to the instruction 'store in accumulator, etc.'. The control block within the processor expects this pattern to be an instruction, so it reads it from the data bus and moves it to the instruction register via the processor's internal bus. Once in the instruction register, the decoder circuit recognises that this is an instruction which causes data to be placed in the accumulator. Moreover, the instruction decoder recognises that the data to be stored in the accumulator is in the memory location after the instruction. The program counter has, whilst this has been happening, been incremented so it now has the address of the data. To complete the execution of the instruction, the control block again places the contents of the program counter on the address bus and indicates a read. The data in that memory location is then put on the data bus. The control block reads this data into the data buffers and then completes the instruction by arranging the

Memory address (hex)	Contents
1000	Binary pattern representing the instruction 'Store in accumulator, etc.
1001	40H
1002	Next instruction

Figure 1.6 A segment of program stored in memory

internal circuits of the processor so as to send 40 (hex) to the accumulator. Virtually simultaneously, the program counter is incremented by the control block so that the processor is ready to fetch the next binary pattern from memory, which it knows must be an instruction since it has finished handling data associated with the previous instruction. The next binary pattern read from memory will be sent to the instruction register so that it can be interpreted and the appropriate control sequence started.

In addition to generating the control signals to be sent from the processor, the control block is also responsible for handling incoming signals such as interrupts and the reset signal. This last signal is used to indicate that the processor should be reset to a known state and is most often used when the processor is first switched on so as to prevent the processor starting the program with unknown data in its registers.

See note in Preface about questions

There are two further signals which are input to the control block and these are two clock signals labelled Φ_1 and Φ_2. These signals serve to synchronise the series of operations listed above.

Q1.1, 1.2, 1.5

1.4 Microprocessor clock signals

These are binary waveforms which are derived from crystal-controlled oscillators so that they can be used for accurate timing within the processor. Typical clock waveforms are shown in Figure 1.7. The frequency of these waveforms is usually a few megahertz for many popular microprocessors but it can be as high as 10 MHz for a few specialised types of processor.

Early types of microprocessor required external circuitry to generate the clock waveforms but now it is quite common to find micro-processors complete with their own clock generating circuits in the same integrated circuit.

Inside the microprocessor these clock signals are used to synchronise all the various operations of the control block. By ensuring that all of the basic operations are instigated by rising or falling edges of the clock waveforms, the control circuitry can ensure that they occur at the correct time, and in the correct order.

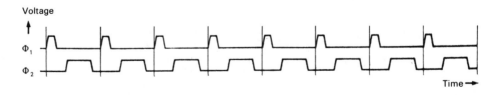

Figure 1.7 Microprocessor clock waveforms

Interfacing hardware to the processor requires careful attention to the timing intervals implied by these clock waveforms, but for the purpose of this book it is not necessary for you to have a detailed knowledge of the processes involved. It is sufficient that you understand the need for such controlling waveforms.

1.5   Three popular microprocessors

There are a great variety of types of microprocessor, but all of them conform to the basic structure outlined in the previous section. One processor which remains popular, despite its relative age, is the Intel 8080. Figure 1.8 shows the block diagram of this processor. You should be able to notice several similarities between this and the general diagram I have been describing up to now. For instance there is an instruction decoder, a control section, an ALU, some data and address buffers, general storage registers and an internal bus connecting them together. Other important features of this processor are that it has eight data bus wires and sixteen address wires. The basic register size within the processor stores eight bits so this

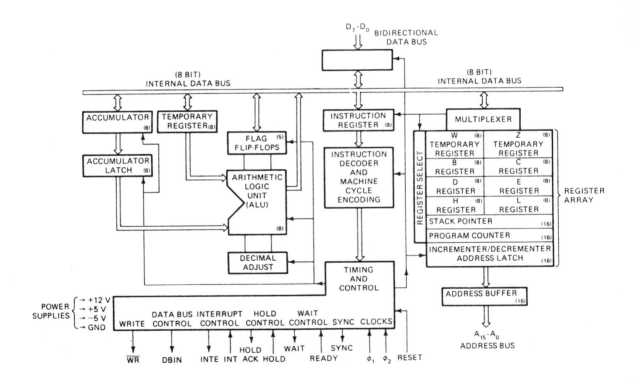

Figure 1.8   The architecture of an Intel 8080 microprocessor

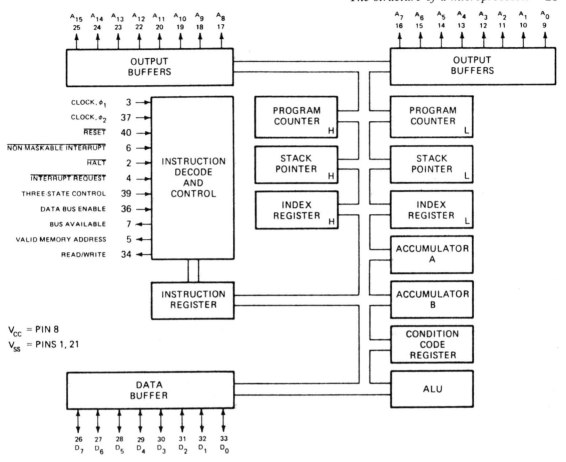

Figure 1.9 The architecture of a Motorola 6800 microprocessor

microprocessor is called an eight-bit processor. It requires two clock signals to be supplied to it from external circuitry and their frequency is around 2 MHz. From the figure you can see that it also requires power supply voltages of $+12$ V, $+5$ V, and -5 V to be connected to it.

Another popular microprocessor is the Motorola 6800 and its block diagram is shown in Figure 1.9. Again, the main features of this processor are similar to the ones I described earlier. Like the 8080 this processor is an eight-bit processor and has a clock frequency of around 2 MHz.

The Z80 microprocessor was first produced some years after the 8080 and 6800 processors and as a result it has a few more features as you can see from Figure 1.10. Its structure is very similar to the 8080 microprocessor but it has twice as many general registers and more special-purpose registers. In addition, its clock frequency may be as high as 4.5 MHz and it only requires a single $+5$ V supply. The effect of all these differences is that the Z80 is generally regarded to be a

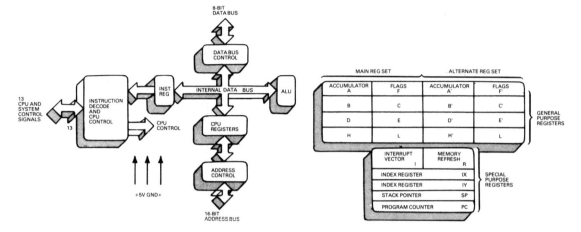

Figure 1.10   The architecture of a Zilog Z80 microprocessor

more powerful microprocessor than the 8080. However, the 8080 processor continues to be a very popular processor because many designers are familiar with it, it is cheap and many applications do not require the extra computing power of microprocessors such as the Z80.

1.6   Choosing a microprocessor

There are many factors which influence the choice of a particular type of microprocessor for a specific application. Amongst the factors involved are the word size used by the processor, i.e. 4,8,16 or more bits, the clock frequency, the architecture and the ease with which the processor can be interfaced to external devices.

The choice of microprocessor is made more difficult because as Appendix 1 shows there is an almost bewildering selection to choose from. The table in this appendix lists several important characteristics for each of the processors. This information would be sufficient for the designer to pick out, say, all of the 16-bit processors but more information would be required before a decision could be made. Instructions used by the microprocessors would have to be compared and manufacturer's data consulted. I have included some of this more detailed information for a few of the more popular microprocessors in Appendix 2.

Microprocessor or microcomputer?

As you should remember a microprocessor requires memory and interface circuits connected to it before it can be used. Such a system consisting of microprocessor, memory and interface device is commonly called a microcomputer. In the last few years, microprocessor manufacturers have started to make integrated circuits which contain, in addition to the microprocessor, RAM, ROM and interfacing circuits. Such integrated circuits are called micro-computers and as Appendix 3 shows there is a great variety of these as well. These microcomputers, or 'all-in-one processors' as they are sometimes called, have varying amounts of RAM and ROM and some of them such as the Texas Instruments TMS2100 have a built-in analogue-to-digital converter.

The choice between using a microprocessor with external memory and interfaces or one of these microcomputers often hinges on the difficulty of the task it has to perform and the likely number of microprocessor-based products to be produced.

In general, if the task to be performed is fairly straightforward and the final product is going to sell in thousands it is likely that a self-contained microcomputer will be used. If, on the other hand, the task to be performed is difficult, requires several analogue-to-digital converters or several other interface systems then the likelihood is that a microprocessor plus external memory and interface circuitry will be used. However, I must add a word of caution: the micro-processor manufacturers are continually introducing new integrated circuits with improved features so that tasks which may be beyond the capabilities of an 'all-in-one' microcomputer one year may be **Q1.3, 1.4** possible the next.

1.7 Summary

1   The internal structure of a microprocessor consists of several basic elements such as ALU, instruction decoder, program counter, status register, general-purpose registers and a control section. All of these various elements are linked together by an internal bus.

2   The control section has an important function in interpreting the instruction and controlling the execution of the instruction.

3   There is a great variety of microprocessors available. The major differences between them concern the number and size of the internal registers. Commonly microprocessors operate on 4, 8, 16 and 32-bit internal registers.

4   Microprocessor manufacturers are tending to include more and more of the elements of a microcomputer system on a single integrated circuit.

Questions

1.1   Draw a block diagram of the structure of a microprocessor.

1.2   Describe the functions of the program counter and the control section of a microprocessor.

1.3   Answer the following for the Zilog 8002 microprocessor and the Intel 8085 processor:

What is their word size?

What is their maximum clock frequency?

What is the number of basic instructions?

What is the number of internal general-purpose registers?

Do they require an external clock signal?

How many connections (pins) do they have?

1.4   What are the features of the Motorola 6805R2 microcomputer which are additional to those present in the Motorola 6800 microprocessor?

1.5   Describe the steps involved when a microprocessor executes an instruction to store the contents of the accumulator in memory location 1000 (hex).

Chapter 2 Programming a microprocessor – machine code and introduction

Objectives of this chapter   *When you have completed studying this chapter you should be able to:*
1. *Describe what is meant by the term 'program' and distinguish between different levels of program language.*
2. *Explain the various addressing modes which are used in microprocessor programs.*
3. *Explain the need for multiple byte instructions.*
4. *Use a microprocessor-based computer system to examine and alter the contents of memory locations.*

2.1   Introduction

The aim of this chapter is to describe what is meant by the term 'program' and how the action of the microcomputer is determined by the contents of the program stored within it. At the end of the chapter I will be suggesting some experimental work involving simple programs, but to begin with I need to explain the basic forms of instruction that are used to form microprocessor programs.

2.2   Microprocessor programs

You should remember from the microprocessor appreciation course that the microprocessor's operation is controlled by a sequence of instructions which form its program. When these instructions are stored in the memory of the microcomputer they are in a binary form with patterns of ones and zeros representing the various actions to be performed by the microprocessor. Superficially they resemble binary patterns representing numbers or characters. However, there is one important difference between instructions and data and this is that the instructions forming the program do not change during the operation of the program but data will. It is because of this property of instructions and data that they are often stored in different types of memory devices; programs being stored in Read Only Memories (ROMs) and data being stored in Read/Write Memories (RAMs). Within a microprocessor system certain addresses will be allocated to ROM-type memory and other addresses to RAM.

One important consideration when examining an existing microprocessor system or designing a new system for a specific application is the amount of ROM available to store the program and the amount of RAM available for the storage of the data generated during the operation of the program.

Because the program and data are stored in different parts of memory, the microprocessor can easily distinguish between binary patterns representing instructions and those representing data. Moreover, the execution of the program consists of the processor logically working step by step from one instruction to the next. The microprocessor keeps track of the address of the next instructions using the program counter register. This register is automatically incremented by the microprocessor so that it always contains the address of the next instruction or part instruction to be executed.

Program languages

The final program stored in memory is always in the form of binary patterns (as explained above), but the program can be written initially by the programmer in a great number of different forms using different programming languages. The languages used are at three levels:

1 *Machine level* Programming at this level involves the programmer in producing a program that consists of a series of binary patterns representing the instructions in the program. A segment of such a program is shown in Figure 2.1. Because this program is already in binary form it can be readily entered into the microprocessor's memory.

2 *Assembly level* Programming at this level involves the programmer in using a programming language closely linked to a particular type of microprocessor and which uses a symbol as shorthand for an instruction. A segment of assembly level program is shown in Figure 2.2. This program needs to be converted into binary form by a special program, called an assembler.

3 *High level* Programming at this level involves the programmer in using a programming language whose notation is very similar to normal mathematical notation. A segment of this type of program is shown in Figure 2.3. Again you should realise that this program language is used to express the program in terms that are relatively easy to understand, but it has to be converted into binary form by a special conversion program.

At the present time (1982) most programs for microprocessor-based systems are written in assembly level languages. This level provides a good compromise in that it is easier to write at assembly level than at machine level and it produces a final binary program that is more compact and faster operating than binary code produced from high-level languages. However, the trend in microprocessor programming is to use high-level languages more and more as the need for compac

Contents	Address
11001110	0
11111111	1
00000100	2
11111110	3
10000000	4
00100000	5
11001110	6
00000000	7
00101001	8

Figure 2.1 A segment of machine language program

```
MVI      A,01110110B
CMA
INR      A
MOV      E,A
```

Figure 2.2 A segment of assembler language program

```
K:=0
for I:=1 to 10 do K:=K+I
```

Figure 2.3 A segment of a high-level language program

and fast programs becomes less important and ease of programming becomes more important.

2.3 Microprocessor instructions

One of the comparisons that can be made between microprocessors is to compare the different sets of instructions available to the assembly level programmer. These instructions will include instructions which allow arithmetical operations such as the addition of two binary numbers, but the comparison which is most often made centres on the way in which the microprocessor can address memory. The various methods of addressing memory are sometimes called the *addressing modes* of the microprocessor.

Addressing modes

You should already be familiar with two memory addressing modes for the 8080 microprocessor. These use the mnemonics MOV and MVI.

What is the result of the following instructions?

```
MVI    B,81H
MOV    E,B
```

The first instruction places the number 81 (hex) into the B register and the second instruction copies the contents of the B register into the E register and leaves the B register unchanged.

The instructions MVI and MOV are examples of two of the five addressing modes available on the 8080 microprocessor.

The addressing modes of the Intel 8080 microprocessor

Immediate addressing   The instruction MVI B,81H is an example of immediate addressing. The data to be placed into the B register is specified in the instruction. In the example the data is 81 (hex). Other examples of instructions which use immediate addressing are LXI and CPI.

LXI is an instruction that is used to place 16 bits of data into two 8-bit registers taken as a pair. For example,

```
LXI    D,20FCH
```

loads the 16-bit number 20FC (hex) into the D and E registers.

CPI is an instruction that compares the contents of the accumulator with the immediate data specified in the instruction. For example,

```
CPI    10H
```

compares the contents of the accumulator with 10 (hex). If the contents are the same the zero flag in the status register is set to one.

Register addressing   The instruction MOV E,B is an example of register addressing. With this instruction the source and destination registers are specified as part of the instruction. The effect of the instruction is to copy the contents of register B into register E.

Register indirect addressing   You should remember from the microprocessor appreciation course that the MOV instruction may be used in a slightly different way. For example,

```
MOV    M,C
```

is an instruction that copies the contents of the C register to the memory location specified by the contents of the H,L register pair. This type of addressing is called *register indirect addressing*.

Direct addressing   In this type of addressing the instruction contains a 16-bit address as part of the instruction. For example,

```
JMP    2100H
```

is an instruction that causes the program to jump to another segment. This is achieved by the JMP instruction exchanging the current contents of the program counter register by the address following the JMP command. In the example this is the address 2100 (hex).

Implied addressing   Some instructions are so specific that their addressing mode is implied by their operation. For example,

```
XCHG
```

is a special instruction which exchanges the contents of the H,L registers with the contents of the D,E registers. No operand is required as the destination and the origin of the data is specified by the instruction.

In addition to the addressing modes mentioned above the Intel 8080 microprocessor has several instructions such as POP and PUSH which are used to address the stack area of memory.

The addressing modes of the Motorola 6800 microprocessor

In many ways the 6800 microprocessor addresses memory in a similar fashion to the Intel 8080 in that it uses 16 address lines, has integral registers within the processor that can be addressed and it uses some addressing modes which are the same as the 8080. However, it also has some addressing modes which the 8080 does not possess and does not use some of the addressing modes of the 8080.

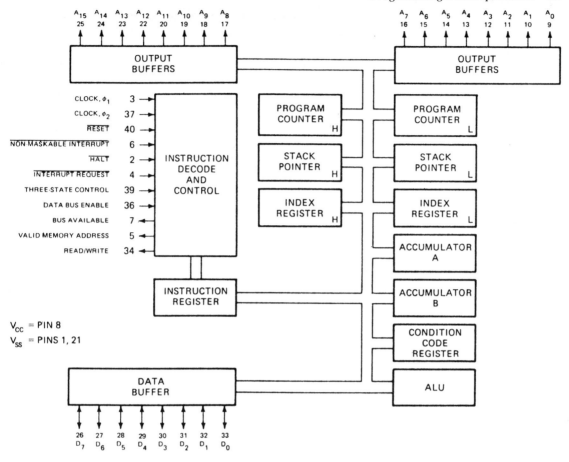

Figure 2.4 The architecture of a Motorola 6800 microprocessor

The addressing modes of a particular microprocessor depend to a large extent upon its architecture. It is thus worth re-examining the architecture of the 6800 as shown in Figure 2.4. It contains fewer internal registers than the 8080 and as a result there are fewer registers to register instructions than the 8080 but it has a special-purpose register called the *Index register*, which is not present in the 8080. This index register allows a form of addressing called *Indexed addressing* which is not available with the 8080.

The addressing modes available with the 6800 are:

Immediate addressing   This allows the loading of, for example, an accumulator with data specified as part of the instruction. For example,

        LDA   A#2

loads the A accumulator with the binary pattern representing the denary number.

Register addressing The 6800 does have a few register-to-register instructions which allow, for example, the movement of data between the two accumulators A and B. For example,

TAB

copies the contents of accumulator A to accumulator B. In the process the former contents of accumulator B are lost.

Direct addressing The 6800 allows addressing of the form used by the 8080 in which a 16-bit address forms part of the instruction. For example,

JMP   2100H

causes the program to jump to a program segment starting at 2100 hex.

In addition the 6800 also allows a shorter form of direct addressing for memory locations 0000 to 00FF (hex). If only two numbers are specified in the operand field the instruction is taken to refer to this range of memory locations. For example,

LDA   A,20H

loads the A accumulator with the contents of the memory location 0020 (hex).

Relative addressing A number of program branching instructions such as BLE (Branch if Less than or Equal to zero) only allow a jump in program control of 128 locations backward or 127 forward relative to the current program counter. This is less restrictive than it may appear because most program branches involve relatively small jumps.

Stack addressing The 6800, like the 8080, has several instructions which are designed to help with transferring data to and from the stack.

Indexed addressing This form of addressing uses the Index register. In the indexed addressing mode the address to which or from which data is to be moved is calculated by the microprocessor during the execution of the instruction. A typical instruction would look like this:

LDA   A 1,X

The X refers to the contents of the index register and the effect of the instruction is to calculate the address of the data to be loaded into the

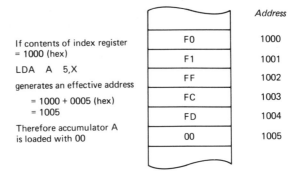

If contents of index register
= 1000 (hex)

LDA   A   5,X

generates an effective address

= 1000 + 0005 (hex)
= 1005

Therefore accumulator A
is loaded with 00

Figure 2.5   An example of index addressing

A accumulator by adding 1 to the contents of the index register then fetching the data from the resulting address and placing it in the A accumulator. Figure 2.5 shows an example of this type of instruction.

Indexed addressing of this type is extremely useful in accessing data which is arranged in the form of a table in successive memory locations.

Addressing modes of other microprocessors

Other more recent microprocessors such as the Zilog Z80 processor have additional addressing modes. The Z80 is a development from the 8080 microprocessor and it has all of the instructions that are available on the 8080 but as it has an index register it is also possible to use indexed addressing such as that used on the 6800 micro-processor. Other instructions on the Z80 allow a block of memory to be searched for a particular binary value. Remember that the 8080 requires the programmer to set the compare instruction inside a loop to perform a search through a block of memory. With the Z80 the block search can be performed with just one instruction.

Other more recent microprocessors such as the Motorola 68000 and the Zilog Z8000 are based on 16-bit word lengths and can address more than 64K memory locations as a result. The instructions that they make available to the programmer enable programs to be written which make use of this extra memory.

Arithmetic instructions

Other useful comparisons of microprocessor instructions centre around the arithmetical instructions available. In general, all of the early 8-bit microprocessors had instructions which enabled the addition and subtraction of binary numbers, but few of them had single instructions which allowed the multiplication or division of such numbers. With the newer and more powerful microprocessors,

Q2.1

such as the Motorola 68000, instructions are available which allow multiplication and division.

2.4   Memory requirements of various instructions

One of the factors that a programmer must consider is how much memory space will be required for a particular program. With experience, a programmer may well be able to guess from the application a likely figure but it is also possible to estimate the memory requirement by examining the program once it is written.

The point is that different instructions will require different numbers of memory locations. For example, the 8080 instruction to complement the accumulator CMA requires just one 8-bit memory location to store the instruction, whereas

```
MVI     B,81H
```

requires two memory locations, one for the instruction and one for the data as shown in Figure 2.6.

Some instructions such as

```
JMP     2100H
```

Q2.2

require three bytes of memory (as shown in Figure 2.7), one byte for the instruction and two for the 16-bit address that the processor has to jump to.

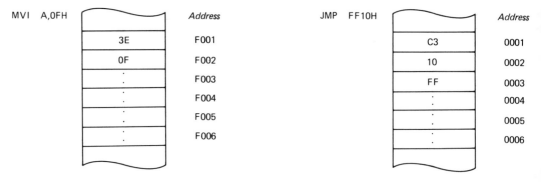

Figure 2.6   Storage of a 2-byte instruction   Figure 2.7   Storage of a 3-byte instruction

2.5   Instruction timings

In addition to specifying the number of memory locations required for instructions, the microprocessor manufacturer will also specify the time taken to execute the various instructions, this last information is particularly useful when calculating the time taken to execute a segment of program.

2.6 Experimental exercises

These suggested exercises are designed to show the effect of individual microprocessor instructions of the type referred to in this chapter. The required operations necessary on any particular microprocessor system so as to be able to perform these experiments will be different but all good systems should have the following features:

1 Commands that allow the contents of the microprocessor's registers to be examined before and after an instruction performed.
2 Commands that allow the CPU registers and RAM locations to be pre-loaded with data.
3 The ability to execute just one instruction at a time.

Exercises

1 Load 0F (hex) into the accumulator, execute an instruction to increment the accumulator (INR A for the 8080/8085) then examine the accumulator again.
2 Load 0F (hex) into the accumulator. Examine the accumulator and flag register, execute an instruction to rotate the contents of the accumulator right using the carry flag, RAR for the 8080. Then examine the new contents of the accumulator and the carry flag.
3 Load FF (hex) into the accumulator and the address of a free RAM location into the H,L register pair. Load 00 (hex) into this memory location then run an instruction

    MOV   M,A

Examine the new contents of the RAM location.
4 Examine the effect on the CPU registers of instructions of the type

    MVI   reg,data

5 Examine the contents of the program counter register before and after a jump instruction of the form

    JMP   address

Note: use an address that is in a free area of RAM.
6 Load the binary equivalent of denary 2 into the accumulator and the C register then execute an ADD instruction of the form

    ADD   C

Where is the result stored?
7 Clear (that is set to 0) the carry flag in the status register by loading 00 (hex). then load F0 hex into the accumulator and 1F (hex) into the C register. Execute an ADD instruction and

examine the result and the contents of the status register to
determine the value of the carry flag.

2.7 Notes for the Hektor microcomputer kit (see note in Introduction)

The Hektor User Manual gives details of the appropriate commands
required to perform these experiments but the following notes should
help.

1 The contents of the registers can be examined and changed using
   the monitor X ('examine') command.
2 The contents of a memory location can be examined and, if it is
   part of RAM, changed with the memory modify command M.
3 One instruction can be executed at a time using the monitor 1
   command.
4 The instruction to be executed must be first stored in memory in
   binary form using the M commands. This means that to perform
   these experiments you have to first look up the binary code for the
   instruction from the User Manual.
5 The procedure to run one instruction on Hektor can be summarised as: enter the code for the instruction into a free location
   or locations in RAM; load the starting address of the instruction
   into the program counter and then enter the 1 command. A
   convenient area of RAM begins at location 3100 (hex), so I
   suggest that you place your instruction there.
6 Another convenient free address for Experiment 3 is 3200 (hex).

2.8 Results of the experimental exercises

1 The accumulator contents should be 10 (hex).
2 The contents of the accumulator will depend on the previous
   contents of the carry flag. If this was 1, the accumulator will
   contain 10000111, if not it will contail 00000111. In either case the
   new value of the carry will be 1.
3 The contents of the memory location will have changed from
   00 (hex) to FF (hex).
4 The register will be loaded by the data specified in the instruction. This is an example of immediate addressing.
5 The contents of the program counter will have been changed to
   the address in the JMP instruction.
6 The ADD instruction adds the contents of the specified register
   to the contents of the accumulator and stores the result in the
   accumulator. After the ADD instruction the contents of the
   accumulator will be 04 (hex).
7 The experiment asks you to add the equivalent of the denary
   numbers 240 and 31 together. The result should be 271 but the
   contents of the accumulator are 0F (hex) which is equivalent to
   15. However the carry flag is now 1 indicating an overflow from

the addition so it is still possible to deduce the correct result by using the carry flag together with the accumulator contents:

carry   *accumulator*
1   00001111

The binary number 100001111 is equal to 271 denary (the carry is equivalent to $2^8 = 256$).

2.9 Summary

1 A microprocessor's operation is controlled by a sequence of instructions which form its program.
2 These instructions are stored as binary patterns in the memory of the microprocessor.
3 Programs can be written in machine level, assembly level or high-level languages.
4 Just as different microprocessors have different architecture so they also may have different instruction sets. General operations are the same for these instructions but the exact form of the instruction may well be different.
5 The way in which a microprocessor addresses memory is referred to as its addressing modes.
6 The amount of memory required by an instruction varies. A simple one such as CMA requires only one memory location, whereas JMP 2100H requires three memory locations.
7 Different instructions require different amounts of time to be executed.

Questions

2.1 List the main differences between the addressing modes of the 6800 and 8080 microprocessors.

2.2 How many locations do the following 8080 instructions require?

```
(a)   JMP   1FFFH
(b)   MOV   M,A
(c)   MVI   A,0FH
(d)   ADD   B
(e)   CMA
```

Chapter 3 Software development – assemblers and editors

Objectives of this chapter *When you have completed studying this chapter you should be able to:*

1   *Describe the uses of editor programs.*
2   *List and describe the usual facilities of an editor program.*
3   *Describe the purpose of an assembler program.*
4   *Explain the purpose of assembler directives and macros.*
5   *Perform practical work using editors and assemblers.*

3.1   Introduction

The aim of this chapter is to describe two of the most important programming aids available to the microprocessor programmer: the assembler and the editor. These aids are, in fact, special-purpose computer programs which can be run on both large and small computers.

An editor is a program that allows, amongst other things, the typing in of characters and numbers to be stored within the computer. These characters, etc., can represent anything such as inventory details or documents but the most important use as far as a microprocessor programmer is concerned is when the editor program is used to input a program written in, say, assembler language. This program when stored within the computer can be used as the source for the assembler program which as you should remember converts the mnemonics and symbols written by the programmer into binary instructions suitable for storing in the memory of a microprocessor.

3.2   Editors

Remember from the last chapter that you have to use very specific operations to input single instructions into a simple microprocessor, this was because there was only a very simple program interpreting your input from the keyboard. In general, editor programs allow easy and flexible entry of all sorts of text, usually from the keyboard. Editor programs also have facilities to allow the storage of the text once it has been entered into the computer. This storage may be in the main memory area of the computer or it could be in some form of backing store such as a tape or disk store. In either case the text can be stored with a code name which allows the text to be recalled from the store by a simple reference to this codeword. This codeword is called a *file name* and the text once it is stored in there is often referred to as a *text file*.

Therefore there are two main aspects of editors: facilities that allow easy input of the text and facilities that allow easy storage and retrieval of the text once it is stored in a file.

3.3 Inputting text using an editor program

There are many different types of editor but all of the good ones have the following features:

Corrections There are many forms in which errors may be corrected. The simplest is a provision which allows the last character typed to be erased and replaced by the correct character. Usually a special key on the keyboard such as 'DEL' or '←' is used for this. Pressing this key erases the previous character from the VDU display and the text stored in the computer. Alternatively there is often a command which allows the erasure of a complete line or section of text.

More sophisticated editors allow a whole set of errors to be corrected at once. For instance, suppose that you had completed typing in a program using assembler mnemonics but that you had mis-spelt the mnemonic JMP as JPM. The editor would allow you to instruct the computer to search the text file for each occurrence of JPM and replace each one by JMP. This last feature can be a big time-saver on large programs.

Combining or appending text files Often, as I shall be explaining in the next chapter, it is advantageous to write programs a small segment at a time, test them, and then combine them to form the final large program. There is usually a special command in an editor which enables small segments of text which have been stored under different file names to be combined or as it sometimes called *appended* together to form one large file which can then be given another file name.

Layout You should remember from the microprocessor appreciation book that it is important when, for example, programming in assembler, to obey certain programming rules such as leaving spaces between the opcode and the operand as shown below:

Label	*Opcode*	*Operand*	*Comment*
START:	MOV	A,B	;Move B register to
			;accumulator

Some editors will help the programmer by automatically skipping the required number of spaces once the opcode has been entered. Of course the programmer must, to obtain this facility, instruct the editor at the start as to the nature of the text being typed in. If an editor has this facility a great many of the silly errors that may occur in a program can be avoided.

3.4   Storing and naming text using an editor

As I explained earlier, an editor program allows text of different sorts to be stored in the memory area of a computer under a unique file name. Typically this name can be chosen by the programmer at the start. Various rules exist regarding the length of name allowed and whether the name should be preceded by a special symbol such as $. The important point is that, once stored, the text can be referred to by its file name. For example, if the text was a program written in assembler language it would be possible to allow an assembler to call a particular program by its file name and convert the program into binary code.

3.5   Line-based and cursor-based editors

Although all good editors have the features outlined above there are in practice two distinct types of editor commonly available: line-based editors and cursor-based editors. Each produces a distinctive type of display on the VDU although I must stress that their purpose is identical and the choice between them is to a large extent a matter of personal preference. Figure 3.1 shows an example of text being produced by both types of editor. With the line-based editor each line is given a number as it is typed and all commands relating to changes to be made to the text are made with reference to the line numbers. For instance, D1 could be the command to delete line number 1 and the text remaining after such a command if it were applied to the example of Figure 3.1 would be as shown in Figure 3.2.

Since the editor program needs a line reference for each of the corrections to be made, this can be given by typing in the line number or by telling the editor to jump a specified number of lines from the current line being edited. For instance, if the current line was line 28 and the programmer typed in 20L the current line would become 48. Then corrections could be made to line 48. Typing –20L would move the current editing position back to line 8. Similar commands are used to move the current position of the editor back and forward along a line.

Cursor-based editors have commands that allow a flashing mark referred to as the *cursor* to move over the VDU screen and text can be inserted or corrected at the position of the cursor. It is as if the VDU screen was a piece of paper and the cursor a pencil which could be moved anywhere to make insertions and corrections. A typical

(a)

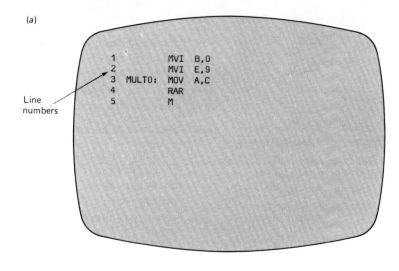

Line
numbers

(b)

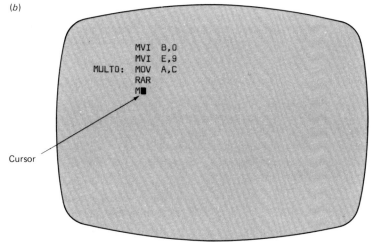

Cursor

Figure 3.1

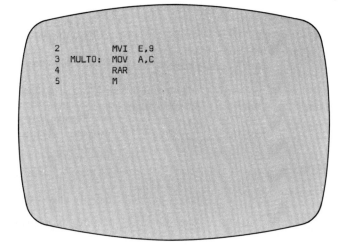

Figure 3.2

operation using one of these editors would involve the programmer typing in text which would be stored in the computer and displayed on the VDU. The text could be entered at any place on the screen by appropriate movements of the cursor and corrections made at this point which would alter the display and the stored text.

What would happen when the screen was full?

When the screen is full such an editor allows the display to be *scrolled*. What this means is that on receipt of a scrolling command the editor moves one line off the top of the display, shifts the rest of the text up one line leaving one line space for extra text at the bottom of the screen. This process is very similar to the method in which a scrolled manuscript is read hence the term 'scrolling'. The command to scroll can be produced by the operator typing a special key or it may be an automatic feature of the editor. The important point to make is that this scrolled text is not lost since it is stored within the computer and can be recalled to the screen for editing by using a command which shifts or scrolls down the display.

Q3.1, 3.2

3.6   Advantages of line- and cursor-based editors

Cursor-based editors are easier to learn to use and for this reason they are often used by microcomputers such as the Commodore PET which is a small microprocessor-based computer whose low cost attracts a large proportion of first-time users of computers.

Line-based editors are by comparison harder to learn to use but they allow much greater flexibility in use so that editing tasks such as combining or appending text files are more convenient. Moreover it is usually more convenient to skip back and forward in text by reference to line numbers than by movements of the cursor.

3.7   Example: entering a piece of microprocessor program into a computer using an editor

For this simple example I am going to enter the piece of assembler program shown in Figure 3.3(a) using a line-based editor with the following commands:

Keying I followed by RETURN begins the process of inserting text into the computer.

Pressing the RETURN key, which is present on most VDU terminals, ends the line and begins the next with a new number.

Keying Dn where n is a line number deletes that line from the store.

Keying Pn,m prints the text between lines n and m.

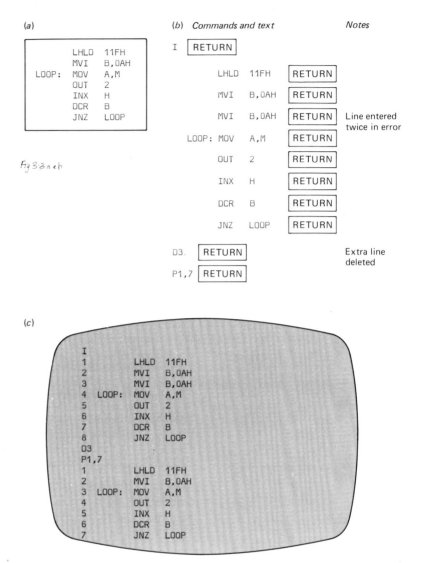

Figure 3.3 *(a)* Program; *(b)* sequence of editing commands; *(c)* printout on VDU

All the editing commands must be terminated by pressing the key marked RETURN.

A possible editing sequence is shown in Figure 3.3(b) and the resulting VDU display in Figure 3.3(c).

Once this program has been successfully entered into the computer the next step may well be to convert the program into binary instructions so that the program can be run on a microprocessor. This could be the same microprocessor that was used to edit the program or the binary code could be transferred to another microprocessor to be executed. In either case the program that converts from a program written in assembler language to binary code is called an assembler.

3.8 Assemblers

By now you should be familiar with the idea that the purpose of an assembler is to convert a source program written using mnemonics and which has been entered into the computer using an editor, into binary patterns representing the instructions in the program. If these patterns are then used to control the same computer as ran the assembler program then the assembler is said to be a *resident assembler*. However if the code is produced by an assembler running on a different type of computer from the one it is finally destined for then the assembler is said to be a *cross-assembler*.

The advantage of producing the code on a large or special-purpose computer and transferring it to the final machine is that the assembler on the larger machine will probably have more facilities designed to make programming easier than the assembler available on a smaller machine. One of these features which is strictly not concerned with the assembler is that the large machine may have a very good and easy-to-use editor.

3.9 Facilities offered by a good assembler

Figure 3.4 shows a segment of program written in assembly language for the Intel 8080 processor and it illustrates probably the most

```
        MVI   B,0     ;Initialise most significant byte of result
        MVI   E,9     ;Bit counter
MULT0:  MOV   A,C     ;Rotate least significant bit of multiplier
        RAR           ;to carry and shift low-order byte of
        MOV   C,A     ;result
        DCR   E
        JZ    DONE    ;Exit if complete
        MOV   A,B
        JNC   MULT1
        ADD   D       ;Add multiplicand to high-order byte of
                      ;result if bit was a one
MULT1:  RAR           ;Carry = 0 here. Shift high-order byte of
                      ;result
        MOV   B,A
        JMP   MULT0
DONE:
```

Figure 3.4

Table 3.1 *Summary of directives*

Format			Function
Label	Opcode	Operand(s)	Comment
Optional label	DB	exp(s) or string(s)	Define 8-bit data byte(s). Expressions must evaluate to one byte
Optional label	DS	expression	Reserve data storage area of specified length.
Optional label	DW	exp(s) or string(s)	Define 16-bit data word(s). Strings limited to 1–2 characters
Optional label	ELSE	null	Conditional assembly. Code between ELSE and ENDIF directives is assembled if expression in IF clause is FALSE. (See IF)
Optional label	END	expression	Terminate assembler pass. Must be last statement of program. Program execution starts at 'exp,' if present; otherwise, at location 0
Optional label	ENDIF	null	Terminate conditional assembly block
Name	EQU	expression	Define symbol 'name' with value 'exp.' Symbol is not redefinable
Optional label	IF	expression	Assemble code between IF and following ELSE or ENDIF directive if 'exp' is true
Optional label	ORG	expression	Set location counter to 'expression'
Name	SET	expression	Define symbol 'name' with value 'expression' Symbol can be redefined

important feature of a good assembler. Notice that symbols have been used to mark the destination of jump instructions. This is not allowed on all assemblers but a good one will automatically recognise such symbols as labels and produce code which produces the required jump.

Another facility that you have met before is the one which enables the programmer to specify data in binary, octal, hexadecimal or denary form.

Most of the other facilities offered by an assembler are controlled by the use of special commands called *assembler directives*. These directives are used to form part of the program that is interpreted by the assembler. Table 3.1 lists some of the directives available on a typical assembler.

The directive EQU could appear at the start of an assembly language as shown in Figure 3.5. Its purpose is to assign a binary value to a symbolic name. In the example shown the name ZERO is made equal to binary zero. Later instructions which require binary zero, for example, to be loaded into the accumulator can as you can see from the example just refer to the symbol ZERO instead of, say, writing 00H. You may not think this is a great advantage but with large

Label	Opcode	Operand	Comment
START	EQU	07DDH	
LOOP	EQU	030AH	
SUBR	EQU	273AH	
ZERO	EQU	00H	

Figure 3.5

programs such a facility clarifies the program and improves its readability.

The DB and DW directives enable data which is to be used by a program to be specified as part of the program. For instance, this data might be a message which the microprocessor has to output to a VDU during the course of its operation. The DB directive handles 8-bit bytes and the DW directive handles 16-bit values. In either case they store fixed data in fixed locations in the memory. Moreover, for ease of programming these locations can be referenced by a symbolic label as the following example (for the 8080) shows:

Label	*Opcode*	*Operand*	*Comment*
EMES:	DB	'Switch off'	;Emergency switch
			;off message

The effect of this assembler directive is to store the binary codes representing the letters in the message SWITCH OFF in successive memory locations and to give the label EMES the value of the address of the first location. (*Note:* the inverted commas" are used to denote a binary pattern representing letters.)

If as a result of some test made by the program this message is required, the following instructions will load the S stored in the first of the memory locations in the accumulator prior to an OUT instruction which is used to send the first letter to the VDU:

```
LHLD  EMES  ;Load H,L registers with start
            ;of message
MOV   A,M   ;Load 'S' into accumulator
```

To load the rest of the message in turn all that is required is to increment the contents of the H,L registers by one each time.

Once again not only has the DB directive performed a valuable function but the facility to label the start of the block of data has improved the readibility of the program.

Other assembler directives allow conditional assembly. These directives can be inserted into the program so that one segment of program is assembled if one condition is met and another segment of program if the condition is not met. This facility is most useful when the program may be run on different configurations of the basic microprocessor. For example, the microprocessor may have different amounts of memory or different peripherals.

The last assembler directive that I am going to describe is so important that it warrants a complete section to itself.

3.10 Macros

A *macro* is a facility that enables the programmer to avoid having to rewrite the same group of instructions several times in the one program. For example, suppose you wanted to write a set of instructions which output a message which has been stored in memory (with the DB directive perhaps). Then later on you wanted to output a different message. The instructions would be the same except for the starting address of the message and the numbers of characters in the message. The macro facility allows you to get the assembler to generate the appropriate instructions given a master or macro set and the new information.

Macros are usually defined at the start of the program. In addition to the instructions it contains, the macro must be named and any dummy parameters such as the starting address of a message mentioned above must be listed. The example shown in Figure 3.6 is of a macro written in 8080 assembler. The purpose of the macro is to output a block of data from memory to an output device. The macro is kept general by allowing the start of the data, the length of the data

```
OPMAC   MACRO   L1,L2,L3   ;Directive indicating start of
                           ;macro definition
        LHLD    L1         ;Load H,L registers with the start
                           ;address of data
        MVI     B,L2       ;Load B register with no. data words
LOOP:   MOV     A,M        ;Fetch first piece of data from
                           ;memory and store in accumulator
        OUT     L3         ;Output to device L3
        INX     H          ;Add 1 to H,L to form address of
                           ;next data
        DCR     B          ;Decrement B register
        JNZ     LOOP       ;If B ≠ 0 more data for OP
        ENDM               ;Signals end of macro definition
```

Figure 3.6

and the output device number to be specified each time the macro is called as part of the assembly program.

In this example a macro is defined which is named OPMAC and has three dummy parameters: L1 the starting address of the data, L2 the number of bytes of data and L3 the number of the output device to which the data is to be sent. The segment of code uses the H,L register pair to store the address of the data to be fetched, the B register to keep track of the amount of data remaining in the memory and the JNZ instruction to test the B register to see if all the data has been output.

Such a set of instructions could be used for several data transfers; all that is required each time is the starting address of the data, the amount of data and the number of the output device. These numbers are provided each time the macro is called during the program proper. The following line of assembly language program illustrates such a call:

```
Opcode        Operand
OPMAC         11FFH,0AH,02H
```

The effect of such a call is for the assembler to insert the segment of program defined in the macro definition with the dummy parameters replaced by the actual numbers in the call. L1, the first dummy parameter, is given the value of the first number in the macro call, 11FF (hex). Similarly, L2 is made equal to 0A (hex) (10 in denary) and L3 is made equal to 02H.

The substitution produced by the assembler results in the following program segment being inserted into the main program:

```
        LHLD   11FH
        MVI    B,0AH
LOOP:   MOV    A,M
        OUT    2
        INX    H
        DCR    B
        JNZ    LOOP
```

Labels within macros

One potential problem with the macro shown in the previous section is that if the macro were called more than once in a program, which is after all the purpose of the macro directive, then the label LOOP: would appear each time the macro is replaced by the code it represents. Clearly the assembler will detect this as an error since a jump instruction using this label as an address would have more than one destination address. To overcome this problem another assembler directive may be used at the beginning of the macro definition.

This directive is the LOCAL directive and it is used as shown in the following example:

```
OPMAC   MACRO   L1,L2,L3     ;Macro definition
        LOCAL   LOOP
          .
          .
          .
```

The assembler interprets the local directive as meaning that the labels defined within the macro are local to that macro and each time the macro is called the assembler inserts a unique label; for example, for the 8080 assembler the effect of the directive

```
LOCAL   LOOP
```

is for the assembler to assign the symbol ??0001 in place of LOOP the first time the macro is expanded, ??0002 the second time it is expanded and so on. In this way no instruction is given the same label.

Summary of the uses of assembler directives

Assembler directives are made available in good assemblers so as to make programs written in assembler language easier to write and as a result less prone to errors. Macros allow a shorthand way of writing blocks of code which appear several times in a program and assembler directives such as EQU and DB for the 8080 allow the use of symbols for numbers and the storage of data in memory.

There are additional directives that I have not mentioned which again help the programmer. These include directives allowing programs

Q3.3, 3.4   that can be easily amalgamated into larger programs to be written.

3.11   The output from an assembler

One of the outputs from an assembler is, of course, the binary patterns representing instructions. These can be stored directly in the memory area of the microprocessor they are intended to control in several ways. For example, if the program is to be run on the same computer that the assembler program was run on, then the easiest thing to do is to instruct the assembler program to load the results of its operation in the appropriate area of RAM. The disadvantage of this is that the program would be lost if the power to the computer were switched off. Alternatively, if the microprocessor the assembler output was destined for is different to the one the assembler was run on, then it is possible to send the binary patterns as electrical voltage over an electrical circuit to the other microprocessor, where the program is loaded into the appropriate area of RAM. Again the program is lost if the power is switched off. However, the advantage of loading programs into RAM is that the program may be run and tested, corrected, reassembled and reloaded into the same memory area for retest.

Once the program is finally tested the usual procedure is to store it in ROM. There are two main ways of doing this:

1   The assembler program can be instructed to produce a listing of all the binary patterns either on magnetic tape or disk or on paper tape. This is then sent to the ROM manufacturer and at the fabrication stage the binary patterns representing the instructions are stored in the appropriate memory locations.
2   A PROM programmer can be used to program those types of ROM which are designed to be electrically programmable. The input to the PROM programmer could be either electrical signals via a wire from the computer producing the binary output or signals read from tape or disk of the type sent to semiconductor manufacturers.

Method 1 is usually preferred if a large number of ROMs are to be produced for a large-volume microprocessor product such as a microprocessor-controlled toy. Method 2 is preferred when the number of final products is relatively small.

In either case the program once stored in ROM is permanent and unaffected by the removal of power supplies.

In addition to producing the binary instructions required all assemblers produce a listing on a printer or VDU such as that shown in Figure 3.7. This contains both the original program listing and the binary codes produced from it along with the addresses of the memory locations in which they are stored.

The listing consists of the original source program and in the two left-hand columns details of the binary code produced. The extreme left-hand column contains the address in which the *first byte* of the instruction on that line is stored. The second gives the complete binary pattern for that instruction (in hex). This binary pattern can consist of one, two or three bytes depending on the type of instruction. As a result the memory address for the start of the subsequent instruction may be one, two or three locations further on.

The printer listing is extremely useful as a record of the original program. This acts as a reference document during any later testing or modification of the program.

```
ISIS-II 8080/8085 MACRO ASSEMBLER, V2.0        MODULE  PAGE   2


  LOC   OBJ         SEQ           SOURCE STATEMENT

                    53 ;
  31D0  F3          54 CRW:       DI
  31D1  E5          55            PUSH      H         ;SAVE PTRS
  31D2  D5          56            PUSH      D
  31D3  21DD07      57            LXI       H,CSMES   ;'SET RECORD'
  31D6  CD0A03      58            CALL      PRMES
  31D9  CD1227      59            CALL      CVINV     ;AWAIT KEY
  31DC  CD9B04      60            CALL      CRON      ;MACHINE ON
  31DF  217332      61            LXI       H,CRWT    ;INT. VECTOR
  31E2  221027      62            SHLD      TRAPV+1        .
  31E5  2A3B27      63            LHLD      CRWDEL
  31E8  2204A4      64            SHLD      TIMLO     ;SET TIMER
  31EB  AF          65            XRA       A
  31EC  323A27      66            STA       CFLAG     ;TO WRITE 0'S
  31EF  37          67            STC
  31F0  CD8F32      68            CALL      TIMON     ;START TIMER
  31F3  3A3927      69            LDA       CRDEL     ;WRITE 0'S
  31F6  CD3A07      70            CALL      DELAY2    ;FOR 10S
  31F9  0E5F        71            MVI       C,05FH    ;SYNC CHAR
  31FB  CD4232      72            CALL      CRWB
  31FE  AF          73            XRA       A         ;ZERO CHECKSUM
  31FF  323F27      74            STA       CHK
  3202  2A4727      75            LHLD      ARG1      ;WRITE SA
  3205  CD3D32      76            CALL      CRWW
  3208  2A4927      77            LHLD      ARG2      ;WRITE EA
  320B  CD3D32      78            CALL      CRWW
  320E  2A2627      79            LHLD      UPC       ;WRITE ENTRY
  3211  CD3D32      80            CALL      CRWW
                    81 ;
  3214  D1          82            POP       D         ;BLOCK PTRS
  3215  E1          83            POP       H
  3216  4E          84 CRW1:      MOV       C,M
  3217  CD4232      85            CALL      CRWB      ;WRITE BYTE
  321A  20          86            RIM
  321B  E620        87            ANI       020H      ;BREAK?
  321D  C22E32      88            JNZ       CRW2      ;(YES, ABORT)
  3220  CD1A02      89            CALL      DCMP      ;LAST?
  3223  23          90            INX       H
  3224  C21632      91            JNZ       CRW1      ;NO, LOOP
  3227  3A3F27      92            LDA       CHK
  322A  4F          93            MOV       C,A
  322B  CD4232      94            CALL      CRWB      ;WRITE CHK
  322E  AF          95 CRW2:      XRA       A
  322F  CD8F32      96            CALL      TIMON
  3232  CDA404      97            CALL      CROFF
  3235  210602      98            LXI       H,TRINT   ;RESTORE TRAP
  3238  221027      99            SHLD      TRAPV+1
  323B  FB         100            EI
  323C  C9         101            RET
                   102 ;
  323D  4C         103 CRWW:      MOV       C,H       ;MS BYTE
  323E  CD4232     104            CALL      CRWB
  3241  4D         105            MOV       C,L       ;LS BYTE
                   106 ;
  3242  3A3F27     107 CRWB:      LDA       CHK
```

Figure 3.7

3.12   A programming exercise – multiplication and division

One of the best ways to become accustomed to the facilities offered by editors and assemblers is to use them to produce a useful program. The actual detailed commands necessary to perform the following programming exercise will depend on the particular computer system that you are using and you will need to read the relevant instruction manuals. If, however, you are using the Hektor kit I will include some specific information to help you.

The programs that I am suggesting you develop are:

1   A program to multiply two 8-bit binary words together.
2   A program to divide a 16-bit binary number by an 8-bit binary number.

A multiplication program

Most 8-bit microprocessors do not have instructions to multiply binary numbers together so the programmer has to produce a segment of program to do this if such a multiplication is required.

The process of multiplying two binary numbers together is similar to ordinary denary multiplication. Figure 3.8 shows the multiplication of two 3-digit denary numbers and the multiplication of two 4-bit binary numbers. The binary multiplication is simpler than the denary case because only multiplication by 1 or 0 is required. The result of these basic multiplications is either the multiplicand or zero.

The basic process of binary multiplication can therefore be described in terms of addition of the partial products. The partial products themselves are shifted versions of the multiplicand with zeros filling the least significant digit spaces left by the shifting process. Unfortunately the process described above is difficult to program

(a)	103	Multiplicand	
	125	Multiplier	
	515	Partial product	
	2,060	Partial product	
	10,300	Partial product	
	12,875	Product = Sum of partial products	
(b)	(5) x	101	Multiplicand
	(6)	110	Multiplier
	30	000	Multiplier bit is 0, partial product is 0
		101	Multiplier bit is 1, shifted partial product is multiplicand
		101	Multiplier bit is 1, shifted partial product is multiplicand
		11110	Product = Sum of partial products

Figure 3.8

with the limited set of registers available in the 8080 microprocessor. Instead an entirely equivalent process can be used as suggested in the Intel 8080 programming manual:

a Test the least significant bit of multiplier. If zero, go to step b. If one, add the multiplicand to the *most* significant byte of the result.
b Shift the entire two-byte result right one bit position.
c Repeat steps *a* and *b* until all 8 bits of the multiplier have been tested.

For example, consider the multiplication: 2AH*3CH=9D8H

Step 1 Test multiplier 0-bit; it is 0, so shift 16-bit result right one bit.

Step 2 Test multiplier 1-bit; it is 0, so shift 16-bit result right one bit.

Step 3 Test multiplier 2-bit; it is 1, so add 2AH to high-order byte of result and shift 16-bit result right one bit.

Step 4: Test multiplier 3-bit; it is 1, so add 2AH to high-order byte of result and shift 16-bit result right one bit.

Step 5 Test multiplier 4-bit; it is 1, so add 2AH to high-order byte of result and shift 16-bit result right one bit.

Step 6 Test multiplier 5-bit; it is 1, so add 2AH to high-order byte of result and shift 16-bit result right one bit.

Step 7 Test multiplier 6-bit; it is 0, so shift 16-bit result right one bit.

Step 8 Test multiplier 7-bit; it is 0, so shift 16-bit result right one bit.

The result produced is 09D8.

An example of this process is shown in Table 3.2.

Figure 3.9 shows a flow diagram for the multiplication shown in Table 3.2 and the program is given in Figure 3.10.

The program uses the B register to hold the most significant byte of the result, and the C register to hold the least significant byte of the result. The 16-bit right shift of the result is performed in the accumulator by two rotate-right-through-carry instructions as shown in Figure 3.11.

Practical exercise

Enter the program given in Figure 3.10 into your computer using its editor, then assemble it. Load two binary numbers in the B and D registers, run the program and check the answer in the register pair D,E.

If you are using the Hektor kit the editor is entered using E followed by RETURN. Once the editor has been entered the program can be entered using the I command. When the program has been

Table 3.2

		Multiplier	Multiplicand	High-order byte of result	Low-order byte of result
Start		00111100(3C)	00101010(2A)	00000000	00000000
Step 1	a				
	b			00000000	00000000
Step 2	a				
	b			00000000	00000000
Step 3	a			00101010	00000000
	b			00010101	00000000
Step 4	a			00111111	00000000
	b			00011111	10000000
Step 5	a			01001001	10000000
	b			00100100	11000000
Step 6	a			01001110	11000000
	b			00100111	01100000
Step 7	a				
	b			00010011	10110000
Step 8	a				
	b			00001001	11011000(9D8)

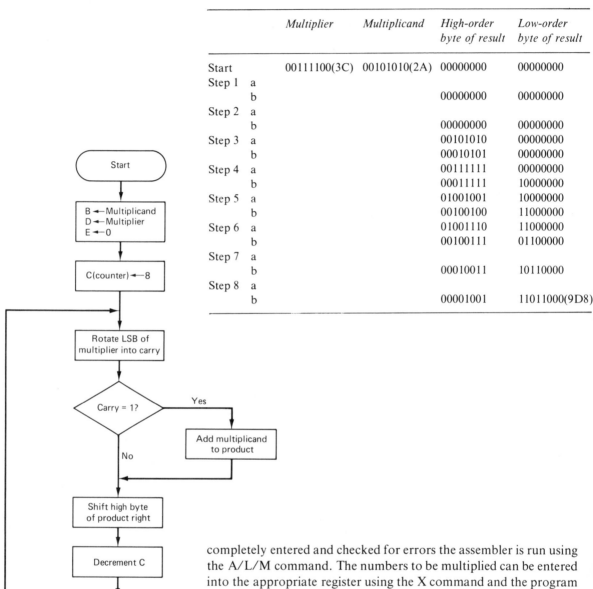

Figure 3.9

completely entered and checked for errors the assembler is run using the A/L/M command. The numbers to be multiplied can be entered into the appropriate register using the X command and the program run using the G starting address command. The result can be determined using the X command.

A division program

The process of binary division is shown in Figure 3.12. This time the process can be performed by shifting and subtraction instructions. A flow diagram for a division program as suggested in the 8080 programming manual is shown in Figure 3.13.

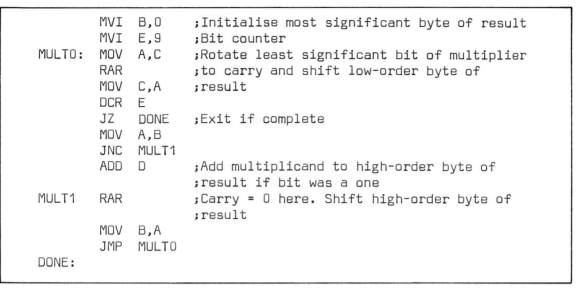

```
          MVI   B,0      ;Initialise most significant byte of result
          MVI   E,9      ;Bit counter
MULT0:    MOV   A,C      ;Rotate least significant bit of multiplier
          RAR            ;to carry and shift low-order byte of
          MOV   C,A      ;result
          DCR   E
          JZ    DONE     ;Exit if complete
          MOV   A,B
          JNC   MULT1
          ADD   D        ;Add multiplicand to high-order byte of
                         ;result if bit was a one
MULT1     RAR            ;Carry = 0 here. Shift high-order byte of
                         ;result
          MOV   B,A
          JMP   MULT0
DONE:
```

Figure 3.10

Zero carry and then rotate B:

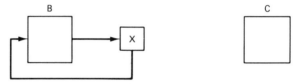

Then rotate C to complete the shift:

Register D holds the multiplicand, and register C originally holds the multiplier.

Figure 3.11

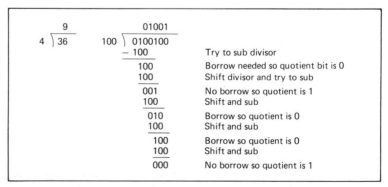

Figure 3.12

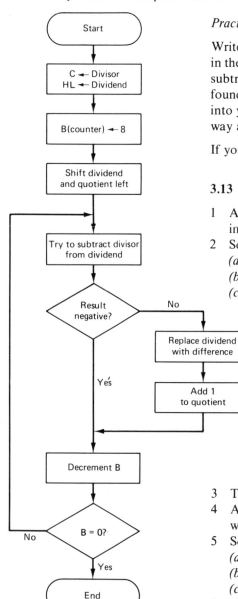

Start

C ← Divisor
HL ← Dividend

B(counter) ← 8

Shift dividend
and quotient left

Try to subtract divisor
from dividend

Result
negative?   No

Replace dividend
with difference

Yes

Add 1
to quotient

Decrement B

No   B = 0?

Yes

End

Practical exercise

Write a program to implement a division program of the type shown in the flow diagram. You will need to find instructions to perform the subtraction and the test to see if the result is negative. These can be found in the Appendices. When you have written the program enter it into your computer, assemble it and run it with test data in the same way as for the multiplication program.

If you get stuck there is a working program in the Appendices.

3.13   Summary

1   An editor program allows the easy input of programs and data into a computer.
2   Some of the features of a good editor are that:
   (a)   it is easy to use;
   (b)   it allows the naming of files;
   (c)   it allows the appending of text.

Figure 3.13

3   There are two main types of editor: line-based and cursor-based.
4   An assembler is a computer program that converts programs written in assembler language into binary code.
5   Some of the features of a good assembler are:
   (a)   it has useful assembler directives;
   (b)   it allows macros;
   (c)   it is easy to use.
6   Assembler directives allow amongst other things the easy storage of data and the use of symbols.
7   A macro is a facility that enables the programmer to avoid having to rewrite the same group of instructions several times in the one program.

Questions

3.1   What are the main differences between line-based and cursor-based editors?

3.2   What are the meanings of the following terms:
- *(a)*   file name;
- *(b)*   text file;
- *(c)*   cursor;
- *(d)*   scrolling.

3.3   Why is the local directive often required when defining a macro?

3.4   Turn the multiplication program into a macro definition and give an example of the use of this macro in an assembler program.

Chapter 4 Elements of good programming and fault-finding

Objectives of this chapter *When you have completed studying this chapter you should be able to:*

1 List the advantages of using subroutines.
2 Explain how to implement subroutines in an assembler language.
3 Explain the function of the stack and stack pointer.
4 Describe a top-down approach to program development.
5 Explain the function of a debugging system.
6 List the facilities offered by a debugging system.
7 Use a debugging system to detect and correct programming errors.

4.1 Introduction

The aim of this chapter is to describe the major tasks involved in producing a good piece of software for a microprocessor. I deliberately use the word software because this implies more than just a listing of the assembly language program.

4.2 Aspects of software development

Among the less obvious aspects of good programming is the need to ensure that the program actually performs the required task. The key to achieving this is a good specification of the task to be performed before the programming proper is started. In addition to performing the required task, the program must be well documented not only in terms of having comments included in the program listing but also it should have a clear statement of the programmer's intention along with flow diagrams and any other aids to program understanding.

Once written the program must be easily testable to ensure that there are no errors in it and easily modifiable at a future date if the specification of the program and the task it is to perform changes.

Specification

This is often the most critical aspect of any software design since it is at this stage that the temptation to begin writing lines of program is at its greatest. However, a clear specification must be obtained first. The programmer and the person describing the task to be performed must go through several stages of communications in which each is encouraged to write down their understanding of the specification. This is never an easy task even when both the programmer and the person requesting the program are both familiar with computers and their limitations but, when, as is becoming the case more frequently since the advent of microprocessors, the person specifying the problem is not familiar with computers the task is particularly difficult.

However, specification must be done and done well or the programmer will hear sooner or later the famous words '. . . well its very nice but its not what we wanted'.

Program design – a top-down approach

By far the most successful way of designing computer programs is to employ a technique called *top-down design*. The essential features of this technique are illustrated in Figure 4.1. The program is first specified in terms of fairly general subprograms which are then further refined themselves into smaller subprograms. This process continues until the subprograms are so simple that their coding, in whatever language is chosen, is a comparatively easy task. To ensure a good final design the program should be examined at each stage in the process to ensure that the divisions into subprograms are sensible.

One of the essential features of this approach is that the program evolves in a modular form so that when the programming proper begins only small segments of program have to be written at a time.

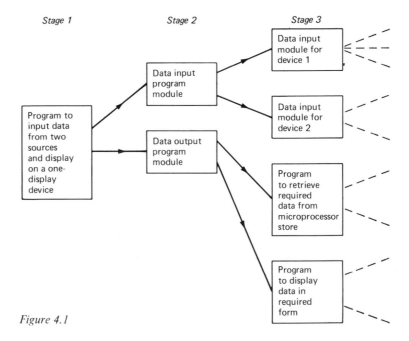

Figure 4.1

This modular approach makes error-free coding easier and also helps during the test phase of program development.

Programming

A top-down approach such as that outlined above will help to simplify the programming task but the programmer should also use techniques which help to ensure error-free and clear programs. One technique is to use flow diagrams of the type shown in Figure 4.2 as described in *Microprocessor Appreciation* to clarify the segment of program before coding begins. However, perhaps a more important technique is for the programmer to employ a technique called *structured programming*.

In structured programming only simple types of program structure are allowed. True/false tests and loops such as those shown in the flow diagrams of Figure 4.3 are allowed, but unconditional jumps such as those implied in the flow diagram shown in Figure 4.4 are not used.

The problem with unstructured programs such as that shown in Figure 4.4 is that program segment P1 can be entered as a result of the true/false test or from anyone of the four segments which jump to P1. If, subsequently, a fault is detected in P1 the error could be in any one of the programs which led to P1 so they would all have to be checked. In the structured case there is only one route to P1; as a result, structured programs are much easier to correct if errors occur.

If the program is ultimately to be written in assembler language then all of the facilities of the assembler should be used to ensure a clear, well commented, modular, structured, well documented and easily

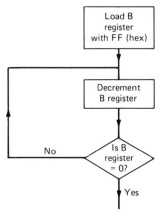

Figure 4.2

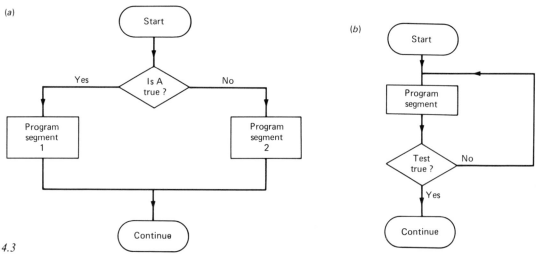

Figure 4.3

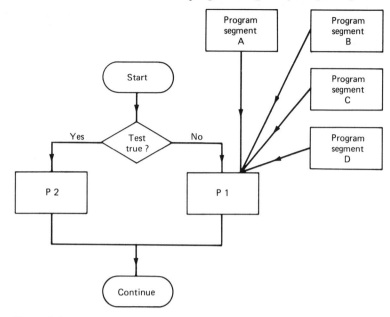

Figure 4.4

testable program. For instance, symbols and labels should be used to aid clarity. Moreover, they should be meaningful, e.g. MAX for a maximum value, DONE for the label marking the end of a test. The labels should be kept as different as possible and the use of the numbers 0, 1 and 2, and the letters O, I and Z in such labels restricted because of the difficulty in distinguishing between these on many types of VDU and printer.

Unfortunately, no matter how carefully a program is pre-prepared and written, it is probable that it will contain errors and the next aspect **Q4.1** of good program design is to ensure that the program is easily testable.

Testing

The testing stage of program development is sometimes called the *debugging stage*. There are several hardware and software aids which can be used during what can be, if the program has not been developed according to the principles outlined above, a frustrating and time-consuming process.

Amongst the hardware aids that can be used are logic analysers, which can display the data and addresses on the data and address buses as the microprocessor executes the program. Perhaps the most frequently used piece of software which is used to track down errors is a special program called a *debugger*. I shall be describing the features and uses of such programs later in this chapter.

The process of program development can be described in almost endless detail but I want to concentrate on just two aspects for the remainder of this chapter. These are the use of subroutines to help to achieve a modular program structure and the use of a debugger to test programs and detect errors.

4.3 Subroutines and their uses

Subroutines are small program segments that can be called repeatedly by the main program. Obviously subroutines lend themselves to programming in a modular fashion, but perhaps their most useful aspect is that they enable frequently used portions of a program to be written just once.

Subroutines are so useful that virtually all levels of program language have instructions that enable their use. For example, a high-level language program would call a subroutine using a statement of this form:

```
CALL AREA  (A1,LENGTH,WIDTH)
```

The purpose of this would be to transfer program control to the subroutine segment named AREA and with the values of the variables A1,LENGTH and WIDTH available to the subroutine. Moreover, when the subroutine has been completed the program control returns to the main program along with the new values of A1,LENGTH and WIDTH. This simple line of program achieves all of the basic requirements of the use of a subroutine. These are that the address of the start of the subroutine has to be specified, values have to be transferred backwards and forwards and the main program should continue after the subroutine has been completed.

When programming at assembler level, many more instructions are required to perform successfully a subroutine call and the transfer of numbers between the subroutine and the main program and *vice versa*. However, because of their usefulness, subroutines are frequently used in assembler programs for the following reasons:

1 The programmer avoids having to write a commonly used sequence of instructions several times over.
2 Corrections to subroutines need only be made once, despite the fact that they may be used several times during a program.
3 Subroutines make programs easier to read and understand.
4 Sometimes subroutines previously written and tested for other programs can be used in a new application.

4.4 Subroutines in assembly language programs

To understand the way in which subroutines can be used in assembly language it is necessary to understand the operation of the program counter register, which controls the sequence in which instructions are performed and the way in which data can be stored in memory using the stack pointer register.

The program counter is the register which automatically keeps track of the address of the next instruction to be executed. When a call is made to a subroutine this address has to be stored so that, on return from the subroutine, the execution of the main program can continue. The subroutine call must also, once the current contents of the program counter have been stored, replace them with the address of the first instruction in the subroutine. This address usually forms part of the subroutine call instruction, for example,

    CALL   0100H

is the 8080 instruction which causes the program to jump to the subroutine which begins at memory location 0100 (hex). Often though for clarity the address of the subroutine will be given a symbolic name as shown in the following example

    CALL   MULT

Of course, MULT must be defined earlier in the program to be equal to 0100 (hex) for the two examples to be equivalent.

In the examples the current contents of the program counter are stored and replaced by 0100 (hex) so that execution of the subroutine can begin.

Notice that the CALL assembly language instruction does not include a list of variables which can be used to pass numbers to and from the subroutine in the way it is possible with a high-level language. In an assembler program the programmer must write specific instructions which allow the transfer of data to and from the subroutine. This is usually done using the same method as that used to store the contents of the program counter, namely by the use of the stack pointer, and the area in memory called the *stack*.

The use of the stack and stack pointer in assembler subroutines

The stack is an area in RAM addressed by the special 16-bit register in the processor called the stack pointer. Often the area reserved in memory begins at the highest memory location – for a reason which should become apparent shortly.

The stack pointer contains the address of the last byte of data stored in this memory area and its operation can best be described by the use of an example. Suppose that the stack pointer has been loaded with the initial address FFFF (hex), the highest available in a typical 8-bit microprocessor, with the instruction:

```
LXI  SP,OFFFFH  ;Load SP with FFFF (hex)
```

Next suppose a call to subroutine is encountered; this, as I have said before, causes the contents of the program counter to be stored on the stack so as the program contains 16 bits it is stored in two successive memory locations. In our example the location FFFF (hex) will be assumed to contain data, so the stack pointer will be decremented by one then the highest-order byte of the program counter stored in location FFFE, the stack pointer decremented by one and the lowest-order byte stored in the next lowest location FFFD.

When the subroutine is completed, this stored address has to be retrieved. This is done by a special instruction at the end of the subroutine, the RET instruction. Its effect is to restore the contents of the program counter from the stack. This can be easily achieved because the stack pointer contains the address of the last data to be stored on the stack. This address is FFFD and it contains the data to be returned to the lowest-order register of the program counter. Once this is done as a result of the RET instruction, the stack pointer is incremented by one to FFFE and the highest-order data returned to the program counter and the main program can continue.

Data can be transferred to and from subroutines using much the same sort of procedure, but this requires the use of instructions which push and pull registers other than the program counter on to and from the stack. The mnemonics for the 8080 instructions that perform these operations are PUSH and POP. They allow pairs of registers to be stored and retrieved from the stack and they have the form:

```
PUSH   reg
POP    reg
```

In the 8080 the registers specified can be B and C, D and E, H and L and the contents of the accumulator and the condition code registers. For example, with

```
PUSH   B
POP    B
```

the first instruction stores the contents of register pair B and C on the stack, the second restores them. The stack pointer controls these operations as can be seen from an extension to the previous examples. Suppose the subroutine in the example has been entered from the subroutine call, the program counter contents will have been stored in locations FFFE and FFFD and the stack pointer will contain the address FFFD of the last byte of data to be stored. If the subroutine begins with a PUSH B instruction, this will cause the stack pointer to be decremented by one to FFFC and the contents of the B register stored in this location; then the stack pointer is decremented by one more to FFFB and the contents of the C register stored in this location.

Now suppose that there are no further PUSH instructions and that the POP B instruction occurs at the end of the subroutine. Then the first effect is to restore the data in the memory location given by the stack pointer to the C register. The stack pointer is incremented by one to contain the address FFFC so that the contents of the B register may be restored. Finally the contents of the stack pointer are incremented by one to FFFD to point to the remaining data which has the lowest address on the stack. In our example this data is part of the original contents of the program counter and will be restored by the RET instruction.

By now you should be getting an idea of why this special storage area in memory is called a stack. Data is stacked up by using instructions such as PUSH and the stack grows downward from high addresses to lower ones; the register which keeps track of the latest data to be placed on the stack is the stack pointer. Data is 'popped' off the stack with POP instructions.

The simplest use for the PUSH and POP instructions is to use them to save the contents of the processor registers so that the subroutine may use these registers. At the end of the subroutines these registers can be restored from the stack to the processor so that the main program may proceed with all its register contents intact. Obviously, the storage of the register must take place before the subroutine begins to use them so the necessary PUSH instructions are usually at the start of the subroutine and the POP instructions at the end. Figure 4.5 is an

```
TIME:  PUSH  PSW   ;Stack acc plus status
       PUSH  B     ;Stack B and C
       PUSH  D     ;Stack D and E
       PUSH  H     ;Stack H and L
         .
         .
         .



subroutine instructions
  .
  .
  .
POP   H     ;Recall H and L
POP   D     ;Recall D and E
POP   B     ;Recall B and C
POP   PSW   ;Recall acc plus status
RET
```

Figure 4.5

example of such a subroutine whose starting address has the label TIME. Notice that as a result of the way in which data is put onto the stack the registers which are first to be stored with the PUSH instruction are the last to be recalled by the POP instruction.

Not all subroutines begin by storing all the registers on the stack. Indeed, data is often transferred between the main program by the use of the processor registers as the following section explains.

Passing data between the main program and subroutine

Often the purpose of a subroutine is to perform operations such as multiplication on data that is in the main program. This can most easily be done using the registers in the processor to pass the data. If the data is placed in the processor's registers prior to the subroutine call and the subroutine does not push it onto the stack then the data in the registers is available during the processing of the subroutine instructions.

For example, if the purpose of the subroutine were to multiply two 8-bit binary numbers together and return the 16-bit result to the main program, the two numbers could be stored initially in the B and C registers. Then when the subroutine was called they would be available and the result could be stored in, say, the H,L register pair. Upon return to the main program, the result of the multiplication would be available in the H,L register pair.

In the 8080 microprocessor the accumulator and the B,C,D,E,H and L registers are available to pass data in this way and microprocessors with more registers can pass more data. If the subroutine has to have access to more data than can be passed via the registers other techniques have to be used.

For example, suppose a list (or as it is sometimes called a table of data) has to be used by the subroutine and that it is too big to be transferred using the registers. Instead of passing the data, all that has to be done is to pass the address of the start of the table and its length. This can be done using the H,L register pair for the address and, say, the C register for its length. Indeed, in some situations it is not even necessary to transfer information concerning the length of the table. Having done this, the subroutine has access to all the information in that table and, if a large amount of data has to be passed back to the main program, the same sort of technique can be used. This time the subroutine loads the H,L register pair with the start address of the table before the return instruction.

Subroutines calling subroutines

A common requirement in a subroutine is to be able to call another

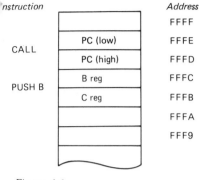

Figure 4.6

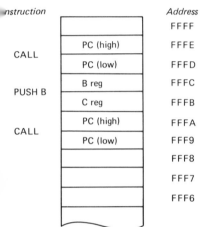

Figure 4.7

subroutine. For example, a subroutine which calculates the length of the hypotenuse from Pythagorus's theorem may well call a subroutine to calculate the square of a number (the length of the sides). Such subroutines are said to be *nested*. Nesting of subroutines is possible in assembly language programs due to the nature of the stack storage and stack pointer systems.

Suppose that the first subroutine has been called and has stored some of the registers on the stack. Then the contents of the stack would be similar to that shown in Figure 4.6. When, during the execution of this subroutine, another subroutine is called, the current contents of the program counter are stored automatically by the call instruction in the manner described previously and the stack would be as shown in Figure 4.7. The new subroutine could save the contents of the first subroutine's registers or accept the data in them as appropriate. In this way no data is lost and the stack area grows in an orderly fashion so that all the data can be retrieved by appropriate RET and POP instructions. Using this process many subroutines may be nested within each other with the second calling a third and so on. The only limit to this process is the memory available for the stack as it grows.

Summary – assembler subroutines

1   Subroutines in assembler or any other language allow efficient and modular programming techniques.
2   High-level languages allow simple subroutine calls in which data can be passed to and from the subroutine as part of the calling instruction. In assembler programming the programmer must make use of the stack and stack pointer to achieve effective subroutine calls.
3   Care has to be taken by the programmer to decide which processor registers are to be stored on the stack. Storage saves their contents for the return to the main program; if they are not stored the data in them is available to the subroutine program.
4   The stack and stack pointer mechanism allows subroutines to call other subroutines provided all the relevant register contents are stored before the second subroutine uses them.

Q4.2–4.4

4.5   Testing – the use of a debugger

Once a program has been written and assembled, the next phase of software development is testing. The assembler program will have indicated any simple errors that are in the program, such as mis-spelt mnemonics, but it is the testing phase that is designed to detect any errors that occur when the program is run. These errors are often produced by the programmer mistaking the original requirements, so that correct code is produced but it does not perform the required task. For example, a wait loop may be the wrong duration, data may have been sent to the wrong output device or the wrong register saved during a subroutine call. None of these errors will be detected by the assembler because they are errors of purpose not of the use of the instructions.

What is needed to detect these errors occurring during the operation of the program is a way of stopping the execution of the program once an error is detected and examining the processor registers at this point in the program. A debugger is a special-purpose test program that allows just this.

Facilities offered by a debugger

Obviously, this depends on the particular debugging program being used, but there are certain basic facilities common to all of them. Perhaps the most basic facility is that the debugger allows the programmer to set break points. *Break points* are points where the programmer wants the execution of the program to stop so that the contents of the processor's registers or memory can be examined.

For example, the programmer could run the debugger program and instruct it to run the program to be tested which begins at, say, memory location 0F00 (hex) and to stop the program when it reaches the instruction stored at the address specified by a break point command. This break point is specified to the debugging program before the instruction to run the program under test is given. If this break point was set at 0F10 (hex), say, then the program under test would run up to memory location 0F10 and then stop. The programmer could then use other commands available in the debugging program, such as:

1   Examine the contents of a memory location.
2   Print out on the current output device the contents of the processor's registers.
3   Change the contents of a memory location or a processor register.
4   Allow the program to proceed at normal speed.
5   Allow the program to proceed one instruction at a time.

If this last option is chosen then all of the debugger commands are available each time execution stops.

More sophisticated debugging programs have extra facilities such as *trace commands* which produce a printout of the instructions and data that led up to an error or a break point.

However sophisticated the debugging program, it is clear that the information that it provides has to be interpreted by reference to the original program instructions and the specification for the software. This being the case, good documentation of the program and the software specification is essential for this test phase of software development to be completed successfully.

4.6 Programming examples

1 Write and run a program in assembler to place two binary numbers in the B and D registers. Multiply them together using a call to a subroutine that contains a multiplication program of the type shown in Chapter 3. On return from the subroutine store the result in memory, increment one of the original binary numbers and repeat the multiplication call followed by storage of the result in a different part of memory.

2 Use the debugging facilities to examine the operation of the program you have just written. This can be done by setting break points at the appropriate places. For instance, the following break points might be sensible:
(a) After the B and D registers have been loaded, so that the examine command can be used to check to see they contain the correct value.
(b) After the return from the subroutine so that the D register pair can be examined for the result.
(c) After the memory store instructions to check the result has been stored in the correct memory location.

Do not forget that the single step or single instruction command can be very useful after a break point is reached.

Notes for using Hektor

The assembly and the running of your program should be familiar to you from Chapter 3. However, you should take a good note of the locations of the instructions as given by the assembly listing. These locations need to be specified as part of the break point instructions.

Remember that the debugging command is part of the monitor program and that when a break point is reached in your program, control reverts to the monitor program so that the examine register and memory commands, X and M, can be used. Only one break point can be specified at a time so you will need to specify the next one after you have finished with the current one and before you instruct the program to continue.

4.7 Summary

1 A piece of software for a microprocessor should consist of more than just a program listing. It should be supported by flow diagrams, program descriptions and other aids to program understanding.

2   One of the best ways of producing good software is to use a top-down approach. This is because this leads to modular programs which are easy to write, test and understand.

3   Subroutines can be used to achieve a modular program structure.

4   In assembler programming the use of subroutines requires a knowledge of the operation of the stack pointer and the stack storage mechanism.

5   The stack is used to store the return address required when a subroutine is completed, as well as the contents of the processor's registers.

6   Once written a program may be tested by a variety of different devices, one of which is called a debugger.

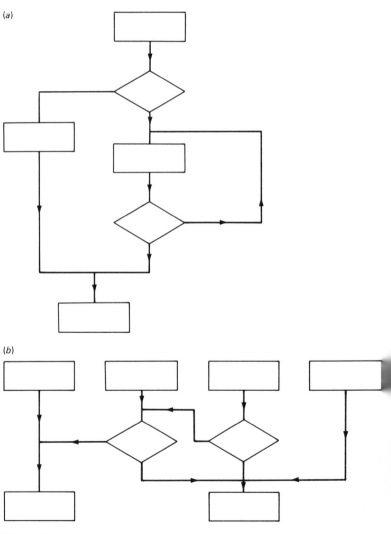

Figure 4.8

7   A debugger is a special test program that allows, amongst other things, the program under test to be halted at a specified point and the processor's registers examined to see if they contain the expected data.

Questions

4.1   Which of the flow diagrams shown in Figure 4.8 would not be used in structured programming?

4.2   What are the similarities and differences between macros and sub-routines?

4.3   Which memory location would contain the contents of the C register following these instructions:

```
PUSH    PSW
PUSH    D
PUSH    H
PUSH    B
```

Given that the content of the stack pointer before these instructions is FFF0 (hex).

4.4   How is data transferred to and from the main program and a subroutine?

Chapter 5 Input and output techniques

Objectives of this chapter *When you have completed studying this chapter you should be able to:*

1. *Discuss the difference between serial and parallel data transmission.*
2. *Draw a block diagram of a programmable parallel interface device.*
3. *Describe the operation of a typical parallel interface device.*
4. *Draw a block diagram of a programmable serial interface device.*
5. *Describe the operation of a serial interface device.*
6. *Discuss the difference between memory-mapped and accumulator input and output schemes.*
7. *Describe the function of handshake signals between an interface and peripheral.*

5.1 Introduction

The aim of this chapter is to introduce you to the ideas of micro-processor input and output, and to show you how simple input and output interfaces can be built up with the aid of general-purpose integrated circuit devices. The chapter falls into two main parts: the first deals with the input and output of single bytes along an 8-bit bus, whilst the second looks at the problem of serial transmission of data.

5.2 Microprocessor input and output

For microprocessor systems to have any real value they must be able to communicate with the outside world. They must be able to gather information about what is happening in order to calculate or determine what events should take place next. For example, suppose we wanted to use a microprocessor to count the number of objects passing a point on a conveyor belt and display the running total. The microprocessor cannot do this on its own; we must design some means for it to count the objects and to display the result.

The object sensor and the display are not part of the microprocessor, but are external units added to the system to meet specific requirements. They are examples of *peripherals*, as are the VDU, paper tape reader and paper tape punch.

Most peripherals are general purpose and are designed to be used with any microprocessor. However, microprocessors differ in many respects; they have different timing requirements and communicate

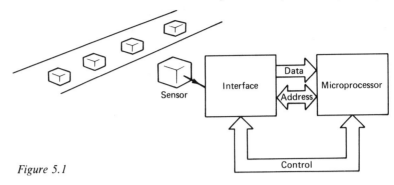

Figure 5.1

with peripherals in different ways. Each peripheral must therefore be mated to the particular microprocessor controlling the total system.

The mating function is achieved by a special electronic circuit called an *interface*. Figure 5.1 shows a block diagram for the counting system described above. The sensor detects the items passing and conveys this information to the interface. The interface in turn must convey this information to the microprocessor by means of the address, data and control busses. We will see how this is done later in the chapter.

Because the range of application of microprocessors is so large, few interfaces are exactly the same. This means that a lot of time and effort must go into the design of new interfaces for each new microprocessor system. The integrated circuit manufacturers quickly recognised this and realised that designers would not use their devices unless the whole problem of interface design was simplified. They responded by producing general-purpose devices that could be used as building blocks in the design of peripheral interfaces.

5.3 Memory-mapped and accumulator I/O

With these interface circuits it is fairly simple to attach all sorts of peripherals to the system. However, we must provide a means for the microprocessor to distinguish between these peripherals otherwise the data transfer may not be directed to the right one.

Two techniques have been developed. The first treats every peripheral as a section of memory so that different peripherals occupy different areas of memory. This technique is referred to as *memory mapping* and has the advantage that all the microprocessor instructions that can be used to read/write or alter memory can be used with the peripherals.

The second technique requires that each peripheral is assigned a unique code and that information must be transferred from the accumulator to the peripheral by means of special instructions. This is referred to as *accumulator input/output*.

The 8080 and Z80 microprocessors have two special instructions for transferring data between an accumulator and a peripheral. Each peripheral is assigned a unique code number, or device code, in the range 00H to FFH, and this code becomes the operand in a special instruction.

For example, to read a byte of data from peripheral 09H, the IN instruction is used. It has the format

```
IN   09H   ;Read data from peripheral 9
           ;into the accumulator
```

To send a byte of data to peripheral 08H the OUT instruction is used. This instruction has the format

```
OUT   08H   ;Transfer contents of accumulator
            ;to peripheral 8
```

The microprocessor addresses all the peripherals by placing the device code on the address bus. The data bus cannot be used because it will be needed for the actual data transfer. The peripheral interface must decode this address in order to determine if the data transfer is directed at its peripheral.

Since the address bus is connected to both the interfaces and the memory, a special signal is provided by the microprocessor to distinguish between a memory read/write and a peripheral read/write.

Interfaces addressed in this way are often referred to as *ports*, since they allow information to be loaded and unloaded from the peripherals, somewhat similar to goods in a shipping port.

Q5.3

5.4   Parallel and serial data transfers

Data can be transferred between the microprocessor and the peripheral in one of two ways. In the first, the data word, be it an 8-bit byte or more, is sent in one operation with all the bits travelling along a set of parallel wires. This is called *parallel data transfer*. In the second, the bits are sent one after the other along a single pair of wires. This is called *serial data transfer*.

The choice between these two methods is not always easy to make, but there are two important questions to answer that influence the decision.

1   Is the transmission to be high speed?
2   Is the transmission over a long distance?

Parallel transfer is generally faster than serial because all the bits of the word are transmitted in one cycle, whereas serial transmission requires n cycles for an n-bit word. So if the application needs high speed, design an interface that uses parallel transfers.

If the data is to be transferred over long distances, as for example temperature readings in a large petrochemical plant, the cost of cabling for parallel transfers can become very expensive. This is because electrical signals degrade with distance travelled, either due to voltage drop in the wires or because other signals are 'picked-up' and contaminate the one we want. Signal degradation can be minimised by using special amplifiers and low-loss cables, but these are expensive. Using serial transmission obviously keeps the cost down because only one pair of wires is needed.

Q5.1

5.5 Modems

A further advantage of serial transmission is that we can make use of existing communications networks for worldwide data transfers. In particular it is possible to use the public telephone network for low-speed serial data transfers.

We cannot just connect our wires to the telephone; it might damage the equipment. Instead the serial data is fed into a special box called a *modem*. This box translates the digital data from the microprocessor into signals that can be transmitted down the telephone. Another modem at the far end of the telephone line is used to convert the tele-phone signal back into digital form.

5.6 Handshake signals

No matter what form of transmission system is used, both the inter-face and the peripheral must know when data is sent or requested. The interface is connected directly to the memory, address and control busses of the microprocessor and so uses the standard timing arrangements for data transfer. The peripheral cannot use these signals, so most systems provide extra signals between the interface and the peripheral to control the timing of data transfers. These signals are usually referred to as *handshake signals*.

In the previous example of sensing objects on a conveyor, the sensor must be able to tell the interface when an object has passed so that this information can be conveyed to the microprocessor. Likewise when the microprocessor wants to display the number of items that have passed, it must be able to tell the display interface that new informa-tion is ready. Other interfaces may require a more complicated set of handshake signals as we shall see later.

5.7 Parallel data transfers

In this section I want to examine some of the devices available for designing parallel transfer interfaces. Let us start by examining an interface for a paper tape punch that is to be connected to a system that uses accumulator I/O.

The sequence of operations required to transfer a byte of data to the punch are:

1   The microprocessor puts the device code of the punch onto the address bus.
2   The microprocessor puts the data byte onto the data bus and indicates to all the interfaces that this is an I/O write operation.
3   The punch reads the data byte on the bus and punches the appropriate holes in the tape.

Storing data in the interface

The punch, being an electromechanical device, will take 10–20 ms to actually punch the holes. During this time the microprocessor will execute several hundred instructions and the data byte destined for the punch will have disappeared from the data bus before the punch is ready. New instructions from memory or data from another peripheral will have replaced the original data word for the punch, and so it may punch the wrong code.

To avoid this problem the punch interface must provide a temporary store for the data word. The storage is provided by a device called a *data register*, which is just a single byte of memory. This single byte is written into during the microprocessor I/O sequence, almost as though it were ordinary RAM.

The interface status register

The relatively slow speed of the punch also means that we must prevent the microprocessor from trying to write a new data word into the register until the previous one is punched. Obviously we can do this by putting a time delay loop into the program, and this is done in many simple systems. However, as we shall see in later chapters, it is useful to add special 'flags' to the interface which indicate the current state of the peripheral. These flags are 1-bit memory elements in the interface device. They store the high (set) or low (reset) voltage levels. For example, when the punch has received a data word, a 'busy' flag is set in the interface to say no more data must be sent. When the current word has been punched this flag can be reset to indicate that a new data word can be sent. Some peripherals need several flags and so a special register is provided in the interface. This register can be read by the microprocessor to determine the current status of the peripheral, hence it is called the *status register*.

Each flag required by the peripheral is associated with one bit of the status register, so depending upon the peripheral this register may be several bits wide. For convenience an 8-bit register is normally used and, like the data register, it looks just like a single byte of memory or an additional I/O port. Of course, not all the bits will be used, so the unused bits are just ignored by the program that reads the peripheral status.

Handshake signals and the status register

The 'flags' or bits in the status register are set and reset by special signals. Some will be generated by the microprocessor, or derived from a combination of the signals on the control bus, others will be generated by the peripheral.

In the case of the punch the 'busy' flag must be set immediately the microprocessor has written a data word into the data register, otherwise a new word may be sent before the current one has been punched.

To minimise the delay between the writing of the data and the setting of the flag, the interface can use the read/write line of the control bus to set the busy flag.

Once the interface has stored the data word it must tell the punch that data is available. A special signal is used for this purpose. It might be called DATA AVAILABLE, and runs along an extra wire between the interface and the punch.

A second special signal is used by the punch to tell the interface that the data has been punched and more can be sent. This signal might be called PUNCH COMPLETE and also runs along a separate wire from the punch to the interface. The interface can use this signal to reset the busy flag in the status register and so inform the micro-processor that a new data word can be sent.

The two signals, DATA AVAILABLE and PUNCH COMPLETE, control the timing of the flow of data between the interface and the punch. They are examples of *handshake signals*, which are used by many peripherals and interfaces to control data transmission.

Figure 5.2 shows a block diagram of the complete microprocessor, interface and punch system. It also shows the two handshake signals and the direction information flows along these two wires. Hand-shake signals for an input device, such as a paper tape reader, work in exactly the same way. However, the DATA AVAILABLE signal will now originate in the peripheral rather than the interface, because the reader must tell the interface that it has read a character. The equivalent of PUNCH COMPLETE will be generated by the interface and is used to inform the reader to get the next character.

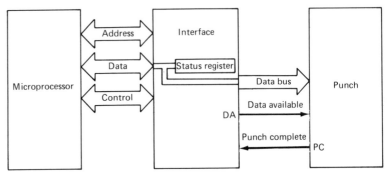

Figure 5.2   Punch

A programmable parallel interface device

Designing interfaces for peripherals is a complicated and a time-consuming task and few interfaces are interchangeable amongst peripherals. To minimise the cost of building interfaces, manufacturers have developed general-purpose integrated circuits that can be used to build an interface for almost any peripheral. The flexibility of these devices is due to the fact that the exact mode of operation is controlled by software rather than hardware – the devices are programmable. A few instructions can change a device from an interface controlling an input peripheral to one controlling an output peripheral.

Figure 5.3 shows a block diagram of a typical *programmable input/ output* device (also referred to as a PIO or PIA) used for parallel transfers. The device contains sufficient registers and flags to control several peripherals. This is achieved by using the latest large-scale integration techniques and has the advantage that the package count for a complete interface is minimised. Because of their flexibility, these devices are made in very large numbers and so the cost can be kept very low.

The two ports labelled A and B can transmit or receive 8-bit data words. The device contains six 8-bit registers, two CONTROL, two DATA DIRECTION and two DATA. The function of each of these registers is described below. Although there are six registers, this device only requires decoding for four registers and so, if used in a memory-mapped system, four memory addresses must be reserved, or in an accumulator I/O system four port numbers.

Two programmable handshake signals are provided for each port, CA1 and CA2 for port A and CB1 and CB2 for port B. These signals can be used to control the transfer of data between the PIO and the peripheral.

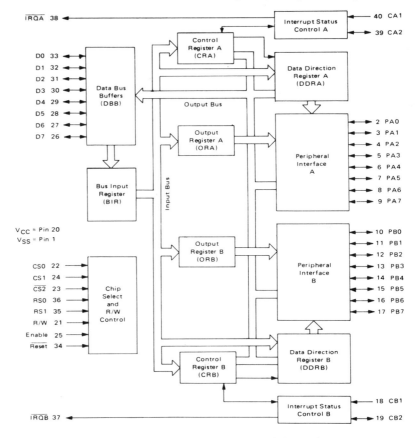

Figure 5.3 Block diagram of the Motorola 6820 Peripheral Interface Adapter

Control register

The·control registers are used to store an 8-bit control word that determines the basic operating mode of the device. Figure 5.4 shows the organisation of the two control registers for the programmable device shown in Figure 5.3.

	7	6	5	4	3	2	1	0
CR A	IRA1	IRA2	CA 2 Control			DDRA Access	CA 1 Control	

	7	6	5	4	3	2	1	0
CR B	IRA1	IRA2	CB 2 Control			DDRA Access	CB 1 Control	

Figure 5.4 Organisation of PIO control registers

The IRA1, IRA2, IRB1 and IRB2 bits of the control registers are the status flags for the interface, and they are set by transitions of the CA and CB handshake signals, respectively. These flags function in a similar way to the 'busy' flag of the paper tape punch interface described in the previous section. I will refer to them as the DATA READY flags. When data is sent to a data register by the microprocessor, these flags are automatically reset to 0. When the peripheral is ready for more data it sets the appropriate flag. A signal connected to CA1 will set IRA1, whilst a signal connected to CA2 will set IRA2. The B port works in the same way with the IRB1 and IRB2 flags.

Because there are six registers in the PIO but only four port numbers reserved, the device needs to use some form of decoding to enable the microprocessor to get at all the registers. The method adopted for this particular device requires that the data direction and data registers share the same port number (or memory address). In order to distinguish between these two registers, an extra flag is provided in the control register. These flags are called DDRA and DDRB for the A and B ports, respectively. So if the DDRA flag is set, any data sent to the common address goes to the A data register. If the flag is reset to 0 the data goes to the A data direction register.

Data direction register

The data direction register is used to set the direction data will travel for each bit of the ports. If a bit of this register is set to a 1, then the corresponding bit of the port will be an output, whilst if set to 0 then that bit will be an input.

The user is therefore free to choose the way the device will function and this is an example of the flexibility of such devices. For instance, one moment the PIO could be used to output values to a display, and the next it could be reading temperatures. In practice one would rarely change the direction of a port within a program, instead one **Q5.2** uses the individual ports of a device for different functions.

Data register

The data registers hold the data word that is to be transferred to/from the peripheral. They function in exactly the same way as the data register described for the punch example.

Handshake signals

The CA1, CA2, CB1 and CB2 lines provide handshake signals between the peripheral and the PIO. Tables 5.1 to 5.4 detail the relationship between the control bits in the control register and the CA1/CA2 and the CB1/CB2 lines. The 'E' signal is the 'Enable' input

Table 5.1

CRA-1 (CRB-1)	CRA-0 (CRB-0)	Data ready input CA1 (CB1)	Data ready flag CRA-7 (CRB-7)
0	0	↓ Active	Set high on ↓ of CA1 (CB1)
0	1	↓ Active	Ser high on ↓ of CA1 (CB1)
1	0	↑ Active	Set high on ↑ of CA1 (CB1)
1	1	↑ Active	Set high on ↑ of CA1 (CB1)

Note 1 ↑ indicates positive transition (low to high).
Note 2 ↓ indicates negative transition (high to low).
Note 3 The data ready flag bit CRA-7 is cleared by an MPU read of the A data register and CRB-7 is cleared by an MPU read of the B data register.
Note 4 If CRA-0 (CRB-0) is low when a data ready occurs (data ready disabled) and is later brought high, IRQA (IRQB) occurs on the positive transition of CRA-0 (CRB-0).

Table 5.2

CRA-5 (CRB-5)	CRA-4 (CRB-4)	CRA-3 (CRB-3)	Data ready input CA2 (CB2)	Data ready flag CRA-6 (CRB-6)
0	0	0	↓ Active	Set high on ↓ of CA2 (CB2)
0	0	1	↓ Active	Set high on ↓ of CA2 (CB2)
0	1	0	↑ Active	Set high on ↑ of CA2 (CB2)
0	1	1	↑ Active	Set high on ↑ of CA2 (CB2)

Note 1 ↑ indicates positive transition (low to high).
Note 2 ↓ indicates negative transition (high to low).
Note 3 The data ready flag bit CRA-6 is cleared by an MPU read of the A data register and CRB-6 is cleared by an MPU read of the B data register.
Note 4 If CRA-3 (CRB-3) is low when a data ready occurs (data ready disabled) and is later brought high, IRQA (IRQB) occurs on the positive transition of CRA-3 (CRB-3).

of the PIO, and is used to determine the length of the output signal when the CA2 and CB2 are used as output handshake signals.

To see how the Enable input is used lets look at a specific example. Suppose a peripheral needs a short pulse to tell it data is available at the B port outputs. Table 5.4, row 2, says that if bits 5, 4 and 3 of the

Table 5.3

CRA-5	CRA-4	CRA-3	CA2	
			Cleared	*Set*
0	0	0	Low on negative transition of E after an MPU read A data operation	High on active transition of the CA1 signal
1	0	1	Low immediately after an MPU read A data operation	High on the negative edge of the next E pulse
1	1	0	Low when CRA-3 goes low as a result of an MPU write in control register A	Always low as long as CRA-3 is low
1	1	1	Always high as long as CRA-3 is high	High when CRA-3 goes high as a result of a write in control register A

Table 5.4

CRB-5	CRB-4	CRB-3	CB2	
			Cleared	*Set*
1	0	0	Low on the positive transition of the first E pulse following an MPU write B data register operation	High when the data read flag bit CRB-7 is set by an active transition of the CB1 signal
1	0	1	Low on the positive transition of the first E pulse following an MPU write B data register operation	High on the positive transition of the next E pulse
1	1	0	Low when CRB-3 goes low as a result of an MPU write in control register B	Always low as long as CRB-3 is low. Will go high on an MPU write in control register B that changes CRB-3 to 1
1	1	1	Always high as long as CRB-3 is high. Will be cleared when an MPU write control register B results in clearing CRB-3 to 0	High when CRB-3 goes high as a result of an MPU write into control register B

control register are set to 101, respectively, then the first positive transition of the Enable input following a write to port B will set CB2 low. The next positive transition will set CB2 high and the whole sequence will produce a short negative pulse on the CB2 line.

To ensure such transitions occur, the Enable input is normally connected to the system clock.

5.8 Example of the use of a PIO – paper tape reader interface

As an example of the use of a PIO, I am going to examine how we can design an interface for a paper tape reader. Before we can make any decisions regarding this interface we must know something of the way the reader functions. Data is transferred between the reader and the interface as an 8-bit data word.

Each data byte is accompanied by a DATA AVAILABLE signal, which can be used to tell the interface to read the data on the data bus. Before any data can be read the tape must be inched forward under the scanning head. This is done by activating another signal called DRIVE; it turns on the motor in the reader. DATA AVAILABLE and DRIVE are two more examples of handshake signals, the former generated by the peripheral, the latter by the interface. A block diagram of the interface is shown in Figure 5.5.

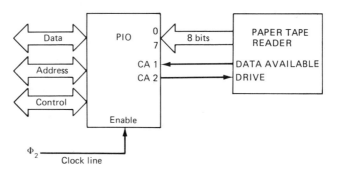

Figure 5.5

I have assumed that port A of the PIO is to be used for the reader, so the data lines can be connected directly to the AD0–AD7 pins of the device. The program must set the bits of the data direction register of the PIO.

What code word should be loaded into the data direction register?

Since all the bits of the port are to be inputs, the codeword must be 00H.

The main problem when using PIOs is to determine which handshake signals to use and how to program the device accordingly. Unfortunately there are no easy rules and one must read through the description of the PIO very carefully. In this example the PIO I have selected is the Motorola M6820 and the device data sheet (see Appendices) indicates that CA1 input can be used as a data 'strobe'. This means that data will be transferred from the bus to the data register when a transition occurs on the CA1 line. Hence if CA1 is connected to DATA AVAILABLE, each data byte will be transferred to the data register as it appears on the bus.

The data sheet for the PIO also indicates that CA2 can be used as an output handshake line and so can provide the signal DRIVE. However, we must remember that DRIVE causes the tape to move forward under the scanning head of the reader, so in order to prevent the tape moving continuously, DRIVE must be a short-duration pulse.

Ideally what we want is to be able to set DRIVE active at the beginning of a read and have it set inactive when the data from the reader has been stored in the data register. Fortunately we can obtain exactly this response by appropriate programming of bits 3, 4 and 5 of control register A.

Assuming DATA AVAILABLE is a high-to-low transition, what bit pattern must be loaded into the CA1 and CA2 control bits?

The values for these bits can be determined from Tables 5.1 and 5.2, which relate the function of the CA1 and CA2 lines to the bits of the control register. CA1 is controlled by bits 0 and 1 and these should be set to 10 to ensure that CAI responds to the high-to-low transition of DATA AVAILABLE.

CA2 is controlled by bits 3, 4 and 5 of the control register and they should be set to 100. This will ensure that CA2 will go high on an active transition of CA1 and it will not be reset until the microprocessor has read the data from the data register.

Under certain conditions it may not be possible to obtain the correct polarity of signal from the PIO directly, or even get an appropriate signal. In such cases it will be necessary to introduce additional logic circuits into the interface.

As well as providing handshake signals between the interface and the peripheral, transitions on the CA1 and CA2 lines will also set the IRA1 and IRA2 flags in the control register. In this example only CA1 will be programmed as an active input, so IRA1 can be used as the data ready flag for the microprocessor. To test if a word has been sent by the reader, the microprocessor must read the control register (which also acts as a status register in this PIO). If IRA1 is set, a data

Q5.4   word has been received, if it is not set no word has been received.

5.9 Software control of the reader interface

So far we have been concerned with the hardware aspects of connecting a peripheral to a PIO and hence the microprocessor. Now I want to examine the software requirements that enable us to program a device to meet a specific need, that of inputting data from the reader.

Paper tape reader program

The program for the paper tape reader (see Figure 5.6) can be divided into two parts. The first part must set the bits of the control register

```
TBLADR:   EQU   2000H     ;Define start of memory storage area for data
CREG:     EQU   1000H     ;Define address of control register
PORTA:    EQU   1001H     ;Define address of port A data direction and
                          ;data registers
          ORG   100H      ;Define starting address of program

START:    LXI   H,TBLADR  ;Load address of storage area into H,L
                          ;register pair
          MVI   A,00H     ;Set accumulator = 00H
          STA   CREG      ;Store 00H into control register to address
                          ;data direction register
          STA   PORTA     ;Set data direction = 00H, i.e. all bits
                          ;are inputs
          MVI   B,FFH     ;Load character count into register B
          MVI   A,26H     ;Load control register data word into
                          ;accumulator
          STA   CREG      ;Set control register
          LDA   PORTA     ;Read port A data register to start paper
                          ;tape reader
LOOP:     LDA   CREG      ;Read control register flags
          ANI   80H       ;Test bit 7 of control register
          JNZ   READ      ;Bit 7 = 1 so read character
          JMP   LOOP      ;Bit 7 = 0 so try again
READ:     LDA   PORTA     ;Read port A data register
          MOV   M,A       ;Store data word in table
          INX   H         ;Increment table pointer
          DCR   B         ;Decrement character count
          JZ    END       ;If character count = 0 jump to END
          JMP   LOOP      ;Not zero so get next character

END:      RET             ;Return to main program
```

Figure 5.6 Paper tape reader program

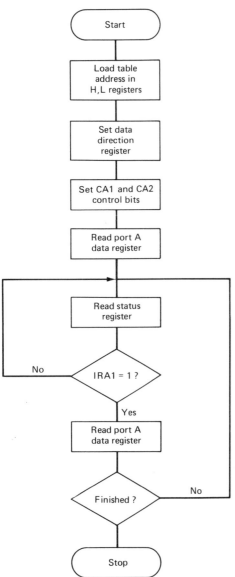

Figure 5.7   Paper tape reader program flow diagram

for the handshake signals, and set the data direction register. This is usually referred to as the *initialisation* stage. The second part of the program is concerned with reading the actual data words from the I/O port.

The microprocessor can test to see if data is available by reading the status register of the PIO. Remember that the transition of CA1 will set IRA1, bit 7 of the control register. When this is set to a 1, data is available; if the bit is a 0, data has not yet been transferred. Interogating the control register in this way is called *polling* the interface.

A simple way to test bit 7 is to read the contents of the control register into the accumulator, then AND it with 80 (hex). The result will be zero if the IRA1 bit was not set, or non-zero if it was.

A flow diagram for the program is shown in Figure 5.7. The program has been written for a memory-mapped system in which the PIO uses addresses 1000 to 1003 (hex). When each data byte is read, it is stored in a table area of memory.

The first few lines of the program are used to equate the addresses of the registers with labels. This makes it much easier to read and understand the program. Next the table address is loaded into the H,L registers.

The control and data direction registers are set by storing hex constants into the appropriate memory locations. Notice that the control register is set to zero first; this ensures that we can load the data direction register with the appropriate codeword.

In order to start the reader we must force the microprocessor to read the data register, even though there will be no data. Remember that the motor in the reader is tied to the CA2 line and this is set to the active state after a read by the microprocessor.

The remainder of the program is a simple loop to read a number of characters from the reader. Normally a fixed number of characters would be read and then the reader halted, otherwise incoming characters could overwrite other parts of the current program.

5.10   Serial data transfers

Perhaps the commonest example of a serial data transmission system is the standard teletype or VDU used as a console for a microcomputer system. The basic purpose of such an interface is the transfer of single characters.

Such characters can be coded in many ways, but the most frequently encountered code is the ASCII code (ASCII stands for American Standard Code for Information Interchange). This code uses 7 bits to

Table 5.5 *ASCII code*

Even parity bit	7-bit octal code	Char.	Even. parity bit	7-bit octal code	Char.	Even parity bit	7-bit octal code	Char.
0	000	NUL	0	053	+	0	126	V
1	001	SOH	1	054	,	1	127	W
1	002	STX	0	055	–	1	130	X
0	003	ETX	0	056	.	0	131	Y
1	004	EOT	1	057	/	0	132	Z
0	005	ENQ	0	060	∅	1	133	[
0	006	ACK	1	061	1	0	134	\
1	007	BEL	1	062	2	1	135	]
1	010	BS	0	063	3	1	136	↑
0	011	HT	1	064	4	0	137	←
0	012	LF	0	065	5	0	140	`
1	013	VT	0	066	6	1	141	a
0	014	FF	1	067	7	1	142	b
1	015	CR	1	070	8	0	143	c
1	016	SO	0	071	9	1	144	d
0	017	SI	0	072	:	0	145	e
1	020	DLE	1	073	;	0	146	f
0	021	DC1	0	074	<	1	147	g
0	022	DC2	1	075	=	1	150	h
1	023	DC3	1	076	>	0	151	i
0	024	DC4	0	077	?	0	152	j
1	025	NAK	1	100	@	1	153	k
1	026	SYN	0	101	A	0	154	l
0	027	ETB	0	102	B	1	155	m
0	030	CAN	1	103	C	1	156	n
1	031	EM	0	104	D	0	157	o
1	032	SUB	1	105	E	1	160	p
0	033	ESC	1	106	F	0	161	q
1	034	FS	0	107	G	0	162	r
0	035	GS	0	110	H	1	163	s
0	036	RS	1	111	I	0	164	t
1	037	US	1	112	J	1	165	u
1	040	SP	0	113	K	1	166	v
0	041	!	1	114	L	0	167	w
0	042	"	0	115	M	0	170	x
1	043	#	0	116	N	1	171	y
0	044	$	1	117	O	1	172	z
1	045	%	0	120	P	0	173	{
1	046	&	1	121	Q	1	174		
0	047	'	1	122	R	0	175	}
0	050	(	0	123	S	0	176	~
1	051	)	1	124	T	1	177	DEL
1	052	*	0	125	U			

represent 96 printing characters, letters, numbers and punctuation marks, plus 32 non-printing characters such as backspace, carriage return, etc. Table 5.5 shows the ASCII codes for all the characters, from which you can see that the character 'A' has the codeword 1000001.

When the characters are transmitted in serial fashion along a single pair of wires, the voltage waveform looks like that shown in Figure 5.8. By convention the least significant bit is always transmitted first and the most significant last. The whole sequence of bits is called a *bit stream*.

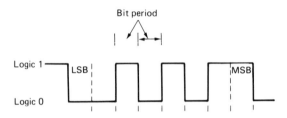

Figure 5.8

The voltage level representing the bit is held on the line for a fixed time interval called the *bit period*, as indicated in Figure 5.8.

The main problem when designing serial interfaces is to ensure that the receiver can interpret the bits in the stream correctly, that is as least significant, most significant bit, etc. If the receiver cannot do this then the characters sent will be misread.

Methods for solving the first problem have led to two types of serial data transmission, *synchronous* and *asynchronous* data transfers, but we will only examine the latter.

Asynchronous data transmission

In the case of asynchronous transmission characters are sent one at a time as and when required. During intervals of no data, the signal line is held in the logic high state, referred to as *marking*.

In order to help the receiver determine when a character has been sent, the bit stream for each character is preceded by a *start bit*. A start bit is defined as a change from the inactive marking state to a low logic level with the low level held for one bit period. What is important is the transition from high to low level, because the receiver can use this to sense the start of a new character.

Of course, such transitions will occur within a bit stream and so the receiver must be able to distinguish between the start bit and any other transition. It does this by detecting the first transition and then counting bit periods until all the bits of the character have been received. Once a complete character has been read it waits for the next transition.

To ensure there is a high-to-low transition at the beginning of each new character, every character is terminated by a *stop bit*. This last bit is always a logic high level.

At the beginning of each character the receiver must detect the change in state, from high to low, caused by the start bit, and then proceeds to sample the bit stream to recover the character. The sampling process works as follows. After the start transition has been detected, the receiver waits half a bit period and then tests the input signal line. If the level is high the receiver will not recognise a start bit because the start bit must be low for at least 1 bit period.

If the level was low the receiver recognises the start of a character. After one bit interval the receiver again tests the level on the input line to determine the value of the first bit of the codeword. The process continues with a one bit period delay between each test of the input until all the bits of the character have been recovered. The initial half bit delay is used to ensure that the receiver tests the input at approximately the midpoint of each bit period of the stream, rather than at either end where transitions may occur.

Transmission speeds

The detection scheme described above requires that the transmitter and the receiver work with a common bit period. This is usually achieved by using a fixed frequency clock at the two ends of the transmission line to control the bit periods of the data stream. The higher the clock frequency, the faster characters can be transmitted.

The speed will depend upon the particular job. For example, a keyboard input need not be very fast because people cannot type quickly, whilst a display system for presenting information to a reader may need a high transmission speed. Over the years several speeds have been standardised. Some date from the time when all typewriters were mechanical and slow, but more recently VDUs have encouraged the adoption of very high transmission speeds.

Table 5.6 lists the most commonly encountered speeds; they vary from 110 bits per second to 19,200 bits per second. Also listed are the number of stop bits used at each speed. The slowest speed uses two stop bits, another remnant of an older, mechanically based technology.

Table 5.6 *Serial transmission speed*

Bits per second	Characters per second	Stop bits
110	10	2
300	30	1
600	60	1
1,200	120	1
2,400	240	1
4,800	480	1
9,600	960	1
19,200	1,920	1

Parity bit

In addition to the start and stop bits, many systems add a *parity bit* to the data bits. This parity bit is used to detect transmission errors in the bit stream for each character. It works as follows. The number of 1's in the data word are counted and the value of the parity bit is set so as to make the total number of 1's (including the parity bit) either even (even parity) or odd (odd parity). When the receiver decodes the bit stream it calculates its own parity bit by counting the number of 1's received, and if this does not agree with the parity received, the receiver flags an error. Unfortunately the parity bit cannot be used for error correction.

Figure 5.9 shows the bit stream for the character 'A' complete with start, one stop and even parity bit.

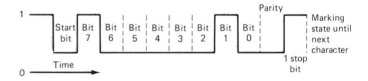

Figure 5.9 Bit stream for ASCII character A

5.11 The ACIA

Designing circuitry to implement serial data transfers can be very time-consuming. This, together with the fact that they are required in vast quantities, has encouraged the manufacturers of micro-processors to produce special-purpose chips that fulfill all the functions of asynchronous transmission.

Figure 5.10 shows a block diagram of the Intel 8251 Programmable

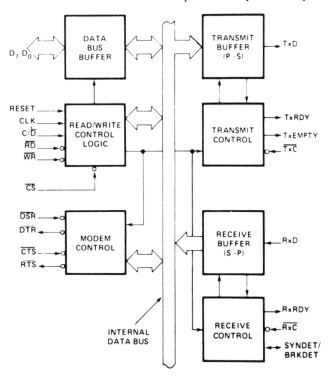

Figure 5.10 Block diagram of the Intel 8251A Programmable Communication Interface

Universal Synchronous/Asynchronous Receiver/Transmitter (USART). The device contains separate receiving and transmitting sections as well as modem control signals and read/write control logic. There are four registers: Command, Status, Transmit Data and Receive Data.

The command register

Transferring data from a microprocessor to a peripheral is not a very Different bits set the transmission speed, the parity (even, odd or none), the number of bits in the data word and the number of stop bits.

To initialise the device requires two, three or four command words to be transmitted from the microprocessor. In the case of asynchronous transmission only two words need be sent. The first of these sets the mode and the transmission parameters. The second is used to enable the transmission and reception of data, reset the data error flags and control one of the modem signals.

Status register

The status register maintains information about the current operational status of the device. When bit 0 goes high the transmit register is empty and a new character can be sent for transmission. Bit 1 high indicates that a complete character has been received and can be read from the receiver data register. Other bits indicate errors in the received character, such as a parity error, and bit 7 is used to indicate the state of one of the modem signals.

Transmit and receive data registers

These two registers are used to hold data either before transmission or after reception.

Programming the USART for asynchronous transmission

As in the case of the PIO, the program for the USART can be divided into an initialisation stage and a data transfer stage. During the initialisation stage two command words must be sent, the first to set the transmission parameters and the second to enable the start of transmission and reset the error flags.

5.12   Input and output on a real microprocessor

Outputting data to a peripheral

Transferring data from a microprocessor to a peripheral is not a very complicated task, provided the right approach is adopted. To begin with we must know how the system is configured and what type of PIO is used. Once the following questions have been answered we should have all the necessary information.

1   Is the system configured for memory-mapped or accumulator I/O?
2   What address/port numbers are to be used for the registers in the PIO?
3   Which address/port is to be used for the output?
4   What codeword must be sent to the control register to set this port for output?
5   How many bits of the port will be used?
6   What handshake signals are required for the peripheral?
7   Which bits of the status register are used by the port?

With this information it should be possible to draw up a flow diagram for the output program. The program will fall into two parts. The first part will be the initialisation stage to set up the control and the data direction registers. This stage is only required once, no matter how many data words are to be transferred to the peripheral, unless the contents of these registers are changed.

For example, the first use of the PIO might be to set port A to all outputs and ignore the other port. Later in the program this second port can be brought into use by sending a new codeword to the control register. If port A is to stay active, then this new codeword must not change the bits that effect the operation of port A.

The second stage of the program is used for the actual data transfer. The data can be sent with the appropriate instruction and then the status register examined to determine when the next value can be sent.

The flow diagram for such a program will look very similar to that of Figure 5.7, except that the read port block will be replaced by a write port block.

The PIO on the Hektor peripheral board

The peripheral board of the Hektor microcomputer system utilises a single Intel 8155 device which, as well as functioning as a PIO, also contains 256 bytes of RAM and a timer. The three ports, A, B and C are configured for accumulator I/O and do not use separate data direction registers. Instead the direction of each of the ports is determined by the four least significant bits of the control register as shown in Table 5.7. This arrangement means that all the bits of the port must transfer data in the same direction.

The code numbers assigned to each of these ports is shown in Table 5.8. Note that two extra ports are allocated for the timer, but this feature will not be described until Chapter 7.

Table 5.7 *Control of I/O port directionally*

Binary contents of control register	*Port A direction*	*Port B direction*	*Port C direction*
XXXX0000	Input	Input	Input
XXXX0001	Output	Input	Input
XXXX0010	Input	Output	Input
XXXX0011	Output	Output	Input
XXXX01XX		Specialised use of I/O ports	
XXXX10XX		(unused in this application)	
XXXX1100	Input	Input	Output
XXXX1101	Output	Input	Output
XXXX1110	Input	Output	Output
XXXX1111	Output	Output	Output

Table 5.8 *8155 port assignment*

Control register	40H
Port A	41H
Port B	42H
Port C	43H
Timer 1	44H low-order byte
Timer 2	45H high-order byte

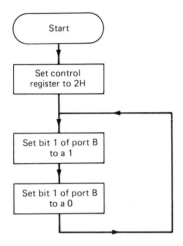

Figure 5.11 Flow diagram for flashing LED program

An example of outputting data on Hektor

The four least significant output bits of the B port of the PIO are each connected to a light-emitting diode (LED). If a 1 is sent to any of these bits the LED will light up, whilst a 0 will turn it off.

A simple example of an output program is one that will turn one of these LEDs on and off, such as might be used in a warning indicator. A suitable flow diagram is shown in Figure 5.11. The first stage is to configure port B for output by loading the control register with 02 (hex); the state of the other two ports can be ignored. The remainder of the program consists of a loop that continuously sets bit 1 of port B to a 1 and then back to 0.

The actual code is given in Figure 5.12. Note that the port numbers have been equated with labels to simplify the writing of the program, and the ORG assembler directive has been used to ensure that the program starts at location 3800 (hex).

The END assembler directive is used to inform the assembler that there are no more instructions in the program. The Hektor assembler allows the END directive to have a label argument, in this case START.

When the program is assembled, the memory address of this label is put into the program counter of the microprocessor, so that to run the program all you have to do is type 'G'. This feature is described in greater detail in the User Manual.

If you type in this program and run it you will find that the LED goes on and stays on. There is nothing wrong with the program, it's just that the LED is flashing on and off so rapidly that it appears to be on all the time. A time delay loop can be used to slow down the switching rate as shown in Figure 5.13. This program uses the CALL instruction to jump to a delay subroutine.

Changing the value stored in location FLASH will alter the flashing rate of the LED.

An example of an input program on Hektor

The four switches adjacent to the LEDs of the peripheral board are

```
CREG:   EQU   40H     ;Define control register port
PORTB:  EQU   42H     ;Define port B data register
        ORG   3800H   ;Set program start address
START:  MVI   02H     ;Load accumulator with 02H
        OUT   CREG    ;Load control register with 02H
LOOP:   MVI   A,01H   ;Load accumulator with 01H
        OUT   PORTB   ;Load port B with 01H, which will turn on LED
        MVI   A,00H   ;Load port B with 00H
        OUT   PORTB   ;To turn off LED
        JMP   LOOP    ;Go back and repeat the cycle
        END   START   ;End of program
```

Figure 5.12   Flashing LED program

```
CREG:   EQU   40H     ;Define control register
PORTB:  EQU   42H     ;Define port B
        ORG   3800H   ;Define starting address
FLASH:  DB    4FH     ;Set delay time
START:  MVI   A,02H
        OUT   CREG
LOOP:   MVI   A,01H
        OUT   PORTB
        CALL  DELAY   ;Jump to delay subroutine
        MVI   A,00H
        OUT   PORTB
        CALL  DELAY   ;Jump to delay subroutine
        JMP   LOOP
DELAY:  LDA   FLASH   ;Load time count into the accumulator
DEL1:   MVI   B,FFH   ;Set register to FFH
DEL2:   DCR   B       ;Decrement register B
        JNZ   DEL2    ;If register B = 0, go to next instruction,
                      ;if not go to DEL2
        DCR   A       ;Decrement the accumulator
        JNZ   DEL1    ;If the accumulator = 0, go to next
                      ;instruction, if not go to DEL1
        RET           ;Return to the main program
        END   START   ;End of program
```

Figure 5.13   Flashing LED program with delay subroutine

connected to the four least significant bits of the port C data register of the PIO, and so can be used as a simple input device. The following example reads these switches and displays the pattern on the LEDs.

A flow diagram for the program (Figure 5.14) is given in Figure 5.15. In order to set port C for input and port B for output, the control register must be set to 2H or 3H, as indicated in Table 5.7. This

```
CREG:    EQU   40H      ;Define the control register
PORTB:   EQU   42H      ;Define port B data register
PORTC:   EQU   43H      ;Define port C data register
         ORG   3800H    ;Define starting address
START:   MVI   A,02H    ;Load accumulator with 02H
         OUT   CREG     ;Set control register to 02H
LOOP:    IN    PORTC    ;Read switch pattern from port C data register
         OUT   PORTB    ;Send switch pattern to the LEDs on the outputs
                        ;of the port B data register
         JMP   LOOP     ;Repeat the cycle
         END   START    ;End of program
```

Figure 5.14　Switch input and display program

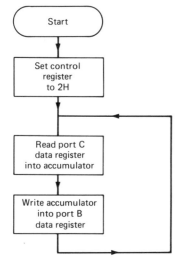

Figure 5.15　Flow diagram for input and output example program

routine does not use the delay subroutine, since the LEDs will only change as rapidly as you can change the switches.

5.13　Summary

1　An interface is an electronic circuit that enables the transfer of data between a microprocessor and a peripheral.

2　A memory-mapped I/O scheme treats every peripheral as a group of memory locations. Data transfers are accomplished using the normal memory reference instructions of the microprocessor.

3　An accumulator I/O scheme requires each peripheral to be assigned a unique set of code numbers that form part of the data transfer instruction. A special set of instructions are required for the data transfers, some for input and some for output.

4　Parallel data transfers send a single codeword to a peripheral in one step along a set of parallel wires. Serial data transfers send a codeword to a peripheral one bit at a time along a single pair of wires.

5　Handshake signals are used to control the timing of the flow of data between an interface and its peripheral.

6　A PIO is a special integrated circuit used in the design of a parallel data transfer interface. The exact mode of operation of such a device is determined by codewords transmitted to special internal registers. The PIO contains several such registers for storing data status and control information.

7　A USART is a special integrated circuit used in the design of serial data transfer interfaces. The device is programmed by a sequence of commands sent by the microprocessor. The USART contains registers for storing data, commands and status information.

Questions

5.1 What factors would you consider when deciding between a parallel or a serial data transmission system?

5.2 Describe the function of the control, data direction and data registers in the Motorola 6820 PIO.

5.3 What are the advantages of a memory-mapped I/O system?

5.4 Why are handshake signals used between an interface and its peripheral?

Chapter 6 Analogue-to-digital and digital-to-analogue converters

Objectives of this chapter *When you have completed studying this chapter you should be able to:*

1 Describe the function of ADCs and DACs.
2 Draw a block diagram of a DAC interface.
3 Draw a block diagram of an ADC interface.
4 Describe the basic operation of one type of ADC.
5 Describe how the polling method of data transfer can be used with several converters.

6.1 Introduction

The aim of this chapter is to introduce you to the devices that enable a microprocessor to monitor and control our everyday environment. I intend to describe the types of devices that can be used and to discuss the most important parameters to examine when selecting a device for a particular application from the many currently available. The chapter falls into two main parts. First there is the design and selection of the hardware and second there is the software, or program, that must be written to control the device.

6.2 The function of conversion devices

A common application of microcomputers is in the control and monitoring of machinery using a variety of sensors called *transducers*. These devices can convert quantities like temperature, flow rate and pressure into electrical voltages, or convert voltages into quantities such as movement or sound. If the output voltage from a transducer varies continuously over a range it is known as an analogue voltage. Unfortunately the microcomputer can only work with digital information in the form of two distinct voltages, so we need some sort of device that will enable us to convert from one form of signal representation to the other.

Such devices do exist: those that convert transducer signals to computer codewords are called *analogue-to-digital converters*, while those that convert a codeword to a voltage are called *digital-to-analogue converters*. (These are normally abbreviated to A/D converter and D/A converter, respectively, or even briefer, ADC and DAC.)

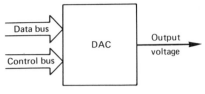

Figure 6.1 Block diagram of DAC

Table 6.1

Input codeword (Binary)	Output voltage/V
0000	0
0001	0.25
0010	0.5
0011	0.75
0100	1.0
0101	1.25
0110	1.5
0111	1.75
1000	2.0
1001	2.25
1010	2.5
1011	2.75
1100	3.0
1101	3.25
1110	3.5
1111	3.75

6.3 Operation of a DAC

First I shall describe the operation of a typical DAC such as that shown in the block diagram of Figure 6.1. The input comes from the data bus and the output goes to an appropriate transducer. The control bus provides the appropriate read/write and timing signals. For each input codeword the device generates a single-valued output voltage, so for an 8-bit input it can generate 256 unique voltage levels.

Although not a true analogue output, remember I said that the quantities that we measure vary continuously, the approximation is good enough for most purposes. If necessary I can increase the number of voltage levels by using more bits in the input codeword.

How many voltage levels can be generated by a 12-bit converter?

A 12-bit codeword can represent 2^{12} states, so in the case of a converter that means 4,096 unique voltage levels. Using these levels to represent an analogue voltage involves the process known as *quantisation*.

Table 6.1 shows one possible relationship between the input codewords and the output voltage for a 4-bit converter. From this table we see that when all the bits are 0 the output is 0 V. The least significant bit, or bit 0, generates an output of 0.25 V. Bit 1 generates an output of 0.5 V, which is twice that of bit 0. Bit 2 generates an output of 1.0 V, which is four times that of bit 0, and bit 3 gives 2.0 V, eight times bit 0. There is the same binary relationship in the output voltage as there is in the bits of the codeword.

If more than one bit is set in the codeword, the output voltage is just the sum of the voltages generated by each bit. For example the codeword 1110 gives an output of 3.5 V, which is equal to $2 + 1 + 0.5$ V.

Effects of quantisation

The 16 possible values of the 4-bit DAC output voltage are called the *quantisation levels* and the difference in voltage between any two adjacent quantisation levels is termed the *quantisation interval*. The quantisation interval is also equal to the voltage output generated by the least significant bit of the input codeword.

Suppose we wanted to generate the sawtooth waveform shown in Figure 6.2(a) to control an actuator. As a first approximation I could try to use the output voltage from the 4-bit converter of Table 6.1, which would produce the waveform shown in Figure 6.2(b), but how good an approximation is it?

Figure 6.3(a) shows a short portion of the two waveforms to a much larger scale. You can see that during the interval t_1–t_2 the sawtooth

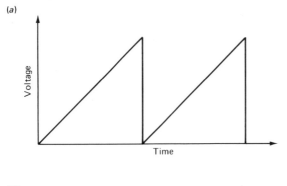

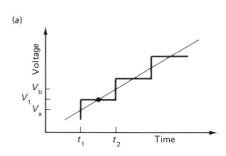

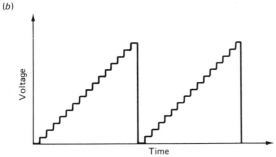

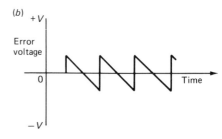

Figure 6.2   Sawtooth waveforms: *(a)* analogue; *(b)* digital

Figure 6.3   Output voltage error due to quantisation

waveform increases uniformly from V_a to V_b but the DAC converter output is constant at V_1. The two waveforms are therefore equal at only one instant during the interval t_1-t_2. This is because the smallest increment in the DAC output is equal to the quantisation interval. In terms of our approximation this difference produces an error, known as the *quantisation error*.

We can see the effects of this error by subtracting the sawtooth from the approximation as shown in Figure 6.3(b). The error voltage alternates about 0 V and has a peak-to-peak value equal to the quantisation interval. We can think of the DAC output as being made up of two parts. The first is the sawtooth waveform we want to generate and the second part is the quantisation error which we do not want. Unwanted signals like this are usually referred to as noise, and since this noise is caused by quantisation, it is called *quantisation noise*.

The magnitude of the quantisation noise can be reduced by increasing the number of bits in the input codeword, since this will reduce the quantisation interval. However, no matter how many bits are used there will always be some error due to the quantisation process.

An alternative measure of the quantisation effects can be found from the *dynamic range* of the converter. This is defined as

$$20 \log_{10} \text{ (full scale/quantisation interval)}$$

and indicates the difference between the smallest non-zero and the largest output voltages that can be generated by the converter. A simple rule of thumb to remember is that each bit of the input codeword adds 6 dB to the dynamic range.

Time response

When the input codeword to the DAC changes, it takes a short but finite time for the output voltage to reach the value represented by that codeword. This delay is caused by the electronic components used in the construction of the converter and the details need not concern us here. However, it is important that you appreciate that such a delay exists. Manufacturers specify this delay in terms of the *settling time*, and often quote it in the form of the time required for the output to settle within half the least significant bit, or half the quantisation interval. Using the example from Table 6.1 and assuming a settling time of 1 ms, when the input codeword changes from 0000 to 1000 the output would be guaranteed to reach a value between 1.875 and 2.125 V within 1 ms.

Bipolar converters

The 4-bit converter used as an example for Table 6.1 only generated positive output voltages. Any converter that generates an output of only one polarity, be it positive or negative, is called a *unipolar converter*. Occasionally we will need to generate outputs of either polarity with a single converter. Converters that can do this are referred to as *bipolar*.

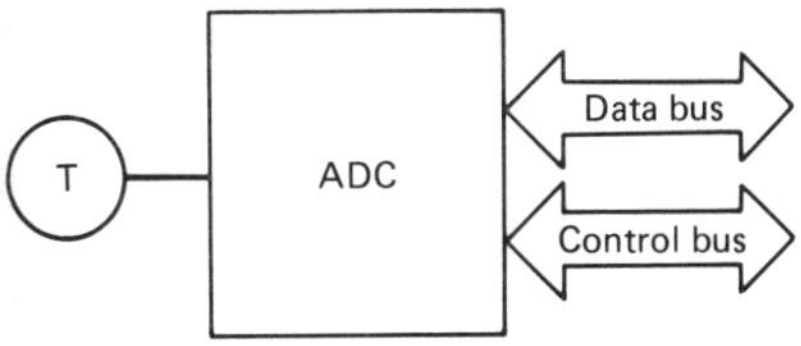

6.4 Operation of an ADC

The basic function of an ADC is to convert an analogue voltage into a binary codeword that can be manipulated by a microcomputer. A simplified block diagram is shown in Figure 6.4. The output voltage from the transducer provides the input to the converter and the binary codeword, or data word, representing that voltage goes onto the data bus. The control bus provides the appropriate read/write and timing signals.

Figure 6.4 Block diagram of ADC

There are several ways of performing the conversion, but most devices do it by comparing the analogue input to a digitally generated voltage. In fact many ADCs do this using an internal DAC. The idea is similar to using a set of balance scales. On one side is the object we want to weigh, equivalent to the unknown input voltage. On the other side of the scales we place a series of known weights of varying size, equivalent to the output of the DAC. The weight of the object is calculated from the sum of weights on the scales when balanced, whilst the voltage is found by reading the codeword that caused the DAC to generate a voltage equivalent to the input voltage.

This whole comparison process is carried out automatically by the converter; there is no need for special programs. All we do is tell the converter to start and wait for it to indicate it has finished.

Obviously in the case of the scales the weight of the object does not vary with time, but the input voltage from a transducer will change as the parameter being measured changes. To overcome this problem the input voltage is *sampled*, i.e. instead of trying to convert the voltage at all possible instants of time, only a few values are taken at uniformly spaced time intervals.

This idea may seem a bit strange, but it can be shown using some mathematics that such samples retain all the essential information contained in the full analogue waveform, provided we take sufficient of them.

There is a simple rule that tells us how frequently a signal must be sampled in order to retain all the information. It is called the *Sampling Rule*. It says that the *sampling rate*, or the number of samples taken per second, must be at least twice that of the bandwidth of the signal.

What is the minimum sampling rate that can be used for a signal with a bandwidth of 5.6 kHz? The sampling rule states that this signal must be sampled at a minimum rate of 11.2 kHz. In practice it is normal to sample at a much faster rate – up to 6 times the bandwidth in some cases.

The actual sampling is carried out by a special device called a *Sample and Hold*. It stores the value of the waveform as a d.c. voltage whilst the ADC completes the conversion.

Alternative types of ADC

ADCs come in various forms, some offering very rapid conversion, others low cost. The two most important types you should remember are *(a)* the *Successive Approximation* and *(b)* the *Dual Slope Integration* converters. The first of these is very fast and gives a conversion time that is independent of the input voltage amplitude, whilst the second provides medium speed with good accuracy.

The successive approximation converter

This converter derives its name from the way the conversion process is carried out, which involves making a series of guesses at the value of the input voltage. Once again the process is carried out by the

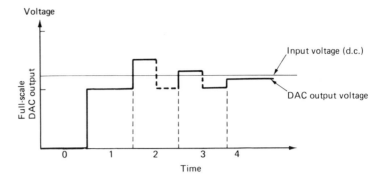

Figure 6.5 Timing diagram for a successive approximation ADC

converter, not the programmer. Figure 6.5 illustrates the conversion for a 4-bit converter. The input voltage is represented by the d.c. voltage stored on the sample and hold.

Since there are four bits in the converter, there are four guesses at the input voltage. Before the guessing process is started the DAC output voltage is set to zero. The first guess is made during interval 1, by comparing the input voltage with the output voltage generated by the most significant bit of the DAC. This is done internally by setting the codeword to 1000, which causes the output to swing to 0.5 of full scale. If the input is greater than this, then the output of the DAC must be increased by setting more of the bits of the input codeword. During interval 2 a second guess is made by adding the voltage generated by the next most significant bit. The DAC output voltage now equals 0.75 of full scale. This is greater than the input voltage, so the next most significant bit is reset to 0.

The third guess is made during interval 3 by setting bit 2 of the codeword, which, together with the most significant bit, sets the output to 0.625 of full scale. This is also greater than the input so bit 2 is reset to 0. The last guess sets bit 1 and so the output becomes 0.5625 of full scale.

The last guess made has produced a DAC output voltage which is just less than the input voltage, so there will be a small error in the measurement. This is due to the quantisation effects of the DAC. Of course, if there were more bits there would be more guesses and so we could obtain a more accurate measurement.

A flow diagram for this algorithm is shown in Figure 6.6. The binary representation of the input voltage is obtained by reading the input register of the DAC after all the bits have been tested.

The dual-slope integration converter

The second way of performing the conversion process is analogue

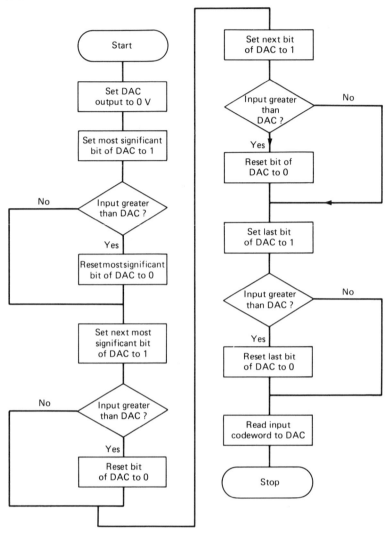

Figure 6.6   Flow diagram for successive approximation converter algorithm

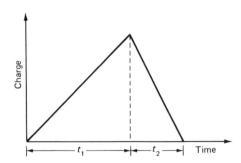

Figure 6.7   Capacitor charge variation for a dual slope integration ADC

integration. Measuring the time it takes for a capacitor to charge to the unknown voltage and to discharge under a known reference voltage forms the basis of this method.

Figure 6.7 shows a graph of charge versus time during a conversion cycle. During interval t_1 the capacitor is charged to the input voltage. During the interval t_1–t_2 the capacitor is discharged by the reference voltage. The ratio of these two intervals is directly proportional to the input voltage. This technique is very accurate because errors due to noise on the input are minimised by the integration process. However the process is rather slow.

Binary coded decimal converters

So far I have only mentioned converters that use binary coding. However, it is possible to buy devices that use alternative coding schemes, and of special importance are those that use binary coded decimal (or BCD) coding.

In this scheme four binary bits are used to represent the decimal numbers from 0 to 9 as shown in Table 6.2. The binary codes from 1010 to 1111 are never used in this coding scheme.

An 8-bit data word can store two BCD digits, so that the number 77 (decimal) would be stored as 01110111. If you treat this codeword as normal binary, you find the result equals 119 (decimal) not 77. To avoid such confusion, think of an imaginary line separating each group of 4 bits, which prevents adding one group to the next until they have been converted to decimal numbers. Once converted the digits are interpreted as tens and units in the normal way for decimal numbers.

What is the value of the BCD codeword 01100010?

The left-hand 4 bits equals 6, and the right-hand 4 bits equals 2, so the number is 62 (decimal).

BCD coding can be extended to any number of bits. For example 12 bits can be used to represent 3 digits which are interpreted as hundreds, tens and units. The coding scheme is particularly useful in cases where data is to be displayed for reading.

The internal workings of a BCD converter follow the same pattern as binary devices, but there are a few new terms to remember. Firstly instead of talking about an *n*-bit converter we use the term *n* digits, each capable of displaying a denary number in the range 0 to 9. For example a 3-digit converter can represent all the numbers from 0 to 999. Often you will see devices referred to as 3 1/2 digits. This means that there is one extra digit that can represent either 0 or 1 but not the full 0 to 9. A 3 1/2 digit converter can represent all the numbers between 0 and 1999.

Table 6.2 *BCD coding*

Binary number	Decimal number
0000	0
0001	1
0010	2
0011	3
0100	4
0101	5
0110	6
0111	7
1000	8
1001	9

How would you determine the resolution of a BCD converter? The resolution of a BCD converter can be determined once we know the number of digits; because that tells us how many codewords exist. The resolution of the 3-digit converter is one part in 1,000 because it can represent all the numbers between 0 and 999.

Specifying the ADC

The very large numbers of converters available can overwhelm most designers when trying to select a device for a particular application, especially as the manufacturers use different terms to specify a particular property of a converter. As an aid to the selection process a few of the most important considerations are examined below.

Analogue input range defines the range of input voltages that can be applied to the converter if the device is to function within the specified limits. In many cases the transducer output will be less than this and so must be amplified before conversion. If it is not some of the quantisation levels will not be used and the effective dynamic range of the converter will be reduced.

Conversion rate defines how many voltage samples can be converted each second. The reciprocal of the conversion rate is the conversion time.

Resolution defines the number of unique voltage levels that can be distinguished by a converter. In theory the resolution is 1 part in 2^n, where n is the number of bits, hence a 12-bit converter has a resolution of 1 part in 4,096, because $2^{12} = 4,096$. However, the resolution over the full working temperature range may be less because of temperature drift.

Accuracy is defined as the difference between the analogue input voltage theoretically required to produce a given codeword and the actual input that produces that codeword.

Q6.1–6.4

6.5   Connecting a converter to the micro

In the previous chapter I introduced the PIO as a general purpose interface device for parallel data transfers between the micro and a peripheral. We can use this type of device for both the DACs and ADCs. Figure 6.8 shows a block diagram of a possible interface for a DAC. The M6820 decodes the peripheral address and transfers the data from the microprocessor to the DAC. Since the output from the DAC takes a short time to settle, the data transfer rate must be limited, either by incorporating a delay loop in the program, or by adding a few extra components to the interface. A very similar circuit

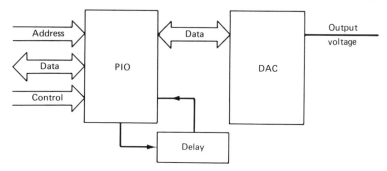

Figure 6.8 DAC interface

can be used for the ADC, but in this case we must provide an extra signal to tell the converter when to start a conversion cycle.

Although the DAC interface looks simple, there are quite a few inter-connections to be made between the individual devices. These inter-connections are expensive to make and can lead to operational faults. Nowadays it is possible to buy DACs specially designed to fit directly onto the microprocessor bus. Figure 6.9 shows a block diagram of one such device, which contains two separate converters. Comparable ADCs are also available.

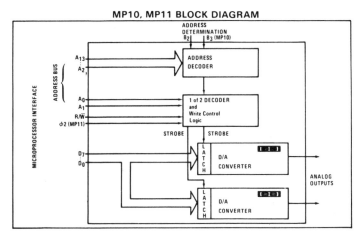

Figure 6.9

Programming a converter

So far I have concentrated on the hardware aspects of converter interfaces, now I want to examine some of the software problems by way of an example.

Let us assume that we need to measure and display the temperature of a liquid over the range 0 to 128 °C, with at least 1 °C resolution. If the

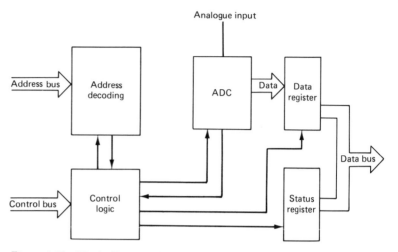

Figure 6.10   Block diagram of microprocessor-compatible ADC

temperature exceeds 100 °C the system must generate an audible alarm and stop measuring.

Since the system must resolve 1 part in 128, we need a converter with a minimum of 7 bits. However, no manufacturer makes 7-bit devices, so I will use an 8-bit device, of the type shown in Figure 6.10, which has a conversion time of 40 µs. The output voltage of the temperature transducer is scaled such that 1 °C equals the voltage of the second least significant bit, hence a temperature of 10 °C generates the binary codeword 00010100.

The selected ADC is memory-mapped and a conversion started by reading the data output register. At the end of the conversion cycle the least significant bit of the status register is set to a 1.

Figure 6.11 shows a suitable flow diagram for this task. The display and alarm functions utilise subroutines and do not form part of the main program. The first step is to start the converter, and then enter a test loop to see if the conversion is complete. When it is, the data word is read and the new temperature is compared to 99 °C. If greater the alarm is sounded, if less the value is displayed and the converter restarted. The assembler program to carry out this sequence is listed in Figure 6.12.

The example above is limited to reading and displaying data from one converter. In many real measurement systems we want to measure and display data from several converters. This can be done very simply by extending the existing program as shown in the flow diagram of Figure 6.13. In this case the first converter is started and when the conversion is completed the result is displayed, then the second converter is started and the result displayed. This technique can be extended to any number of converters.

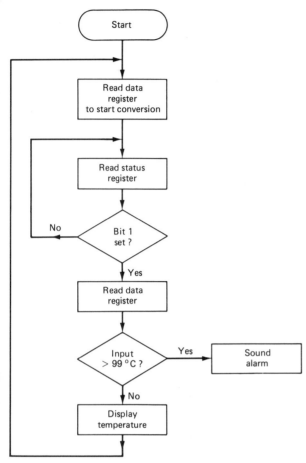

Figure 6.11 Flow diagram for the temperature monitoring program

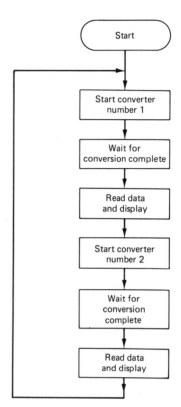

Figure 6.13 Flow diagram for a multiple ADC program

```
START:  MOV   A,80    ;Read data register to start conversion
WAIT:   MOV   A,81H   ;Read status register
        ANI   A,01H   ;Test if bit 1 set by ANDing with 01H
        JZ    WAIT    ;If result is zero then conversion is
                      ;incomplete, so wait
        CPI   63H     ;Test if input greater than 99°C
        JNC   ALRM    ;If carry = 0, temperature too hot so
                      ;sound alarm
        CALL  DISPL   ;Display temperature
        JMP   START   ;Start next conversion
```

Figure 6.12 Temperature monitoring assembler program

Although very simple this method is not the best, especially if the converters have different conversion times. In such cases the fast converter has to wait for the slow ones; this limits the maximum sampling rate. One solution is to duplicate the code for the fast converter in between the code for the slow converters, but a better one is to use the interupt capability of the microprocessor. However, I shall leave this until the next chapter where interrupts are discussed in detail.

6.6   Experimental examples

The Hektor DACs and ADCs

The Hektor peripheral board contains a single 8-bit DAC (device number ZN425E) which is connected to the port A data register. This converter differs slightly from those described earlier in the chapter in as much as it has two modes of operation.

The first mode is quite conventional. Any codeword appearing at the inputs is used to generate an analogue voltage. The range of output voltage is 0–4 V, corresponding to the codewords 00H and FFH, respectively. I will refer to this as the D/A mode of operation.

The second mode enables the converter to generate a sawtooth wave-form. Instead of using the port A data register to obtain input code-words, the DAC uses an internal binary counter. The output voltage increments from zero to maximum in small steps as shown in Figure 6.2(b).

The other important difference with this mode of operation is that the counter outputs are connected to the port A data register. If port A is configured as an input port, the counter outputs can be read by the microprocessor. The whole point of this mode is that the DAC, together with a few other components, can be used to implement an ADC. How this is achieved will be explained later.

Experiments with the DAC

The first experiment is one that will simply transfer a codeword from the microprocessor to the DAC to produce a d.c. output voltage. You can use a voltmeter, set to 5 V full scale, to measure the output, which appears on the pin marked DAOUT.

The initialisation stage of the program must configure the PIO port as follows:

Port A	output
Port B	output
Port C	don't care

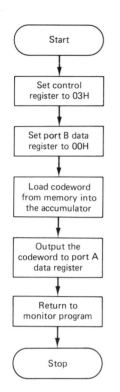

Figure 6.14 DAC test program flow diagram

This is achieved by setting the control register to 03H.

To enter the D/A mode, bit 6 of port B must be set to 0. The other bits have no effect, so the data register can be set to 00H. Once this is done any data word sent to port A will produce an output voltage.

Figure 6.14 shows a flow diagram for a suitable program. This program does not use the move immediate instruction (MVI) to load the accumulator with a data value to be transferred to port A, because to change the value requires that the program is reassembled. Instead the load accumulator instruction (LDA) is used to transfer the contents of location DAOUT into the accumulator for output to the port. Using this technique means that the D/A converter output codeword at 3800H can be changed with the monitor command M and no reassembly is required. The test program is listed in Figure 6.15.

The next experiment uses the DAC to generate a slowly increasing then decreasing output voltage. This voltage will be used to control the speed of the small motor on the peripheral board, by connecting the pin labelled DAOUT to the one labelled MOTIN.

The control register and port B data register are set as for the previous program.

The increasing voltage is obtained by setting the accumulator to zero and then incrementing it in a loop. On each pass through the loop the contents of the accumulator are sent to the DAC. When the accumulator equals 255, the increment loop is left and the decrement loop entered. The accumulator decrements to zero and then the program stops. A flow diagram for this example is shown in Figure 6.16 and the program is listed in Figure 6.17. If you type in this program and

```
CREG:   EQU   40H     ;Define control register
PORTA:  EQU   41H     ;Define port A data register
PORTB:  EQU   42H     ;Define port B data register
        ORG   3800H   ;Define starting address of program
DAOUT:  DB    00H     ;Reserve storage location for DAC codeword
START:  MVI   A,03H   ;Load accumulator with 03H
        OUT   CREG    ;Write command word into control register
        MVI   A,00H   ;Load accumulator with 00H
        OUT   PORTA   ;Set port B data register to 00H
        LDA   DAOUT   ;Load DAC codeword into accumulator
        OUT   PORTA   ;Write DAC codeword to port A data register
        JMP   57H     ;Return to monitor program
        END   START   ;End of program
```

Figure 6.15 DAC test program

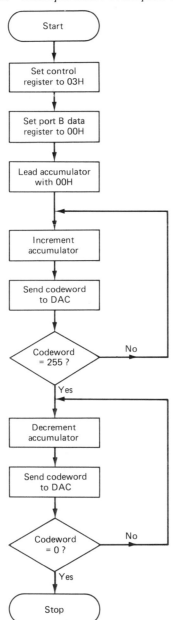

```
          ┌─────────────┐
          │    Start    │
          └─────────────┘
                 │
          ┌─────────────┐
          │ Set control │
          │register to 03H│
          └─────────────┘
                 │
          ┌─────────────┐
          │Set port B data│
          │register to 00H│
          └─────────────┘
                 │
          ┌─────────────┐
          │Lead accumulator│
          │  with 00H   │
          └─────────────┘
                 │
          ┌─────────────┐
          │ Increment   │
          │ accumulator │
          └─────────────┘
                 │
          ┌─────────────┐
          │Send codeword │
          │   to DAC    │
          └─────────────┘
                 │
          ╱ Codeword ╲    No
          ╲ = 255 ?  ╱──────
               │Yes
          ┌─────────────┐
          │ Decrement   │
          │ accumulator │
          └─────────────┘
                 │
          ┌─────────────┐
          │Send codeword │
          │   to DAC    │
          └─────────────┘
                 │
          ╱ Codeword ╲    No
          ╲  = 0 ?   ╱──────
               │Yes
          ┌─────────────┐
          │    Stop     │
          └─────────────┘
```

Figure 6.16   Flow diagram of motor speed control program

try to run it nothing appears to happen. Just like the flashing LED example of Chapter 5, things are changing too quickly. What we need is a short time delay after each of the OUT PORTA instructions.

The delay subroutine of Chapter 5 cannot be used, because this changes the contents of the accumulator. The subroutine given in Figure 6.18 uses register C instead of the accumulator, but otherwise is exactly the same. Changing the initial value of register C will alter the rate of change of motor speed. 2FH is a good starting value.

Operation of the ADC

The Hektor ADC is intended to demonstrate the principles of conversion and was not designed for high-speed sampling. As such it should only be used to measure either d.c. voltages or voltages derived from slowly changing quantities such as room temperature.

A block diagram of the converter is shown in Figure 6.19. Bit 6 of port B of the PIO is used to select the 'generate sawtooth' mode of the DAC as described earlier. Bit 7 of this port is initially set low to place the system into a 'ready to convert state' which holds the DAC output voltage at 0 V. This causes the output of the block labelled 'comparator', connected to bit 5 of port C, to change to a logic 0.

The signal to be measured is connected to the pin labelled ADIN1 and the DAC output is connected to the pin ADIN2.

The operation of the ADC is best explained with the aid of the timing diagram of Figure 6.20. To start the conversion, bit 7 of port B is changed from 0 to 1, which causes the DAC output to start increasing. At some point in time the DAC output will just exceed the analogue input voltage and this causes the output of the comparator to change from 0 to 1. The DAC output voltage stops increasing, because the change in state of the comparator stops the internal binary counter. Bit 5 of port C can therefore be used to indicate the end of a conversion cycle.

Since the binary counter outputs are connected to the port A inputs, the binary equivalent of the analogue input voltage can be obtained by reading the port A data register.

Before the next conversion can be started, bit 7 of port B must be reset to 0. Note that bit 6 of port B must always be held at a logic 1 for the ADC to function properly.

An experiment with the ADC

The following experiment uses the ADC to measure the d.c. voltage produced by the potential divider on the Hektor peripheral board. The results of the measurement are displayed on the TV screen using

```
CREG:    EQU   40H     ;Define PIO control register
PORTA:   EQU   41H     ;Define port A data register
PORTB:   EQU   42H     ;Define port B data register
         ORG   3800H   ;Define starting address of program
START:   MVI   A,03H   ;Load accumulator with 03H
         OUT   CREG    ;Write command word into control register
         MVI   A,00H   ;Load accumulator with 00H
         OUT   PORTB   ;Set port B data register to 00H
         MVI   A,00H   ;Load accumulator with 00H
LP1:     OUT   PORTA   ;Write codeword to DAC
         INR   A       ;Increment the accumulator
         CPI   0FFH    ;Compare accumulator with 255
         JNZ   LP1     ;If Z flag = 0, go to next instruction
                       ;If Z flag = 1, go to LP1
LP2:     OUT   PORTA   ;Write codeword to DAC
         DCR   A       ;Decrement the accumulator
         JNZ   LP2     ;If Z flag = 0, return to monitor
                       ;If Z flag = 1, repeat loop
         JMP   57H     ;Return to monitor program
         END   START   ;End of program
```

Figure 6.17

```
DELAY:   MVI   C,2FH   ;Set C register to 2FH
DEL1:    MVI   B,FFH   ;Set B register to FFH
DEL2:    DCR   B       ;Decrement B register
         JNZ   DEL2    ;If Z flag = 1, repeat inner loop
                       ;If Z flag = 0, exit inner loop
         DCR   C       ;Decrement C register
         JNZ   DEL1    ;If Z flag = 1, repeat enter loop
                       ;If Z flag = 0, exit delay subroutine
         RET           ;Return to main program from delay subroutine
```

Figure 6.18 Delay subroutine

two of the special subroutines provided as part of the Hektor monitor.

The initialisation part of the test program must configure the PIO ports as follows:

Port A   input
Port B   output
Port C   input

which is achieved by setting the command register to 02H. Bits 6 and

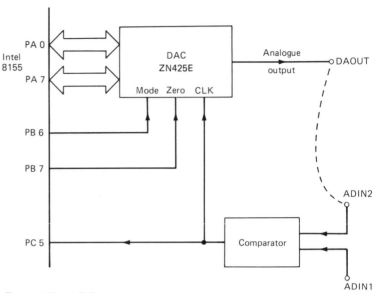

Figure 6.19   ADC block diagram

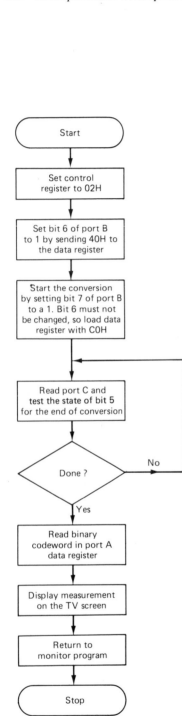

Figure 6.21   Flow diagram for ADC test program

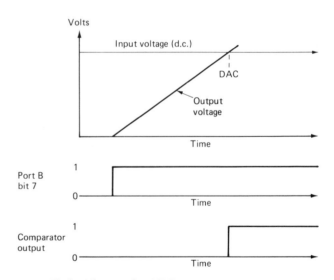

Figure 6.20   Timing diagram for ADC

7 of port B must be set to 1 and 0 respectively, before a conversion can commence.

A flow diagram for the program is given in Figure 6.21, and the listing is given in Figure 6.22. When the potential divider is turned to the limit in the anti-clockwise direction, the displayed result will be 30H. At the clockwise extreme it will be FA.

```
CREG:    EQU    40H      ;Define PIO control register
PORTA:   EQU    41H      ;Define port A data register
PORTB:   EQU    42H      ;Define port B data register
PORTC:   EQU    43H      ;Define port C data register
PRB:     EQU    035AH    ;Define print binary subroutine
PRNL:    EQU    02DAH    ;Define print new line sequence subroutine
         ORG    3800H    ;Define start of program
START:   MVI    A,02H    ;Load accumulator with 02H
         OUT    CREG     ;Write command word into control register
         MVI    A,40H    ;Load accumulator with 40H (bit 7 = 0,
                         ;bit 6 = 1)
         OUT    PORTB    ;Write data word to port B
         MVI    A,0C0H   ;Load accumulator with C0H (bits 7 and
                         ;6 = 1)
         OUT    PORTB    ;Write data word to port B
WAIT:    IN     PORTC    ;Read port C data register
         ANI    20H      ;Test if bit 5 = 1
         JZ     WAIT     ;No, so try again
         IN     PORTA    ;Conversion complete, so read port A
                         ;data register
         CALL   PRB      ;Print result as two hex digits
         CALL   PRNL     ;Print carriage return and line feed
         JMP    57H      ;Return to monitor program
         END    START    ;End of program
```

Figure 6.22   ADC test program

6.7 Summary

1   A DAC is a device that converts a binary codeword into an analogue voltage. The number of discrete voltage levels that can be generated is related to the number of bits in the codeword. For a binary converter it is 2^n where n is the number of bits.

2   An ADC is a device that converts an analogue voltage into a binary codeword. The number of codewords that can be generated equals 2^n where n is the number of bits in the codeword.

3   The resolution of a DAC or an ADC is defined by the number of unique voltage levels that can be generated or measured.

4   A DAC can be specified in terms of
    (a)   resolution;
    (b)   output voltage range;
    (c)   settling time;
    (d)   input codeword format (binary, BCD, etc.).

5 An ADC can be specified in terms of:
   (a) resolution;
   (b) dynamic range;
   (c) conversion time/conversion rate;
   (d) input voltage range;
   (e) output codeword format (binary, BCD, etc.).

Questions

6.1 Describe the function of DACs and ADCs.

6.2 Explain why quantisation errors arise in a successive approximation ADC.

6.3 What is the resolution and quantisation interval of a 10-bit DAC with a full scale output range of ± 10 V.

6.4 Explain how a dual-slope integration ADC functions.

Chapter 7 Interrupt I/O systems

Objectives of this chapter *When you have completed studying this chapter you should be able to:*

1 Define the terms 'polled interrupts' and 'vectored interrupts'.
2 Draw a flow diagram for a multiple interrupt service routine.
3 Explain the difference between non-maskable, software and I/O interrupts.
4 Describe the function of an interrupt priority scheme.
5 Explain the use of an interrupt mask register.

7.1 Introduction

The aim of this chapter is to introduce you to the ideas of interrupts, explain what they are and how they function. I will describe some of the advantages and disadvantages of interrupts and show how they can be implemented in a system with several I/O devices. The first half of the chapter examines polled interrupts, whilst the latter half looks at vectored interrupts and priority networks. The last section of the chapter is devoted to some programming examples.

7.2 The function of interrupts

In Chapter 5 we saw how the microprocessor can handle its data transfers with peripherals by polling (interrogating) the status register of a PIO or similar device. One of the major disadvantages of this system is the amount of time wasted by the microprocessor waiting for devices to complete the transfer. For example, a keyboard that can transmit 10 characters per second will set its DATA READY flag every tenth of a second. During this interval the microprocessor will read the status register several thousand times. Obviously this is very inefficient, but suppose another device needs attention, perhaps a faster device. This device may lose data because the microprocessor is busy with the keyboard.

An alternative scheme to polling is to provide each device with a special signal that when activated will cause the microprocessor to alter its sequence of operation. Such signals are called *interrupts*, and act like a telephone bell. When the bell rings you answer the phone, otherwise you ignore it. Polling, on the other hand is like picking up the phone every few minutes to see if anyone is there. The interrupt signal is connected to a special pin on the microprocessor chip called the interrupt input.

Using this scheme the microprocessor starts the data transfer by reading or writing to the peripheral interface and then continues processing existing data. When the device is ready for more data it sets the interrupt signal to inform the microprocessor to suspend the present program and send more data to the peripheral. This is called an *interrupt request*.

Figure 7.1 shows a timing diagram for the microprocessor activity using polling and interrupt data transfer schemes. In the case of polling considerable time is spent waiting for the peripherals to respond, whilst the interrupts waste little microprocessor time.

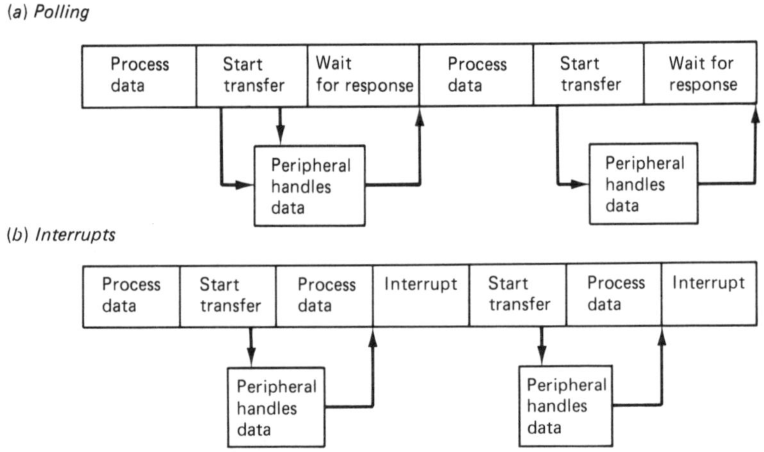

(a) Polling

(b) Interrupts

Figure 7.1 Microprocessor activity during polling and interrupt data transfers

The major disadvantage of interrupts is that because they can occur at any instant of time, it is very difficult to write and test the appropriate programs. Moreover, if there is more than one source of interrupt we need a means of organising and controlling the system to avert the potential chaos that can arise. However, to begin with let us examine the role of the microprocessor and peripheral interface in a single interrupt system.

7.3   The microprocessor's response to interrupts

In order to determine whether an interface is generating an interrupt, the microprocessor tests the state of the interrupt input line during every instruction executed. If the line is high, then the current instruction is completed before any response is made. The microprocessor then enters what is known as an *interrupt acknowledge* cycle, the nature of which depends upon the actual microprocessor.

The Motorola M6800 microprocessor always completes execution of the current instruction before responding to the interrupt request. It then loads the program counter register with the contents of memory locations FFF9H and FFF8H, to form the address of the next instruction to be executed.

This interrupt acknowledge is very simple and can be implemented without any additional hardware, but it does have certain limitations as will be shown later.

The Intel 8080 also completes execution of the current instruction, but it gets its next instruction from the interface itself. This instruction, similar to CALL, tells the microprocessor to start executing a new program sequence at a pre-defined address.

Whichever method is used, the new address obtained as a result of the interrupt acknowledge provides the starting location of a special piece of program that will respond to the needs of the peripheral interface. This program is called an *interrupt service routine*.

The interrupt acknowledge sequence and the interrupt service routine enable the microprocessor to respond rapidly to the needs of an individual peripheral, but once these needs have been satisfied how can the interrupted program sequence be continued?

The technique adopted by most of the microprocessors is to save the contents of all the registers and the program counter on the stack during the interrupt acknowledge cycle. At the end of the interrupt service routine all the registers and the program counter can be restored to the values they had before the interrupt occurred, by reading the values from the stack. Some micros provide a special RETURN FROM INTERRUPT instruction or use a RETURN FROM SUBROUTINE instruction to restore these values.

The 8080 microprocessor does not save any of the working registers onto the stack. The interrupt service routine must save any registers using the PUSH instruction and then restore them with the POP instruction.

7.4 Generating an interrupt signal from a PIO

The control register of the PIO described in Chapter 5 contained two data ready flags, IRA1 and IRA2. These bits of the register are set by the CA1 or CA2 lines. Bit 0 of the control register can be set to enable an interrupt from the PIO whenever the IRA1 bit it set. Bit 0 is called the interrupt enable bit, since if this bit is set by the program, an interrupt will be generated when the IRA1 flag is set. Bit 3 of the control register is the interrupt enable for the CA2 line. The PIO can generate two interrupt signals, one for the A port and one for the B port. These signals appear on two of the output pins of the PIO, which are connected to the interrupt input line of the microprocessor.

7.5   Multiple interrupts

Many microcomputer systems contain more than one device capable of requesting interrupt service from the microprocessor. This presents the programmer with two problems. The first is how to determine which device generated the interrupt, and the second is to determine what happens when an interrupt service routine is interrupted by another device. Let us look at the first of these problems in more detail.

Coping with multiple interrupt sources

When a device generates an interrupt request, one of the IRA/IRB flags of the PIO will be set. In order to determine which device interrupted, the interrupt service routine can read the control register flags of all the devices, until it finds one with an IRA/IRB bit set. This is similar to the normal polled data transfer technique and so is called *polled interrupts*. The main disadvantage of this method is that processor time is wasted testing devices that are not requesting service.

Vectored interrupts

To overcome this problem some microprocessors enable the peripheral to direct program flow to a particular memory address which is the start of their own special interrupt service routine. Such a system is said to possess *vectored interrupts*. Although this method gives a very rapid response to each peripheral, it does increase the complexity of the software and hence testing.

The 8080 microprocessor uses the RST (restart) instruction, a special version of the CALL instruction sequence, to implement vectored interrupts. During the interrupt acknowledge cycle, the interface hardware provides a 3-bit code that selects 1 of 8 possible service routine addresses. The instruction and associated addresses are shown in Table 7.1.

This system can cope with eight separate peripherals with minimal extra hardware, as shown in Figure 7.2. The 8 interrupt signals form the inputs to an 8-to-3 encoder and the three outputs are connected to the microprocessor. The encoder produces a binary number at the outputs corresponding to the active input signal line. For example if input 1 is active the output would be 001, whilst if input 6 is active the

Table 7.1

RST instruction	Address vector
RST 0	0000H
RST 1	0008H
RST 2	0010H
RST 3	0018H
RST 4	0020H
RST 5	0028H
RST 6	0030H
RST 7	0038H

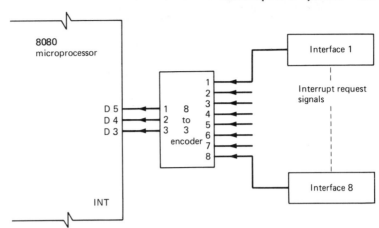

Figure 7.2   Use of an 8-to-3 encoder to generate the restart instruction vector

Q7.1   output would be 110. This is exactly the form of input required by the restart instruction.

Coping with interrupts during the service of an interrupt

Vectored interrupts enable the system to respond to a device's request for service very rapidly. However, there is still the problem that one device may try to interrupt whilst the microprocessor is completing an interrupt service request for another device. If the new interrupt is from a fast peripheral then it may be necessary to transfer to the new interrupt routine. If the new peripheral is slower than the one being serviced, then it may be necessary to prevent a transfer to the new interrupt service routine until the current one is completed.

Occasionally two peripherals may interrupt at exactly the same instant in time and so we will need some way of selecting which peripheral to service first.

Both these difficulties can be overcome by using a *priority interrupt* system. This means that each device is assigned a unique position in a hierarchy of peripherals. Normal practice would ensure that the fastest device has the highest priority and can interrupt the service routine of any other peripheral. Slow devices have a low priority and cannot interrupt higher priority devices.

The extra hardware required to implement a priority interrupt system can be very complicated to design. However, several manufacturers have produced special integrated circuits to provide all the essential features under program control. (A data sheet for the Intel 8259 Programmable Interrupt Controller is included in the Appendices.)

Disabling interrupts in the microprocessor

Most microprocessors enable the programmer to decide whether or not interrupts are to have any effect upon the normal sequence of events. Like the PIO, the microprocessor contains an interrupt enable bit. If this bit is set to 0 interrupts will not be acknowledged; if set to 1 they are.

The state of this enable bit after power-on varies with the microprocessor, but in general all will start with interrupts disabled. It is up to the programmer to change the state of this bit if interrupts are to be used.

The 8080 has two special instructions to control the state of the interrupt enable bit. Interrupts are enabled by issuing the instruction

```
EI    ;Enable interrupts
```

and disabled by the instruction

```
DI    ;Disable interrupts
```

Interrupt service routines

The basic purpose of an interrupt service routine is to respond to the needs of the system peripherals. In many cases this will be limited to transmitting a new data value or reading a data word from the peripheral.

Most microprocessors automatically disable interrupts as part of the interrupt acknowledge cycle. This is to ensure that they can execute sufficient instructions to get to the interrupt service routine before another device can generate an interrupt. In such systems the service routine may need to re-enable interrupts to allow higher priority devices to interrupt the current one. Of course they must re-enable interrupts before returning to the main program.

Other sources of interrupt

A few processors, including the M6800 and the 8085, have one source of interrupt that cannot be disabled internally, called a *non-maskable interrupt*. These are normally reserved for special power-fail detection circuits or emergency shut-off procedures, which must take precedence over all other sources of interrupt.

The 8085 also provides three other interrupt inputs called RST 7.5, RST 6.5 and RST 5.5. Unlike the RST 0-7 instructions, these inputs act directly upon the program flow by causing the execution of a CALL instruction. This CALL instruction is not read from the data bus, instead the address for the CALL routine is stored in fixed locations of memory, as shown in Table 7.2. The response to these
Q7.2, 7.3 interrupts is very much like that of the M6800 to its interrupt input.

Table 7.2

RST instruction	*Address vector*	*Interrupt register mask bit*
RST 5.5	002CH	0
RST 6.5	0034H	1
RST 7.5	003CH	2

An additional feature of these interrupt inputs is that they can be individually disabled. Each input has its own interrupt enable bit, or flag, which can be set or reset by special instructions. These flags reside in a special 8-bit register of the 8085 microprocessor called the *Interrupt Mask Register*.

The bit/flag for each of the RST X.5 instructions in this mask register is shown in Table 7.2. If we want to enable RST 7.5, the accumulator is loaded with the appropriate bit pattern and the following instruction executed:

```
SIM   ;Set interrupt mask
```

The interrupt mask can be read into the accumulator using the instruction

```
RIM   ;Transfer contents of mask
      ;register to accumulator
```

Q7.4

7.6 Interrupt programming example

Input/output timing often presents many problems for a programmer. This book has used a short program to generate a timing delay in the program examples. However, this method is not very efficient and is totally unsuitable for systems that use interrupts. The problem is that an interrupt will cause an exit from the delay loop to a service routine and so the timing of the delay becomes erroneous.

One way round this problem is to use hardware to generate the timing information. A special peripheral can be used to interrupt the microprocessor at predetermined intervals, with the duration under software control.

Such peripherals are referred to as *real-time clocks* and can be used for simple timing loops or even to provide a time-of-day clock. They consist of a pre-setable counter and crystal-controlled oscillator. The counter is loaded at the beginning of each timing loop and each clock pulse causes the counter contents to be decremented by one. When the count reaches zero an interrupt is generated. The counter is just a convenient way to divide the clock frequency down to a low rate, yet retain the accuracy and stability of the crystal oscillator.

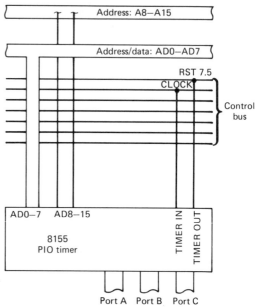

Figure 7.3 Timer interface

Although it is relatively simple to build a basic real-time clock from discrete components, there are several PIO-type devices that incorporate timing functions. These devices also provide additional features, such as pulse or square-wave generation.

The Hektor kit uses the timer element of an 8155 PIO as a real-time clock. The interrupt output is connected to the RST 7.5 input on the CPU chip. A block diagram for the timer interface is shown in Figure 7.3. In this case the timer clock input is derived from the system clock which runs at 3.072 MHz.

As explained in Chapter 5, the 8155 PIO contains six registers and is configured for accumulator I/O. The timer section will accommodate a 14-bit count and will either give a short pulse output, or a square-wave output. The device codes and function of these registers are given in Table 7.3. Further details of the 8155 and its control can be found in the Appendices.

Table 7.3

Device code	Register	Function
40H	Control	Set mode of device
41H	Port A	Port A data register
42H	Port B	Port B data register
43H	Port C	Port C data register
44H	Timer1	Low byte of timer
45H	Timer2	Mode and high byte

Initialisation of the timer

Before the real-time clock can be started the timer must be set to an appropriate mode and loaded with a count. This is done by loading the two timer registers. One of these stores the two mode bits and the most significant 6 bits of the count and the other stores the lower 8 bits of the count. Using the full 14-bit count, the minimum interrupt rate will be 3.073 MHz/2^{14} or 187.5 per second.

The counter is started by setting both bits 6 and 7 of the command register to 1.

Timer interrupt experiment

The object of the following experiment is to write an interrupt service routine for the real-time clock and to see the effect of an external interrupt on normal program flow.

The program is quite complicated and so is broken into two parts. The first part examines the initialisation of the timer and the interrupt service routine; no other processing occurs. The second part adds a separate processing task which runs continuously, but is interrupted by the timer once every second. Be very careful when typing the program, because if you get something wrong all sorts of peculiar things may happen. Using interrupts is not easy and it takes a lot of time to write and test new programs. However, once you have mastered them, the potential for new and exciting applications is enormous.

The timer initialisation program

The initialisation program is used to load the timer count register, set the mode of the timer and then start it.

The timer count register is treated just like any other of the data registers on the PIO, but in this case there are two bytes to transfer. The counter uses 14 bits, the least significant 8 bits are sent to port 44H using the OUT instruction. The most significant 6 bits are sent to port 45H, along with the 2 timer mode bits. For these experiments both these 2 bits will always be set to 1.

The 2 mode bits must be added to the 14-bit count. This can be done in several ways, but the example uses the 16-bit add instruction DAD, which adds either the B or D register pair to the H register pair. After the addition the H and L registers can be sent separately to the two timer registers.

The timer interrupt service routine

The timer generates an interrupt on the RST 7.5 input and so causes the microprocessor to execute the instruction whose address is stored at locations 003CH and 003DH. The locations are part of the monitor program ROM, so it is not possible for you to enter an interrupt service routine address. Instead these locations point to another pair of locations in RAM where the address of the interrupt service routine can be stored. In the case of the timer these addresses are 2F0DH and 2F0EH.

When the timer is set to its maximum count, interrupts will occur at the rate of about 200 per second. This is much too fast for humans to observe what is happening, so we need some way of slowing things down. The simplest method is to make the interrupt service routine count several hundred interrupts before initiating an external visible event. The interrupt count must be saved in a register and must not be altered by other parts of the program. This example uses the D register pair to count 1,000 interrupts.

Experiment 1

The flow diagram for this program has been divided into two, the initialisation stage and the interrupt service routine. These are shown in Figures 7.4(a) and 7.4(b).

The program listing (see Figure 7.5) is not split and the initialisation and interrupt service routines form a single program. Some of the instructions used may be new to you, if they are you can look them up in the Appendices.

The important point to notice is that although the interrupt service routine and the main program are entered as one program, they are independent modules. There are no instructions in the main program that call the interrupt routine to print out the hex number.

When the contents of the D register equal 0, the interrupt service routine forces a hexadecimal number to be displayed on the TV screen. The example will print '32', but any 8-bit number could be used. Before exiting from the routine the D register must be reloaded with the interrupt count.

Experiment 2

In the last experiment the main program was used only to initialise the timer and the interrupt service routine vector. This experiment requires the main program to execute a real task in addition to the initialisation.

The task is to count from 0 to 15 in binary and display the count on the four LEDs connected to port B. It is very similar to the flashing LED program of Chapter 5. This task has no effect upon the interrupt service routine, so there is no change to this portion of the program.

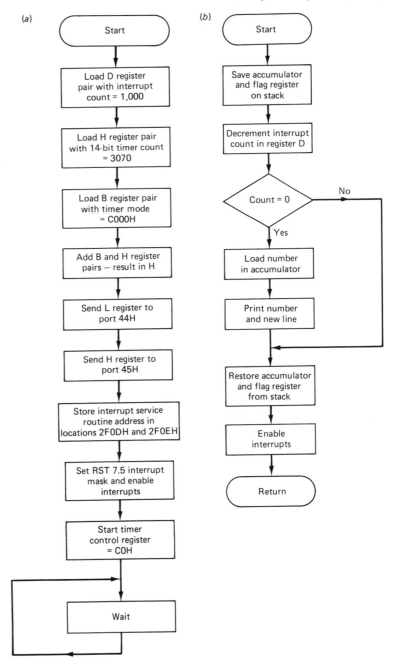

Figure 7.4 Initialisation program *(a)* and interrupt service routine *(b)*

```
Timer test program

CREG:   EQU   40H       ;Define PIO control register
PORTB:  EQU   42H       ;Define port B data register
TIM1:   EQU   44H       ;Define timer counter low-byte data register
TIM2:   EQU   45H       ;Define timer counter high-byte and mode
                        ;data register
IVECT:  EQU   2F0DH     ;Define RST 7.5 vector address
TCVAL:  EQU   3070      ;Define timer count value
TMODE:  EQU   0C000H    ;Define timer mode (single pulse)
PRB:    EQU   035AH     ;Define print binary subroutine address
PRNL:   EQU   02DAH     ;Define print new line subroutine address
        ORG   3800H     ;Define starting address of program

Interrupt service routine

INTS:   PUSH  PSW       ;Save accumulator and flags register on
                        ;stack
        DCX   D         ;Decrement D register pair
        MOV   A,E       ;Test result for 0
        ORA   D
        JNZ   CONT      ;If result non-zero, jump to CONT, else
        MVI   A,32H     ;Load number to print into accumulator
        CALL  PRB       ;Print number
        CALL  PRNL      ;Print new line
        LXI   D,1000    ;Reset interrupt count in D register pair
CONT:   POP   PSW       ;Restore accumulator and flags register
        EI              ;Enable interrupts
        RET             ;Return to main program

Main program

START:  LXI   D,1000    ;Load interrupt count into D register pair
        LXI   H,TCVAL   ;Load timer count into H register pair
        LXI   B,TMODE   ;Load timer mode into B register pair
        DAD   B         ;Add mode bits to count, result into
                        ;H,L register pair
        MOV   A,L       ;Move low byte of result into accumulator
        OUT   TIM1      ;Output byte to timer counter
        MOV   A,H       ;Move high byte of result into accumulator
        OUT   TIM2      ;Output byte to timer counter
        LXI   H,INTS    ;Load interrupt service routine into
                        ;H,L register pair
        SHLD  IVECT     ;Store address in vector location
        MVI   H,19H     ;Load interrupt mask into accumulator
        SIM             ;Set interrupt mask
        EI              ;Enable interrupts
        MVI   A,0C0H    ;Load PIO control word into accumulator
        OUT   CREG      ;Output word to control register to
                        ;start timer
LOOP:   JMP   LOOP      ;Do nothing loop
        END   START     ;End of program
```

Figure 7.5 Timer test program

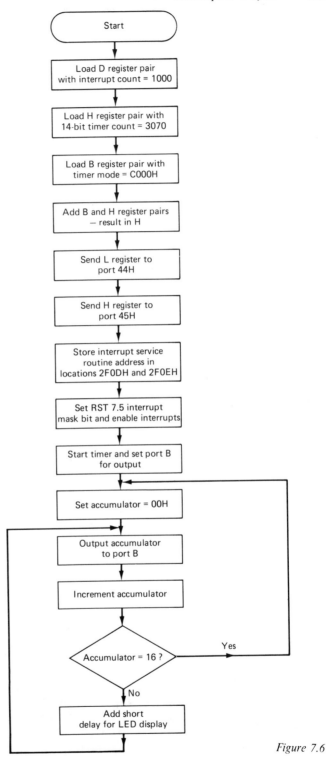

Figure 7.6

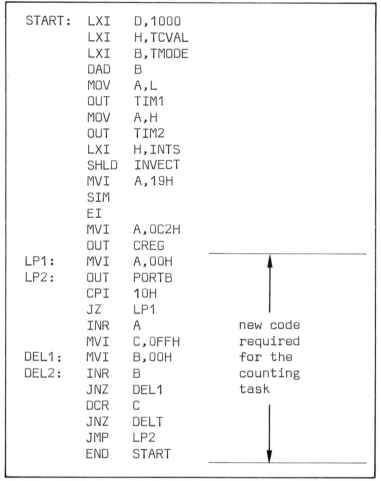

```
START:    LXI     D,1000
          LXI     H,TCVAL
          LXI     B,TMODE
          DAD     B
          MOV     A,L
          OUT     TIM1
          MOV     A,H
          OUT     TIM2
          LXI     H,INTS
          SHLD    INVECT
          MVI     A,19H
          SIM
          EI
          MVI     A,0C2H
          OUT     CREG
LP1:      MVI     A,00H
LP2:      OUT     PORTB
          CPI     10H
          JZ      LP1
          INR     A             new code
          MVI     C,0FFH        required
DEL1:     MVI     B,00H         for the
DEL2:     INR     B             counting
          JNZ     DEL1          task
          DCR     C
          JNZ     DELT
          JMP     LP2
          END     START
```

Figure 7.7

The main program must be modified to incorporate the new task, as shown in the flow diagram of Figure 7.6. Although the whole of the listing for the new program is shown, only the last few lines have been altered. The new main program is listed in Figure 7.7.

7.7 Summary

1   An interrupt is a signal generated by an I/O interface to indicate to the microprocessor the need for some form of attention.
2   The use of interrupts increases the processing capability of a microcomputer system because it minimises the time wasted testing the status registers of the interfaces.
3   Upon receipt of an interrupt the microprocessor enters an interrupt acknowledge cycle, which saves the contents of the

program counter and then starts a special interrupt service routine.

4   In a multiple interrupt system the microprocessor must be able to determine which device generated an interrupt. This can be done either by polling each device, or by use of vectored interrupts.

5   The use of an interrupt priority scheme ensures that the interrupt requests of high-speed peripherals take precedence over those of low-speed peripherals.

6   All interrupts can be disabled and enabled by means of special instructions, or selected interrupts can be disabled by means of an interrupt mask.

Questions

7.1   What are the main advantages of a vectored interrupt system over a polled interrupt system?

7.2   What is the function of an interrupt priority system?

7.3   Explain what is meant by the term non-maskable interrupt and describe one possible use of such an interrupt.

7.4   Why might an interrupt mask register be used in a multiple-interrupt computer system?

Chapter 8 Transducers and controllers

Objectives of this chapter *When you have completed studying this chapter you should be able to:*

1 *Draw a block diagram of a transducer measurement system.*
2 *Discuss the characteristics used to specify the operational performance of a transducer.*
3 *Describe the function of a signal conditioning unit.*
4 *Discuss the need for buffering and isolation of digital control signals.*

8.1 Introduction

The aim of this chapter is twofold: first, to show you how to select a transducer and connect it to a measurement system; secondly, to show you how we can use a microprocessor to control external devices. The first half of the chapter uses the problem of temperature measurement to illustrate the methods of selecting a transducer and shows how the output from the transducer can be adapted to suit the requirements of the microprocessor. The second half of the chapter looks at the problem of a control system and shows how a PIO can be used for switching low- and high-voltage power sources using solid-state switches.

8.2 Basic function of transducers

The basic function of a transducer was introduced in Chapter 6. It is a device for converting variables such as pressure, temperature and flow into electrical signals suitable for use in a measurement or control system. There are two broad classes of transducer: *passive* and *active*. A passive transducer requires no external power supply for its operation, whilst an active one does.

This broad classification has considerable significance for the instrumentation designer because when dealing with passive transducers one must accept certain inherent limitations, particularly in respect of sensitivity. For example, a crystal microphone will produce a fixed output voltage for a given sound pressure, over a limited range of frequencies. One cannot increase the efficiency with which the acoustic energy is converted to electrical energy.

Active transducers on the other hand do provide some flexibility, so that the output from a strain-gauge bridge can be increased by increasing the excitation voltage. Hence one of the important decisions to be made by the designer in selecting a transducer will be whether to choose an active or passive device.

8.3   Common transducers

The number and type of available transducers makes it impossible to list or describe them all in this chapter. However, there are some that are used more frequently than others and these are summarised in Tables 8.1–8.5. The tables cover those transducers commonly available for the measurement of temperature, force, pressure, flow and level.

Table 8.1   *Temperature transducers*

Type	Electrical I/O characteristics	Comments
Thermoswitches	Switch closure. Simple on-off output	Many types available, covering a wide range of temperatures, contact configurations, and current-handling capabilities
Thermocouples	Low source impedance, typically 10 Ω. Voltage-output devices. Output shift is 10's of microvolts/°C. Outputs typically in the millivolts at room temperature	Low voltage output requires low-drift signal conditioning. Small size and wide temperature range are advantages. Requires reference to a known temperature. Non-linear response
Platinum and other RTDs	Resistance changes with temperature. Positive temperature coefficient. Typical impedance (0°C) 20 Ω to 2 kΩ. Typical sensitivities 0.1 to 0.66%/°C, depending on material	Highly repeatable. Good linearity over wide ranges. Requires bridge or other network for typical interface
Thermistors	Resistance changes with temperature. Negative temperature coefficient. Typical impedance (25°C) of 50 Ω to 1MΩ available. Sensitivity at 25°C is about 4%/°C. Linearised networks available with 0.4%/°C sensitivity	Highest sensitivity among common temperature transducers. Inherently non-linear (exponential function) but accurate linearised networks available
Semiconductor sensors	Voltage, current, or resistance functions. Voltage types (diodes) require excitation current. Current types require excitation voltage. Resistive types (bulk silicon) may use either type of excitation	Many devices are uncalibrated and require significant signal conditioning

Table 8.2   *Force transducers*

Type	Electrical I/O characteristics	Comments
Strain gauges (metal)	Resistance shifts with applied strain. Almost always used in bridge configuration. Typical impedence levels of 120 and 350 Ω. Typical change is 0.1% over the whole range	Resistance change with strain small compared with initial value of device resistance. Requires high-quality low-level signal conditioning
Strain-gauge bridge, load cell	Voltage output with applied strain. Requires excitation potential or current to drive the bridge. Typical excitation is from 5 to 15 V	Small voltage outputs require low-drift signal conditioning with good common mode rejection to achieve any degree of precision. Output is linear
Semiconductor strain gauges	Bridge types are assembled from individual gauges and have a voltage output. Bridge requires excitation, typically 5 to 15 V	More output than metal strain gauges, but with increased non-linearity and sensitivity to temperature
Piezolectrics	True charge output device. Modelled as voltage source in series with capacitor. Physical input change produces corresponding charge. AC and transient response only. Typical upper frequency limit is 20 to 50 kHz. Typical output is 10^{-7} coulombs full-scale	Requires low-bias-current charge amplifier configurations for signal conditioning. Responds to a.c. signals only

Table 8.3   *Pressure transducers*

Type	Electrical I/O characteristics	Comments
Rheostat/potentiometer	Resistance or ratio-of-resistance output. Requires voltage or current excitation. Typical impedance 500 Ω to 5 kΩ	High-level easy-to-condition outputs are typical due to significant resistance or ratio
Strain gauge	Resistance shift (single gauge) or voltage output (strain-gauge bridge). Requires excitation potential or current	Small resistance change. Low-level signal requires good signal-conditioning amplifiers
Piezoelectric	Charge output (see Table 8.2)	See Table 8.2

Table 8.4 *Flow transducers*

Type	Electrical I/O characteristics	Comments
Pressure-based	See Table 8.3	Pressure types measure flow by measuring $\triangle P$ between static and flow-caused pressure, or pressure drop across a constriction. Differential pressure transducers are used to avoid common-mode pressure errors. Response is non-linear
Frequency-output types: paddle wheels, rotary types, vortex types	Digital output derived from frequency output are common. Optical or magnetic pickups provide non-invasive measurements. Photo-cell has 100 Ω to 100 MΩ on-to-off ratio. Magnetic employs switching or open-collector transistor	Some types are directly logic-level compatible. Others require impedance and/or voltage amplification, level-shift, and buffering before signal is usable
Force-based	Typical forms use strain-gauge bridges or potentiometer outputs. See Tables 8.2 and 8.3	See Tables 8.2 and 8.3
Thermal	Use active temperature sensors to measure temperature changes caused by flow	See Table 8.1

Table 8.5 *Level transducers*

Type	Electrical I/O chatacteristics	Comments
Float	Resistor or potentiometer output. 100 Ω to 2 kΩ typical impedance	Requires excitation (current, voltage) to achieve voltage output. High-level output due to large resistance swings
Thermal	Resistive. Typical impedances 500 Ω to 2 kΩ	Self-heated temperature sensor (thermistor) is used to detect discrete level changes. Abrupt resistance changes occur when liquid level drops to allow thermistor to be uncovered
Optical	Resistive. Typical on-off impedances 100 Ω to 100 kΩ	Optical occlusion or scattering blocks an opto-electronic path
Pressure	See Table 8.3	Level information obtained by measuring pressure in unoccupied area in top enclosed tank versus pressure in liquid-covered area
Load cell	Contents of container measured by weighing	See Table 8.2

8.4   A transducer measurement system

Table 8.1 shows that the electrical output signal of a transducer can take the form of volts, current, resistance or charge. In general the last three types of signal must be converted to a voltage for use with the ADCs described in Chapter 6. Furthermore the range of the output signals must be scaled to match the input range of the converter. The conversion and scaling functions are carried out by special circuits.

The transducer and special circuits make up what is known as a transducer measurement system, which can be broken down into three basic units as shown in Figure 8.1. The first unit is the transducer itself, followed by a signal conditioning unit and an amplification unit. Breaking the system down in this way helps us to specify the performance of each unit and hence simplify the overall design problem. The basic characteristics and functional performance of each of these units is discussed below.

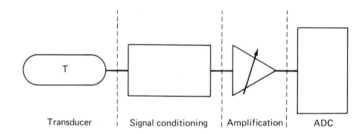

Figure 8.1   Transducer measurement system

The transducer

Sensitivity is defined as the ratio of the change in the transducer output to the change in the measured variable. For a temperature transducer this might be expressed as mV/°C.

Accuracy is a term used to relate the transducer output to the true value of the measured variable and is normally defined in terms of a percentage of full scale or a deviation. The accuracy of a temperature transducer might be expressed as 1% of the working range.

Working environment is a global term used to encompass all the operating and handling restrictions placed upon the transducer by the manufacturer. These might include maximum supply voltage, humidity, measurement range and soldering temperature, etc. Failure to observe these restrictions could result in total destruction of the device.

Speed of response is a term used to describe how quickly the trans-

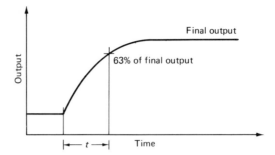

Figure 8.2   Response time of a transducer

ducer output will respond to a change in the measured variable. In some cases manufacturers will specify the time required for the output to reach within a small error of the final output. Alternatively a time constant will be given, which defines the time for the output to reach 63% of the final value, as illustrated in Figure 8.2.

Signal conditioning

The function of this unit is to convert the output of the transducer into a form suitable for the ADC. The main functions to be performed are:

Linearisation   Many transducers do not produce an output that is directly proportional to the measured variable, so that a graph of input *versus* output will not be a straight line. The departure from the straight line is called the non-linearity of the transducer. In many cases the non-linearity is very small and can be ignored, but for those cases where it is not, special electrical circuits can be used to minimise the errors.

Offsetting   This involves introducing a level shift in the output signal of the transducer and it is normally achieved by adding or subtracting a d.c. voltage. This facility is often required for the calibration of individual transducers to correct for small manufacturing inconsistancies. For example, an offset may be required to ensure that a temperature transducer produces 0 V output for 0°C.

Filtering   In Chapter 6 it was shown that when an ADC is used to measure analogue signals, a filter must be used to remove all the frequencies above a certain value. Such filters are referred to as anti-aliasing filters. Another use of filters is the removal of the electrical noise induced in signal leads by mains power cables.

Signal conversion   This involves changing the output signal of the transducer into a voltage. There are many standard circuits for converting one form of electrical signal to another, but the details are beyond the scope of this book.

Amplification

This last unit provides the voltage gain required to ensure that the output of the signal conditioning unit matches the input range of the ADC. Most commercial converters have input ranges between ± 2.5 and ± 10 V. If the input signal to the converter is only a few millivolts, then only a few of the possible quantisation levels will be active and **Q8.1, 8.2** the measurement will have poor resolution.

8.5   Designing a measurement system

In this section I want to examine the characteristics and functional requirements for a real system to measure temperatures using a thermocouple transducer. In all cases it helps to have a basic understanding of the operating principles of the transducer, so let us start with a brief review of thermocouples.

Thermocouple transducers

Basic principles   A thermocouple is a temperature transducer consisting of two different metals joined at both ends. If the two junctions between the two metals are at different temperatures an electric current will flow around the circuit. This phenomenon is called the Seebeck effect and is illustrated in Figure 8.3.

Across the junction of any two dissimilar metals there always appears a difference in electric potential called the contact potential. In Figure 8.3 the contact potentials are labelled V_1 and V_2. This contact potential varies with the temperature of the junction and increases with increasing temperature.

If the temperature of the two junctions is the same no current flows, because the two contact potentials are equal and opposite. This fact is important because if we introduce a voltmeter into the circuit, two

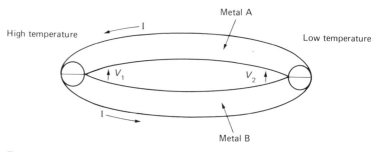

Figure 8.3   Seebeck effect

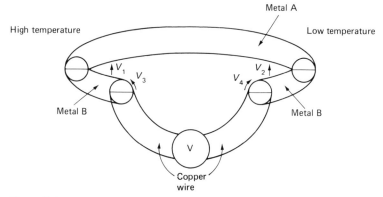

Figure 8.4

new junctions are added as shown in Figure 8.4. These junctions will add their contact potentials to the total of the circuit and therefore increase the current flowing. However, if these new junctions are held at the same temperature the net effect will be zero, because the contact potentials V_3 and V_4 will cancel.

When a thermocouple is used to measure temperature, one of its two junctions is placed in contact with the material whose temperature is to be measured. Since the total voltage at the voltmeter terminals depends upon the temperature of both junctions, the temperature of the second junction must be known. This second junction is usually referred to as the *reference junction* or *cold junction*.

The temperature of the reference junction can be established by placing it in some apparatus in which the temperature is accurately controlled. One method is to use an ice–water mixture to maintain a temperature of 0°C. Alternatively one can use a small commercial oven to keep the junction at some convenient temperature.

Sensitivity   The sensitivity of thermocouples is very low, ranging from about 7 to 75 µV/°C . The total output voltage swing is only a few tens of millivolts even for a temperature change of 1,000°C, as shown in Figure 8.5.

Accuracy   Thermocouple accuracies range from +0.25 to +1%, depending upon the type used and the measurement range.

Working environment   Economic and rugged, thermocouples have reasonably long-term stability and are available to cover the range –200 to 2,000°C. Some of the alloys used in their construction will not withstand corrosive environments, in which case the wires can be protected by placing them in a resistant metal sheath. Such devices are known as *thermocouple probes*.

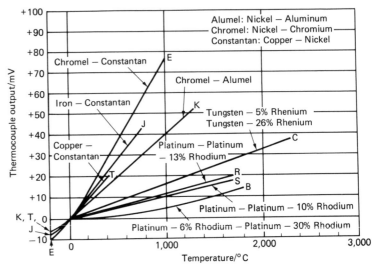

Figure 8.5 Output characteristics of thermocouples

Speed of response Small special high-speed thermocouples can have time constants as short as 10 µs, but probes are more likely to have values around the 0.5 to 5 s mark.

Choosing a thermocouple

The wide use of thermocouples has led to the development of both national and international standards covering the manufacture and operational performance of thermocouples.

Table 8.6 lists the metals and alloys used in the construction of those thermocouples covered by British Standard BS 4937 (1973). Included in this document are tables detailing the output voltage as a function of temperature, for a given reference junction temperature, over the full working range of the thermocouple.

Once we know the range of temperatures to be measured, we can select an appropriate sensor from those covered by the standard. Furthermore, we have the added advantage that devices can be purchased from several manufacturers and readily interchanged because they meet a common standard.

Signal conditioning requirements for a thermocouple

Linearity is poor in some of the standard types of thermocouples, especially at low temperatures. Corrections can be applied to the output signal either by adding special compensation circuitry or by using the mathematical capabilities of the microprocessor. However, over small temperature ranges the errors due to non-linearity can often be ignored.

Table 8.6 *Thermocouple materials to BS 4937 (1973)*

Type	First wire	Second wire
S	Platinum	Platinum 90% Rhodium 10%
R	Platinum	Platinum 87% Rhodium 13%
J	Iron	Constantan (Copper 57%, Nickel 43%)
K	Nickel 90% Chromium 10%	Nickel 94% Manganese 3% Aluminium 2% Silicon 1%
T	Copper	Constantan
E	Nickel 90% Chromium 10%	Constantan
B	Platinum 70% Rhodium 30%	Platinum 94% Rhodium 6%

Offsetting can be used to improve measurement resolution particularly at high temperatures. For example the Type K thermocouple output is 16.4 mV at 400°C and the sensitivity is 40 μV/°C. If the measurement range is only 350 to 450°C, then the 16.4 mV can be subtracted from the output signal and the gain of the system increased.

Another form of offsetting associated with thermocouples is the so-called electronic cold-junction. Instead of using an ice bath or oven to control the reference junction temperature, it is possible to leave this junction at ambient temperature and then correct the measurement. The ambient temperature must be measured with another transducer to determine the correction. Although this method may seem complicated, it has enabled the development of compact and portable electronic thermometers.

Filtering can be used to minimise errors due to unwanted noise in the measurement system. Electric power cables can induce voltages into the signal wires either at the supply frequency of 50 Hz or short transients caused by switching power on and off. Fortunately many temperature sensors are used to measure very slow changes and so the induced signals can be removed by a low-pass filter.

Amplification

The amplification stage in a thermocouple system is used to match the output voltage from the signal conditioner to the input of the

ADC. The gain can be determined by comparing the transducer sensitivity to the quantisation interval for a given measurement resolution.

Suppose for example we want to use a Type K thermocouple to measure temperatures over the range 0–200°C, to a resolution of 1°C. An 8-bit converter has sufficient resolution (1 part in 256), but most devices have an input range between ±2.5 and ±10 V. For the former the quantisation interval will be 19.8 mV and for the latter 78 mV.

Over the range 0–200°C the sensitivity of the Type K thermocouple is almost constant at 40 μV/°C.

If the thermocouple were connected directly to an 8-bit converter, with an input range of ±2.5 V, what would be the smallest temperature change that could be measured? Since the quantisation interval for the converter is 19.8 mV and the sensitivity of the thermocouple is 40 μV/°C, the smallest change would be 19.8 μV/40 μV or approximately 495°C.

The gain of the amplification stage should be sufficient to ensure that a 1°C change in temperature produces an output voltage at least equal to the quantisation interval. The minimum gain will be 19.8 mV/40 μV = 495, say 500.

The very large gains required for thermocouples can introduce errors into the measurement process, unless great care is exercised to minimise them. Fortunately it is now possible to buy special-purpose thermocouple amplifiers whose characteristics have been optimised **Q8.3** by the manufacturers.

8.6 A control system

Many potential applications for microprocessor systems require some means of controlling external devices, such as displays, amplifiers or just simple on-off functions.

A typical block diagram for the output stage of such a control system is shown in Figure 8.6. The PIO acts as the interface between the microprocessor and the controlled device. The buffer module is used to protect the outputs of the PIO either from excess power dissipation, or from high voltage levels in the controlled device.

These control systems can be divided into two groups. The first are typified by switching applications where only one output bit of the PIO is required to change the state of the controlled device from on to off or *vice versa*. The other group consists of those systems that require several output bits. The DAC is an obvious example, but others include seven-segment displays and stepping motors.

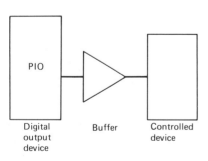

PIO

Digital   Buffer   Controlled
output   device
device

Figure 8.6 Block diagram for a digital control system

Since the techniques for designing the output stage for either group are very similar, the remainder of this chapter will concentrate on the simple single-bit controller used for switching applications.

Electronically controlled switches

There are many types of switching device. The on-off power or light switch in the home is a familiar example. The major difference between this type of switch and one that can be used in a control system is that the latter must be operable by an electrical signal.

Electromagnetic relays are an example of a controlled switch. The contacts are opened or closed by passing current through a coil. Normally the current required to operate the switch is much less than the contacts can handle, so a low-level digital signal can often be used to control the switch. The main disadvantages of relays are that they are slow in operation and have a relatively short life.

The transistor can also be used as a switching device. A small current applied to the base terminal enables a much larger current to flow between the collector and emitter terminals. Transistors will turn on and off very quickly and have a long life, but at the present time they cannot handle high power and high voltages.

Another type of solid-state switch is the thyristor or silicon controlled rectifier (SCR). The device has three terminals and behaves as a diode that can be switched into conduction by applying a control signal to a third terminal. SCRs can be switched very quickly and will handle hundreds of amps. Unfortunately, current can only be conducted in one direction.

The triac is very similar to the SCR, but will pass current in either direction and so is very useful for controlling a.c. power. Like the SCR, devices are capable of handling hundreds of amps at high voltage levels.

Protecting the outputs of a PIO

When using a PIO output bit to generate the signal to control a switch, great care must be taken to ensure that the electrical performance of the PIO output is not exceeded. The output usually consists of one or two transistors and these are not designed to handle more than a few milliamps at 5 V. If more current is required then the output must be protected by including some sort of 'buffer' device.

In many cases the buffer will consist of a single transistor which can handle the necessary current or voltage. In this case the transistor is acting as an amplifier rather than a switch, because the small current from the PIO results in a much larger current from the transistor.

The buffer device normally prevents damage to the digital circuits when they are used for generating a control signal. The other possible cause of damage is when the high voltages get back into the digital circuits because of a faulty component. One way to avoid this problem is to electrically isolate the low-level control signal from the higher voltage on the switch.

This isolation can be achieved by using a light source and detector.

Special devices called 'opto-isolators' are available for just this purpose. The digital signal is used to illuminate the source and the light is detected by a phototransistor across a short air gap between the two devices. Such 'opto-isolators' are capable of providing several kilovolts isolation.

A low voltage switching application

Light emitting diodes (LED) are often used in instruments or control panels to indicate the present state of a signal or switch. When the signal is high or the switch in the 'on' position, the LED is illuminated. LEDs are also used as light sources in opto-isolators.

The amount of light emitted by the LED is determined by the current flowing through it and is typically about 20 mA for maximum illumination. Unfortunately this is greater than that available from a PIO output bit.

Sufficient current can be obtained by using a single transistor buffer as shown in Figure 8.7. When the PIO output bit goes high a small current flows into the base of the transistor (marked *b*). This current allows the transistor to conduct a much larger current, maybe 100 times more, between the collector and the emitter (marked *c* and *e*). Resistor R1 is used to limit this current to a safe value for the LED.

Since the transistor and light source are connected to the same low-voltage power supply as the PIO, there is no need for any isolation.

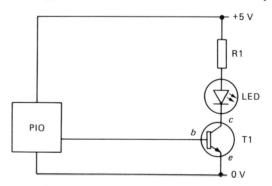

Figure 8.7 Controlling the LED with a PIO output bit

A mains voltage switching application

There are many examples of mains voltage switching applications in household electrical equipment such as washing machines, refrigerators, ovens and immersion heaters. The basic requirement in such applications is a switch capable of handling about 10 amps at 240 V.

Consider for example the temperature control system required for an electric oven. The user will specify the time the cooker must turn on, the length of time to cook and the temperature of the oven during this period. The system must read the time information and apply power to the heating elements in the oven as appropriate.

Once this problem would have been solved using two switches, one controlled by a time-clock and the other by the temperature. Now it is possible to use a single solid-state switching device such as the triac for both functions, in conjunction with a single-chip microcomputer.

A clock within the microcomputer can be used to determine the start and finish of the cooking period, and a temperature transducer within the oven enables the microcomputer to regulate the power delivered to the heating elements.

In such an application it is obviously advisable to isolate the micro-computer from the mains power. This can be achieved either by optical isolation or by transformer coupling.

Although isolation protects the microcomputer from direct contact with mains voltages, it cannot reduce the effect of switching transients. As mentioned earlier, when the mains is switched on and off so as to control the heat, spurious voltages are induced into nearby wires. If these occur on the microcomputer address or data lines they can be misinterpreted as valid data and so cause errors. A more familiar example might be the annoying 'clicks' or 'burps' heard on a hi-fi system, when the refrigerator turns on and off.

The transients caused by switching can be minimised by controlling the time at which switching occurs. Figure 8.8 shows a cycle of mains

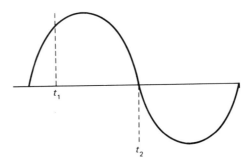

Figure 8.8   Switching off mains voltage to minimise transients

voltage. If the switch is opened at time t_1 lots of interference will be created, whereas if it is opened at time t_2 very little occurs; t_2 is called a zero crossing because the voltage passes through zero at this point in time.

The preceding discussion has highlighted the basic requirements of a digitally controlled mains switch; they are:

1   Control signal compatible with output from a PIO, i.e. low voltage and low current.
2   The control signal must be electrically isolated from the mains voltage.
3   Switching should occur only at a zero crossing of the mains voltage.

Building up this type of switch can be quite complicated, but in fact there is no need – one can buy a ready-made unit with all these features. Such devices are often referred to as solid-state relays since they have the same characteristics as relays but contain no moving parts.

Q8.4

8.7   Summary

1   Transducers can be broadly classified into passive and active devices. Passive devices do not require an external power supply, active ones do.
2   A transducer measurement system comprises three units, the transducer, a signal conditioning unit and an amplification unit.
3   The important characteristics of a transducer are:
    (a)   sensitivity;
    (b)   accuracy;
    (c)   working environment;
    (d)   speed of response.
4   The function of a signal conditioning unit is to convert the output of the transducer into a form suitable for an ADC. The main operations are:
    (a)   linearisation;
    (b)   offsetting;
    (c)   filtering;
    (d)   signal conversion.
5   Amplification is used to ensure that the voltage output range of the signal conditioner matches the input range of the ADC.
6   Digital control systems can be divided into two groups, those that require single-bit control signals, such as switches, and those that require multiple-bit signals such as displays.
7   Digital signals should be buffered and isolated from high-voltage power sources.

Questions

8.1 Draw a block diagram of a transducer measurement system and state the functions of each block.

8.2 Explain the function of a signal conditioning unit in a measurement system.

8.3 A thermocouple with a sensitivity of 100 μV/°C is to be used with an 8-bit converter with ±5 V input range. What gain will be required to ensure that the system can resolve a 2°C change in temperature.

8.4 Explain the function of a buffer block in a digitally controlled mains switch.

Chapter 9 Testing and maintenance of a microprocessor-based system

Objectives of this chapter *When you have completed studying this chapter you should be able to:*

1 *Recognise that faults in an installed system can be hardware- or software-induced.*
2 *Appreciate that the provision of software designed especially to detect faults will be a great advantage in the efficient maintenance of a product.*
3 *Write an assembler program to test the ADCs and DACs and the memory of an 8080/8085-based microprocessor system.*
4 *Appreciate that faults can occur due to incorrect software even after the system has been running satisfactorily for some time.*

9.1 Introduction

The aim of this chapter is to describe aspects of testing and maintenance of microprocessor-based systems that have to be performed after the system has been sold to and installed by the final user. This topic is such an important one that there are several books written on this subject alone. Indeed it is often this last stage of microprocessor product development that determines whether a microprocessor-based product will make a profit for its manufacturer. A poorly maintainable product will waste long periods of the maintenance engineer's expensive time.

9.2 Tasks involved in microprocessor-based product maintenance

On delivery of the system checks have to be made to see that it functions satisfactorily. Often a specially written piece of software will be run that checks all of the major parts of the system. This may well be followed by a program that tests all of the components working together as a system. Such a series of tests are called *commissioning tests* and are designed to prove to the customer's and the manufacturer's satisfaction that the system is working as required.

Once installed it is good practice to test the system every so often to see that all is well. Commonly this is done automatically each time the system is switched on. What happens is that when the system is switched on first, a test program stored in ROM is executed and any faults found listed on an output device. Because this test program is stored in ROM it probably will have to be small so as to leave adequate space for the main programs concerned with running the system.

Certainly a test program of this type will not be as extensive as the test programs used to commission the system which were probably entered into the microprocessor memory from a backing memory such as a cassette tape. However, they will probably be sufficient to detect any major errors before the system begins its main task. In this way expensive malfunctions of the system or equipment it controls can be avoided.

Any faults that become apparent during this regular check or are deduced to be present by a system malfunction will probably require a visit from a maintenance engineer. The maintenance engineer will have extensive and powerful diagnostic programs which will, when run on the system under test, allow the isolation of the fault. These programs will not only test for faults in hardware but also to see if the program stored in the microprocessor has been altered, possibly as a result of a memory malfunction or as a result of an undetected error in the program.

Hardware tests could, for example, include a test of any ADC or DAC present in the system. This might involve running a program which is designed to produce a specific voltage from a DAC and checking with a voltmeter to see if this is produced. Similarly an ADC can be checked by a program that 'reads' the output of the ADC whilst a known voltage is applied to it. This time the engineer would apply the voltage, run the program and examine the appropriate memory location to see that the correct value has been stored.

Undetected program errors are far more difficult for the maintenance engineer to detect. One of the reasons is that they are probably not obvious, otherwise the programmers would probably have detected them during the software testing phase. Also these faults may be specific to the particular application. For example, suppose that the system was a general-purpose system to control some apparatus using interrupts, then this particular application may produce a unique combination of interrupts which expose the fault in the software whereas other installations do not. If this is the case, extensive testing may be necessary to determine the fault.

Correcting software faults at the maintenance stage is extremely expensive which is why it is extremely important to produce good, well documented and well tested software so that the errors detected after the equipment is installed are reduced to a minimum.

9.3   Upgrading microprocessor-based equipment

One of the major advantages of microprocessor-based products is that they can often be upgraded or improved by a change of program. Provided that the designer of the product keeps further developments of the product in mind as the original design proceeds, then extra facilities can be provided at little extra cost to the manufacturer or the user. Moreover, this upgrading can often be performed on the user's premises and can be as simple as removing the original ROM chips and replacing them with ones containing the new program.

9.4   Hardware testing – example programs

Example 1   Testing RAM

Random access memory can be quite simply tested by writing a fixed codeword into memory and then reading it back and comparing the received codeword with the transmitted codeword. If an error is detected the address of the faulty memory location can be displayed.

The codeword used with this type of test must be selected carefully. If a codeword of all 1s is used, this may not detect an error, because the fault may be such that a word of all 1s is returned no matter what word is written. A better test would be to write a 0 and then a 1 into every bit of every memory location.

Although an alternating pattern appears to overcome the objections of a single codeword test, it is by no means ideal. The problem is that there are too many types of memory error. Some are due to timing faults, i.e. the codeword on the data bus may not appear at the right time, so the actual pattern is never correctly entered into the memory.

It is very difficult for the user of a microcomputer system to thoroughly test all aspects of RAM. The best to hope for is the detection of consistent read and write errors. The user must rely on the manufacturer of the system to carry out comprehensive tests using purpose-built equipment.

Nevertheless it is a good policy for the user to execute some form of simple testing on a regular basis. The write-then-read test can be run very quickly, either as part of a system test every time the power is applied, or run overnight when the equipment is not used.

A flow diagram for the write/read test for an 8080/8085 system is shown in Figure 9.1. The number of memory locations to be tested is stored in the D register pair, and the H register pair is used as an index address register. At the beginning of the test the H register pair will contain the address of the first location to be tested.

The test writes two patterns, one after the other, into every memory location, so that every bit is set to both a 0 and a 1. If an error is detected, an error message is printed to indicate the address of the faulty location. In practice, it might be more useful to indicate in

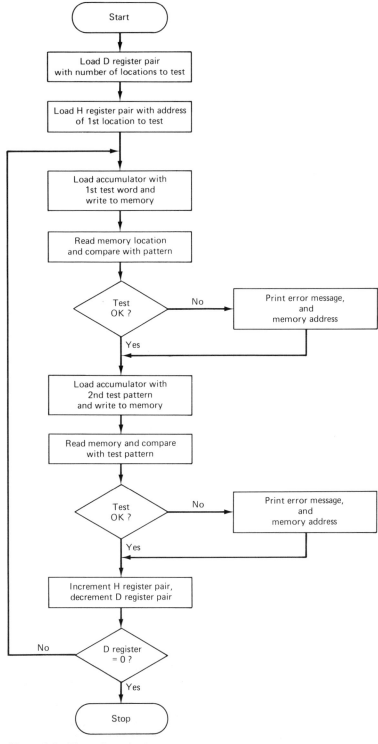

Figure 9.1   Flow diagram for memory test program

which integrated circuit the fault lies, since this can often be changed very easily by the user, rather than sending the whole system away for repair.

The H register pair is used by the monitor program to print the error message and the address of the faculty location. This means that the contents of this register pair must be saved before writing the message, and then restored before returning from the print subroutine to the main program. One way to save the contents of the H register pair is to place them in the B register pair which is unused in this program example.

Example 2   Testing a peripheral

Fully automatic testing of peripherals is not always possible. For example, to test the character generator of the VDU on Hektor, the microprocessor must be able to both generate the character and read the result. Unfortunately it cannot read the result and must rely on human intervention. The best that can be achieved is to generate a test pattern and then wait for the user to indicate whether the pattern is correct.

The Hektor system uses this type of test for both the TV display and the keyboard. For the display all the printing characters are generated in a fixed sequence. If the sequence is incorrect or some of the characters not produced correctly, the user must determine the error. Likewise with the keyboard. When the user hits a key the microprocessor reads the character and displays it on the TV. The user must determine any inconsistency such as a mismatch between keyed and displayed character.

Sometimes it is possible to use two peripherals to test each other, so that one produces a test signal and the other measures it. An obvious example of this type are DACs and ADCs. A codeword sent to the DAC will produce a given voltage, which can be converted back to binary by the ADC and so complete the measurement loop.

The sent and received codewords can then be compared and an error detected automatically. Of course if an error is detected it is essential to test one of the peripherals on its own, otherwise it will not be possible to tell which converter caused it.

One possible technique is to use a fixed reference voltage signal to test the ADC. If a microprocessor-controlled switch is used, the whole process can be made automatic because the microprocessor can switch between test signal, DAC output signal and normal transducer signal as shown in Figure 9.2.

The first test would use the fixed voltage reference signal to test the ADC. If the result was satisfactory, indicating that the ADC was

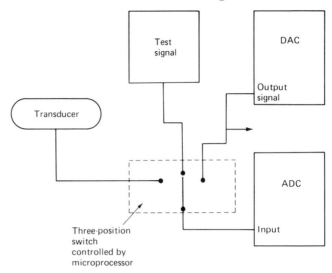

Figure 9.2 Signal sources for automatic testing of DACs and ADCs

working properly, then the second test would connect the DAC output, and both devices would be tested over the full working range. If all the tests were satisfactory the microprocessor would then reconnect the transducer.

Q9.1, 9.2

9.5 Summary

1 Good microprocessor programs are designed from the start with testing and maintenance in mind.
2 Various stages of testing are involved before the microprocessor-based systems are installed, but once they are installed they have to be commissioned to prove to the customer's and manufacturer's satisfaction that the system works.
3 Maintenance programs can be used to detect malfunctions in the system and to indicate the cause of such faults.

Questions

9.1 Write out a program to test the RAM in the Hektor peripheral board. There are 256 bytes available in the 8155 device starting at location 4000H.

If an error is encountered, the message 'ERROR LOCATION' should be printed along with the memory address. The following

Monitor routines can be used:

```
PRNL:    02DAH    ;Print new line sequence
PRWD:    0351H    ;Print 16-bit number in
                  ;H register pair as four
                  ;hex digits
PRMSG:   030AH    ;Print ASCII text starting
                  ;at the location stored in
                  ;the H register pair. The
                  ;message is terminated by
                  ;a zero byte
PRSP:    02E7H    ;Print a space
```

9.2   Draw a flow diagram for a test program that will check out the operation of a DAC and an ADC. A separate signal is available to test the operation of the ADC, which is selected by a three-position switch controlled by the microprocessor.

Appendix 1 General-purpose microprocessors

General-purpose microprocessors

Word size (data/instruction)	Original source manufacturer	Processor	Process technology	Direct addressing range (words)	Number of basic instructions	Maximum clock frequency (MHz)/phases	Instruction time shortest/longest[2] (µs)	TTL compatible	BCD arithmetic	On-chip interrupts/levels	Number of internal general-purpose registers	Number of stack registers
1/4	Motorola	MC14500	CMOS	0	16	1/1	1/1	Yes	No	Yes/1	1	0
4/8	Fujitsu	MB8849	NMOS	2048	70	2	3/6	Yes	Yes	Yes/2	128	4
4/8	Intel	4004	PMOS	4 k	46	0.74/2	10.8/21.6	No	Yes	Yes/1	16	3×12
4/8	Intel	4040	PMOS	8 k	60	0.74/2	10.8/21.6	No	Yes	Yes/1	24	7×12
4/8	National Semiconductor	COP402	NMOS	1 k	49	1/1	.4	Yes	Yes	Yes/3	64×4	RAM
4/8	National Semiconductor	COP402M	NMOS	1 k	49	1/1	4	Yes	Yes	No	64×4	RAM
4/8	National Semiconductor	COP404L	NMOS	2 k	49	0.25/1	16	Yes	Yes	Yes/3	128×4	RAM
4/8	NEC Microcomputers	µPD556	PMOS	2 k	80	0.44/1	4.5/9	Yes	Yes	Yes/2	96×4	3
4/8	OKI	MSM5840E	CMOS	4 k	98	2/1	16/32	Yes	Yes	Yes/2	128×4	4
4/8	Panasonic	MN1498	NMOS	1 k	66	0.3/1	10/20	Yes	Yes	Yes/1	64×4	RAM
4/8	Panasonic	MN1499	NMOS	2 k	75	0.3/1	10/20	Yes	Yes	Yes/1	64×4	RAM
4/8	Panasonic	MN1499A	NMOS	2 k	75	0.3/1	10/20	Yes	Yes	Yes/1	128×4	RAM
4/8	Panasonic	MN1599	NMOS	4 k	125	1/1	2/4	Yes	Yes	Yes/4	256×4	RAM
4/8	Texas Instruments	TMS1099SE	PMOS	1 k	43	0.40/1	15/15	Yes	Yes	No	66×4	1×10
4/8	Texas Instruments	TMS1098SE	PMOS	2 k	40	0.40/1	15/15	Yes	Yes	No	130×4	1×11
4/8	Texas Instruments	TMS1097SE	PMOS	4 k	41	0.55/1	11/11	Yes	Yes	No	130×4	3×12
4/8	Texas Instruments	TMS1096JL	PMOS	2 k	45	0.55/1	11/11	Yes	Yes	Yes/1	130×4	4×11
4/8	Toshiba	TMP4300	NMOS	2 k	67	1/1	33/360	Yes	Yes	Yes/1	128×4	8
4/8	Toshiba	TCP4600	CMOS	4 k	52	0.1/1	20/40	Yes	Yes	Yes/2	160×4	2
4/10	NEC Microcomputers	µPD555	PMOS	1920×10	72	0.2/1	10/20	Yes	Yes	Yes/2	96×4	4
8/8	Fairchild	2 chip F8 (3850)	NMOS	64 k	69	2/1	2/13	Yes	Yes	Yes/1	64	RAM
8/8	General Instrument	8000	PMOS	1 k	48	0.8/2	1.25/3.75	No	Yes	Yes/1	48	0
8/8	Intel	8008	PMOS	16 k	48	0.8/2	12.5/37.5	No	Yes	Yes/1	6	7×14
8/8	Intel	i8031	NMOS	128 k	111	12	1/4	Yes	Yes	Yes/2	128	RAM
8/8	Intel	8035/8039	NMOS	64 k	96	6/1	2.5/5	Yes	Yes	Yes/1	64	RAM
8/8	Intel	8080A	NMOS	64 k	78	2.6/2	1.5/3.75	Yes[3]	Yes	Yes/1	8	RAM
8/8	Intel	8085	NMOS	64 k	80	5.5/1	0.8/5.2	Yes	Yes	Yes/4	8	RAM
8/8	Intersil	80C35	CMOS	64 k	96	6/1	2.5/5	Yes	Yes	Yes/1	64	RAM
8/8	MOS Technology	MCS-650X	NMOS	64 k	56	4/1	0.5/3.5	Yes	Yes	Yes/1	0	RAM
8/8	MOS Technology	MCS-651X	NMOS	64 k	56	4/2	0.5/3.5	Yes	Yes	Yes/1	0	RAM
8/8	Mostek	MK38P70/02	NMOS	4 k	70+	4/1	1/6.5	Yes	Yes	Yes/4	64	RAM
8/8	Mostek	MK38P73/02	NMOS	4 k	70+	4/1	1/6.5	Yes	Yes	Yes/4	64	RAM
8/8	Motorola	M6800	NMOS	64 k	72	2/2	1/2.5	Yes	Yes	Yes/1	0	RAM
8/8	Motorola	6802/6808	NMOS	64 k	72	2/1	2/5	Yes	Yes	Yes/1	128/0	RAM
8/8	Motorola	6803	NMOS	64 k	82	3.58/1	2/12	Yes	Yes	Yes/1	128	RAM
8/8	Motorola	M6809	NMOS	64 k	59	2/1	2/5	Yes	Yes	Yes/1	0	RAM
8/8	National Semiconductor	INS8060	NMOS	64 k	46	4/1	5/22	Yes	Yes	Yes/1	8	RAM
8/8	National Semiconductor	INS8040	NMOS	64 k	96	11/1	1.4/2.8	Yes	Yes	Yes/1	256	RAM
8/8[7]	National Semiconductor	INS8070	NMOS	64 k	74	4/1	3/1000[8]	Yes	No	Yes/2	9	RAM
8/8	National Semiconductor	INS8073	NMOS	64 k	see comments	4/1	3/1000	Yes	Yes	Yes/2	64	RAM
8/8	National Semiconductor	NSC800	CMOS	64 k	150+	8/1	0.5/2.88	Yes	Yes	Yes/5	14	RAM
8/8	NEC Microcomputers	µPD7800	NMOS	64 k	140	1/1	2/4	Yes	Yes	Yes[5]	128+16	RAM

On-chip clock	DMA capability	Specialized memory & I/O circuits avail.	Prototyping system avail.	Package size (pins)	Voltages required (V)	Assembly language development system	High-level languages	Time-sharing cross software	Comments
Yes	No	No[4]	No	16	3 to 18	No	No	No	Needs external program counter
Yes	No	No	Yes	64	5	Yes	No	Yes	ROM-less emulator chip for MB8840 family of all-in-one processors
No	No	Yes	No	16	15	Yes	Yes	Yes	Superseded by 4040
No	No	Yes	Yes	24	15	Yes	Yes	Yes	General-purpose 4-bit μP
Yes	No	Yes	Yes	40	4.5 to 6.3	Yes	No	Yes	ROM-less version of COP420 and 440
Yes	No	Yes	Yes	40	4.5 to 6.3	Yes	No	Yes	single chip μC w/serial I/O, 20 I/O lines, event-counting
Yes	No	Yes	Yes	40	4.5 to 9.5	Yes	No	Yes	
Yes	No	No	Yes	64	−10	Yes	No	Yes	ROM-less version of μPD546
Yes	No	Yes	Yes	42	5	Yes	No	Yes	ROM-less evaluation chip; includes 30 I/O lines, 8-bit timer/counter, and draws 0.8 mA
Yes	No	Yes	Yes	40	5	Yes	No	Yes	ROM-less version of MN1402, but 66 instructions and comes in a 40-pin package
Yes	No	Yes	Yes	64	5	Yes	No	Yes	ROM-less version of MN1400
Yes	No	Yes	Yes	64	5	Yes	No	Yes	ROM-less version of MN1405, but 128 nibbles of on-chip RAM
Yes	Yes	Yes	Yes	64	5	Yes	No	Yes	ROM-less version of MN1564; chip has 12 4-bit I/O ports
Yes	No	Yes	Yes	64	−9	Yes	No	Yes	ROM-less version of TMS1000/1200 microcomputer
Yes	No	Yes	Yes	64	−9	Yes	No	Yes	ROM-less version of TMS1100/1300 microcomputer
Yes	No	Yes	Yes	64	−9	Yes	No	Yes	ROM-less version of TMS1400 microcomputer
Yes	No	Yes	Yes	64	−9	Yes	No	Yes	ROM-less version of TMS2100/2300 microcomputer
Yes	No	Yes	Yes	64	5	Yes	No	Yes	ROM-less evaluator chip; uses a 24-bit control word
Yes	No	Yes	Yes	64	5	Yes	No	Yes	ROM-less evaluator chip for TCP 4600 microcomputer family
Yes	No	No	Yes	64	−10	Yes	No	Yes	ROM-less version of μPD548
Yes	No	Yes	Yes	40	5,12	Yes	Yes	Yes	Usually used with program storage unit
No	No	Yes	Yes	40	5,−12	No	Yes	Yes	Predecessor of F8
No	No	Yes	Yes	18	5,−9	Yes	Yes	Yes	Predecessor of 8080, still in wide use
Yes	No	Yes	Yes	40	5	Yes	No	Yes	ROM-less version of 8051 all-in-one processor
Yes	Yes	Yes	Yes	40	5	Yes	Yes	Yes	ROM-less versions of 8048/8049
No	Yes	Yes	Yes	40	5,12,−5	Yes	Yes	Yes	By and large, still the most popular
Yes	Yes	Yes	Yes	40	5	Yes	Yes	Yes	8080 code compatible, has built-in clock
Yes	Yes	Yes	Yes	40	5	Yes	Yes	Yes	ROM-less version of 80C48 all-in-one processor
Yes	No	Yes	Yes	40	5	Yes	Yes	Yes	Provides 13 addressing modes
No	No	Yes	Yes	40	5	Yes	Yes	Yes	Similar to 650X but needs 2φ clock
Yes	No	Yes	Yes	40+	5	Yes	Yes	Yes	ROM-less piggyback package version of MK3870/12 all-in-one processor
Yes	No	Yes	Yes	40+	5	Yes	Yes	Yes	ROM-less piggyback package version of MK3873/12 all-in-one processor
No	Yes	Yes	Yes	40	5	Yes	Yes	Yes	Available in depletion-load version
Yes	Yes	Yes	Yes	40	5	Yes	Yes	Yes	6802 has 128x8 on chip RAM; 6808 has no RAM
Yes	Yes	Yes	Yes	40	5	Yes	Yes	Yes	ROM-less version of 6801 single-chip μC
Yes	Yes	Yes	Yes	40	5	Yes	Yes	Yes	Enhanced 6800 command set
Yes	Yes	No[4]	No	40	5	Yes	Yes	Yes	Has handy daisy-chain capability
Yes	Yes	Yes	Yes	40	5	Yes	Yes	Yes	ROM-less version of INS8050 single chip μC
Yes	Yes	Yes[4]	Yes	40	5	Yes	Yes	No	ROM-less version of INS8072; 64 bytes of on chip RAM
Yes	No	Yes	Yes	40	5	Yes	Yes	Yes	On-chip ROM contains Tiny Basic interpreter (nibble 2); 74 assembly-level commands also available
Yes	Yes	Yes	Yes	40	3 to 12	Yes	Yes	Yes	Executes Z80 instructions and has 8085 bus structure
Yes	Yes	Yes	Yes	64Q	5	Yes	No	Yes	ROM-less version of μPD7801 microcomputer

General-purpose microprocessors (Continued)

Word size (data/instruction)	Original source manufacturer	Processor	Process technology	Direct addressing range (words)	Number of basic instructions	Maximum clock frequency (MHz)/phases	Instruction time shortest/longest[2] (µs)	TTL compatible	BCD arithmetic	On-chip interrupts/levels	Number of internal general-purpose registers	Number of stack registers
8/8	RCA	1802	CMOS	64 k	91	5/1	3.2/4.8	Yes	No	Yes/1	16	RAM
8/8	RCA	CPD1805	CMOS/SOS	64 k	113	8000/1	2/3	Yes	No	Yes/1	16×8	RAM
8/8	Signetics	2650A	NMOS	32 k	75	2/1	1.5/6	Yes	Yes	Yes/1	7	8×15
8/8	Zilog	Z80B	NMOS	64 k	150+	6/1	0.7/4.2	Yes	Yes	Yes/1	14	RAM
8/8	Zilog	Z8602	NMOS	126 k	47	8/1	1.5/3.75	Yes	Yes	Yes/6	144×8	RAM
8/8	Zilog	Z8603	NMOS	126 k	47	8/1	1.5/3.75	Yes	Yes	Yes/6	144×8	RAM
8/8	Zilog	Z8681	NMOS	126 k	47	8/1	1.5/3.75	Yes	Yes	Yes/6	144×8	RAM
8/16	Signetics	8X300	Bipolar	8 k	NA[10]	5/1	0.2	Yes	No	No	8	0
12/12	Intersil	6100	CMOS	4 k	81	3.3/1[12]	2.5/5.5	Yes	No	Yes/1	0	RAM
12/12	Toshiba	T3535	PMOS NMOS	4 k	108	2.5/1	10/30	Yes	No	Yes/8	8	RAM
16/16	Advanced Micro Devices	Am29116	ECL	64 k	30+	10/1	0.1/0.2	Yes	No	No	32	32
16/16	Data General	mN601	NMOS	32 k	42	8.33/2	1.2/29.5	Yes	No	Yes/1	4	RAM
16/16	Data General	mN602	NMOS	64 k	82	8.3/2	2.4/53	Yes	No	Yes/16	4[6]	RAM
16/16	Fairchild	9445	I³L	64 k	100	20/1[9]	0.3/5.7	Yes	No	Yes/16	4	RAM
16/16	Ferranti	F100L	Bipolar	32 k	153	14/1	1.19/14	Yes	No	Yes/1	RAM	RAM
16/16	General Instrument	CP1600/1610	NMOS	64 k	87	4/2	1.6/4.8	Yes	No	Yes/1	8	RAM
16/16	Intel	iAPX86/10	NMOS	IM[5]	97	5/1	0.4/37.8	Yes	Yes	Yes/1	8	RAM
16/16[1]	Intel	iAPX88/10	NMOS	64 k[5]	97	5/1	0.4/37.8	Yes	Yes	Yes/1	8	RAM
16/16	Motorola	MC68000	NMOS	16M[5]	61	8/1	0.5/NA[10]	Yes	Yes	Yes/1	16	RAM
16/16	National Semiconductor	INS8900	NMOS	64 k	45	2/1	2.5/5	Yes	Yes	Yes/6	4	10×16
16/16[1]	National Semiconductor	NS16008	NMOS	64 k[5]	78/100+	NA[10]	NA[10]	Yes	Yes	Yes	8	RAM
16/16	National Semiconductor	NS16016	NMOS	64 k	78/100+	NA[10]	NA[10]	Yes	Yes	Yes	8	RAM
16/16	National Semiconductor	NS16032	NMOS	16M[5]	100+	NA[10]	NA[10]	Yes	Yes	Yes	8	RAM
16/16	Panafacom	MN1610	NMOS	64 k	33	2/2	2/6	Yes[3]	No	Yes/3	5	RAM
16/16[1]	Texas Instruments	TMS9980/9981	NMOS	8 k	69	4/4	3.2/49.6	Yes[3]	No	Yes/4	16	RAM
16/16[1]	Texas Instruments	TMS9995	NMOS	32 k	72	6/1	1/40	Yes	No	Yes/7	256×8	RAM
16/16	Texas Instruments	TMS/SBP9900	NMOS/I²L	32 k	69	4/4	2/31	Yes[3]	No	Yes/16	16	RAM
16/16	Western Digital	WD-16	NMOS	64 k	116	3.3/4	2.1/780	Yes	Yes	Yes/16	6	RAM
16/16	Western Digital	Pascal Microengine	NMOS	64 k	150+	3/4	2.4/300[8]	Yes	Yes	Yes/4	RAM	RAM
16/16	Zilog	Z8001	NMOS	48M[5]	110+	8/1	0.75/90	Yes	Yes	Yes/1	16	RAM
16/16	Zilog	Z8002	NMOS	354 k	110+	8/1	0.75/90	Yes	Yes	Yes/1	16	RAM
80/16	Intel	i8087	NMOS	1 Mbyte	46	5	9/100	Yes	No	Yes/1	8×80	8×80

1. Has 8-bit external buses and 16-bit internal buses. 2. With maximum clock. 3. Except clock lines.
4. Standard TTL or MOS circuits will suffice. 5. Range in bytes. 6. Frame Pointer too.
7. Double-precision 16-bit operations available. 8. String search.
9. Clock internally divided by 4 or 6 depending on instruction. 10. Not applicable. 11. 9980 only.
12. At 5 V; as supply voltage increases, clock freq. can increase.

On-chip clock	DMA capability	Specialized memory & I/O circuits avail.	Prototyping system avail.	Package size (pins)	Voltages required (V)	Assembly language development system	High-level languages	Time-sharing cross software	Comments
Yes	Yes	Yes	Yes	40	4 to 10.5	Yes	Yes	Yes	On-chip DMA counter
Yes	Yes	Yes	Yes	40	4 to 10.5	Yes	Yes	Yes	ROM-less version of CDP1804; has 64 bytes of RAM on chip and an 8-bit counter/timer
No	Yes	Yes	Yes	40	5	Yes	Yes	Yes	There are 1.25 and 2 MHz versions
No	Yes	Yes	Yes	40	5	Yes	Yes	Yes	8080 instructions are a subset
Yes	No	Yes	Yes	64Q	5	Yes	Yes	Yes	ROM-less version of Z8601 microcomputer; all ROM address and data lines available on the 64 pins of the QUIL package
Yes	No	Yes	Yes	40	5	Yes	Yes	Yes	Piggyback ROM-less package, otherwise same as 8602
Yes	No	Yes	Yes	40	5	Yes	Yes	Yes	ROM-less and RAM-less version of Z8 microcomputer; still has two counter/timers, serial I/O port, 32 I/O lines
Yes	No	Yes	Yes	50	5	Yes	No	Yes	Intended for high speed controllers
Yes	Yes	Yes	Yes	40	4 to 11	Yes	Yes	Yes	Emulates PDP-8 instruction set
Yes	Yes	Yes	Yes	36	5,−5	Yes	Yes	Yes	Has multiply and divide inst.
No	Yes	Yes	Yes	48	5	Yes	No	Yes	Control-oriented microprogrammable CPU, can generate CRC bits
Yes	Yes	Yes	No	40	5,10,14,−4.25	Yes	Yes	Yes	Emulates NOVA instruction set
No	Yes	Yes	Yes	40	3,12,±5	Yes	Yes	Yes	Executes the NOVA instruction set and addresses double the memory of the mN601
No	Yes	Yes	Yes	40	5	Yes	Yes	Yes	Executes NOVA 3 and 4 instruction sets; in devel.
No	Yes	Yes	Yes	40	5,1.2	Yes	Yes	Yes	Can do double word operations
No	Yes	Yes	Yes	40	5,12,−3	Yes	Yes	Yes	All internal registers can be accumulators
Yes	Yes	Yes	Yes	40	5	Yes	Yes	Yes	Has 24 addressing modes
Yes	Yes	Yes	Yes	40	5	Yes	Yes	Yes	8-bit bus version of 8086 microprocessor
No	Yes	Yes	Yes	64	5	Yes	Yes	Yes	Has 32-bit wide internal structure
No	Yes	Yes	Yes	40	5	Yes	Yes	Yes	Architecture intended for data handling
No	Yes	Yes	Yes	40	5	Yes	Yes	No	8-bit bus version of dual language (8080/native) CPU, has internal 16-bit bus
No	Yes	Yes	Yes	40	5	Yes	Yes	No	Full 16-bit version, offers 8080A and native instruction sets
No	Yes	Yes	Yes	48	5	Yes	Yes	No	Expanded 16-bit version with eight 32-bit registers, six 24-bit registers and two 16-bit registers; can address 16 Mbytes
No	Yes	Yes	No	40	5,12,−3	Yes	No	No	
Yes	Yes	Yes	No	40	5,12,−5[11]	Yes	Yes	Yes	The 9980 requires external clock
Yes	Yes	Yes	No	40	5	Yes	Yes	Yes	CPU has 256 bytes of RAM on-board to speed context switches
No	Yes	Yes	No	64	5,12,−5	Yes	Yes	Yes	Emulates 990 mini instructions
No	Yes	Yes	Yes	40	5,12,−5	Yes	Yes	No	Very similar to DEC LSI-11
No	Yes	Yes	Yes	40	±12,±5	Yes	Yes	Yes	Five-chip set directly executes Pascal p-code
No	Yes	Yes	Yes	48	5	Yes	Yes	Yes	Address space is divided into segments
No	Yes	Yes	Yes	40	5	Yes	Yes	Yes	Nonsegmented version
No	Yes	Yes	Yes	40	5	Yes	Yes	Yes	Numeric processor does IEEE floating-point calculations as well as trig, log, and exponential operations

Appendix 2 Data sheets for various microprocessors

8-bit microprocessor, NMOS
MCS-80 (8080A)

Intel Corp.
3065 Bowers Ave.
Santa Clara, CA 95051
(408) 249-8027

Alternate sources: Advanced Micro Devices, Mitsubishi, National Semiconductor, NEC Microcomputers, Siemens, Signetics (Philips) and Texas Instruments.

The 8080A is an 8-bit parallel processor designed for use in general-purpose computing applications. Fabricated with silicon-gate NMOS technology, the 8080A contains six general-purpose 8-bit registers, and 8-bit accumulator, four testable flag bits, an 8-bit parallel-processing arithmetic and logic unit, a 16-bit stack pointer and a 16-bit program counter. The processor can handle vectored interrupts and can directly address up to 512 I/O ports. Arithmetic and logic instructions can set or reset four flags and a fifth flag is used for decimal arithmetic only.

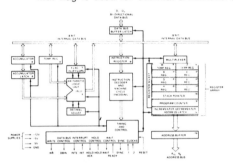

The typical 8080A system consists of a processor, a clock, a bus controller, some memory and a memory decoder. Both the data and address buses are TTL compatible and have three-state capability. All but the clock lines are TTL-compatible.

Specifications

Data word size:	8 bits
Address bus size:	16 bits
Direct addressing range:	65,536 words
Instruction word size:	8 to 24 bits
Number of basic instructions:	78
Shortest instruction/time (Add reg. to accum.):	2μs, typ.
Longest instruction/time (Swap H&L with top of stack):	9μs, typ.
Clock frequency (min/max):	0.5/3 MHz
Clock phases/voltage swing:	2/9 V
Dedicated I/O control lines:	None
Package:	40-pin DIP
Power requirements:	12 V/40 mA
	5 V/60 mA
	−5 V/10 μA

Comments

The 8080A has 78 basic instructions divided into five groups: Data transfer, Arithmetic, Logic, Branch and Stack, and I/O and Machine control. There are also four addressing modes—direct, indirect, register and immediate. The move, load and store instruction groups can transfer either 8 or 16 bit data words between memory, the six working registers and the accumulator.

Software support for the 8080A includes a relocating macroassembler, a text editor and PL/M—all available on the company's own development system. There is also a program library (Insite) available to Intel customers that contains well over 200 programs submitted by users.

The basic software of the 8080A is designed for rapid stack manipulation and flexible jumps from the main program to subroutines. The ability to increment or decrement memory locations, the six general-purpose registers or the accumulator as well as register pairs or the stack pointer provides simple program looping capability.

Hardware support is available in several forms—from the low cost SDK-80 prototyping kit to the larger Microprocessor Development Systems in the Intellec family. Also available is a large range of 8080A-based computer boards from general-

Hardware

Model	Description	Price (100 qty)
8080A	CPU (commercial)	$6.75
8080A	CPU (MIL level C)	35.95
JAN 8080A	CPU, Full MIL version	85.00
8205	1-of-8 decoder	2.80
8212	8-bit latch/buffer	2.45
8214	Priority Interrupt controller	4.65
8216	4-bit bidirectional bus driver	2.25
8224	Clock driver	3.95
8226	Inverting version, 8216	2.25
8228	Bus controller	6.10
8251A	USART	6.70
8253	Counter/timer	15.00
8255A	Parallel I/O	5.00
8257	DMA controller	11.40
8259	Interrupt controller	12.15
8279	Keyboard/disp. control	9.80

purpose CPU boards to multichannel analog-input boards. The large prototyping and development system, the Intellec-MDS, offers the most flexibility—the system comes with a CPU, 16 k of RAM, 2 k of ROM, and software and hardware interfaces for terminals, printers and other equipment. For in-circuit emulation an ¹CE-80 module is available.

8-bit microprocessor, NMOS
MCS-85 (8085A, 8085A-2)

Intel Corp.
3065 Bowers Ave.
Santa Clara, CA 95051
(408) 246-7501

Alternate sources: Siemens and Advanced Micro Devices by mask exchange. Also NEC by independent development.

The 8085A processor is a software-compatible upgrade of the 8080A processor. It offers two more instructions and has many of the peripheral circuits originally needed built right onto the same chip as the processor. With five levels of vectored interrupt, a serial I/O line and a clock speed of 3 MHz, the 8085A offers 8080A users a simple way to upgrade existing systems without losing any software. And, since the clock is on chip, all signal lines are TTL compatible, with the address and data buses having three-state capability. A higher speed version, the 8085A-2, is also available.

Specifications

Data word size:	8 bits
Address bus size:	16 bits
Direct addressing range:	65,536 bytes
Instruction word size:	1, 2 or 3 bytes
Number of basic instructions:	80
Shortest instruction/time	1.3 μs (8085A)
(Move data):	0.8 μs (A-2)
Longest instruction/time	5.2 μs (8085A)
(Double add):	3.2 μs (A-2)
Clock frequency (min/max):	0.5/3 MHz (A)
	0.5.5 MHz (A-2)
Clock phases/voltage swing:	1/TTL
Dedicated I/O control lines:	None
Package:	40-pin DIP
Power requirements:	5 V/170 mA

*8085A uses partially multiplexed address bus—eight lines are direct and eight are shared with the data bus.

Hardware

Model	Description	Price (100 qty)
P8085A	CPU (commercial temp)	$15.00
D8085A	CPU (industrial temp)	18.75
P8085A-2	5 MHz CPU	19.50
P8155	256 byte RAM, I/O & timer	14.00
P8156	Same as 8155	14.00
P8355	2 kbyte ROM & 16 line I/O	consult factory
C8755-A	2 k UV EPROM & 16 line I/O	50.00
P8205	1 of 8 binary decoder	2.80
P8212	8-bit I/O port	2.45
P8214	Priority interrupt	4.65
P8216	Bidirectional bus driver	2.25
P8226	Inverting version 8216	2.25
P8253	Programmable timer	15.00
P8259	Interrupt controller	12.15
P8279	Kbd/display interface	9.80

Comments

The instruction set of the 8085A contains all of the 8080A's instructions plus two more—RIM (read interrupt mask) and SIM (set interrupt mask)—for a total of 80 basic commands. The RIM and SIM instructions are used in conjunction with the interrupt capability built into the 8085A to provide four vectored interrupts, three of which are maskable.

Available software support for the 8085A includes all the existing 8080A software available through Insite—the company's user's software program library—and the many companies and private organizations that offer 8080A and 8085A software. An 8085A macroassembler can also be purchased,

as well as PL/M when an MDS system with floppy disc is used.

Special features of the two new instructions permit the 8085A to handle serial inputs and outputs, and set up special masking bits to set or reset flags for the levels of vectored interrupts. Otherwise, all 8080A instructions can run on the 8085A without modification. The only adjustment that may have to be made is in any timing loops that use the 2 MHz clock frequency of the 8080A to compensate for the new 3 MHz clock (or 5 MHz clock of the 8085A-2).

Hardware support for the 8085A includes the ICE-85, an in-circuit emulator; the SDK-85 low-cost prototyping system; and the UPP 955 and EPROM programmer. Also, most of the development hardware available for the 8080A can be used to develop 8085A circuits and programs. The entire Intellec MDS microprocessor development system can be used, with just a few changes.

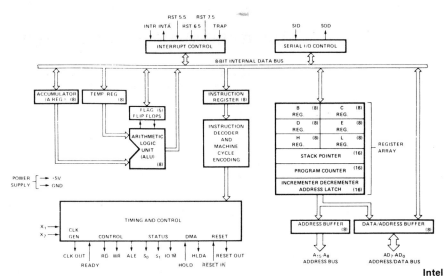

Intel

The basic architecture of the 8085A is the same as that of the 8080A. The only differences are the built-in clock generator, the built-in system control circuit and the multiplexed address/data bus structure. These differences make available several pins for additional control.

8-bit microprocessor, NMOS

MC6800

Alternate sources: American Microsystems, Fairchild, Hitachi and Sescosem/Thomson CSF.

Motorola, IC Div.
3501 Ed Bluestein Blvd.
Austin, TX 78721
(512) 928-6000

Designed as a general-purpose central processor, the MC6800 provides 8-bit computational capability with an instruction set of 72 commands. The processor has a bidirectional data bus, a full 16-bit address bus and can operate from a 5 V supply. There are three versions of the MC6800 available—the original MC6800 with a 1 MHz clock rate, the MC68A00 with a 1.5 MHz clock, and the MC68B00 with a 2 MHz clock. All versions are pin compatible.

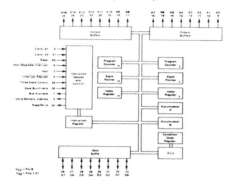

A minimum system for the MC6800 will typically consist of the processor, some ROM and RAM, a clock circuit and some I/O circuits. All lines except the clock lines are TTL compatible and the address bus, data bus and R/W line also have three-state capability. The 6800 has two accumulators, but all stack space is in the user-supplied RAM—there are no auxiliary registers on the processor chip.

Comments

The basic instruction set consists of 72 commands that contain binary and decimal arithmetic operations, logic instructions shift and rotate functions, branch and stack manipulation commands and memory transfer operations. I/O commands are stored in the memory address space. Most instructions operate on both the ALU and memory.

The basic software support includes an assembler, editor, macro-assembler, a disc-based operating system and several high-level languages—Basic and Fortran. The user program library contains more than 65 programs.

Software features include direct page memory addressing and relative branches that allow position independent code to be written. A read/modify/write instruction can be used to modify the contents of a memory location without bringing the contents into the accumulator.

Hardware support for the MC6800 comes in several forms. For the circuit designer there are several evaluation board systems available from Motorola and the alternate sources. And, for the program

Specifications

Data word size:	8 bits
Address bus size:	16 bits
Direct addressing range:	65,536 words
Instruction word size:	8 bits
Number of basic instructions:	72
Shortest instruction/time (Load accumulator A):	1 μs
Longest instruction/time (Software interrupt):	6 μs
Clock frequency (min/max):	0.1/2 MHz
Clock phases/voltage swing:	2/ Vcc − 0.6 to Vss+ 0.4 V
Dedicated I/O control lines:	9
Package:	40-pin DIP
Power requirements:	5 V/100 mA

Hardware

Model	Description	Price (100 qty)
MC6800	CPU (commercial)	$ 8.95*
MC6800	CPU (industrial)	N/A
MC6800	CPU (military)	N/A
MC6821	PIA	4.20
MC6840	Programmable timer	13.00
MC6843	Floppy-disc controller	25.00*
MC6844	DMA controller	23.50*
MC6845	CRT controller	25.00*
MC6847	Video display generator	15.70
MC6849	Double density FDC	N/A
MC6850	ACIA	3.95
MC6851	UCIA	N/A
MC6852	Sync. serial data adapter	4.40*
MC6854	Data link controller	17.00
MC6860	600 bps modem	8.00
MC6862	2400 bps demodulator	13.15
MC68488	GPIB adapter	14.00
F6856 (Fairchild)	Sync. protocol comm. controller	10.00
*(25 to 99)		

development engineer, the EXORciser system, consisting of a CPU board, a 2-k static RAM board, a 16-k dynamic RAM board, a baud-rate board, serial and parallel interfaces, a PROM programmer and a PROM/EPROM board can be used with the floppy-disc operating system. Also available is a user system evaluator (USE) that can help with the early prototyping efforts.

8-bit microprocessor, NMOS

Z80-CPU

Alternate sources: Mostek, NEC, SGS-ATES and Sharp.

Zilog Inc.
10460 Bubb Rd.
Cupertino, CA 95014
(408) 446-4666

Based on the architecture of the 8080, the Z80 can perform the 78 instructions of that processor plus 80 additional instructions. The ion-implanted NMOS device is offered in two versions — the Z80 with 2.8 MHz maximum clock and the Z80A with a 4.5 MHz clock. Operating from a single 5-V supply and a single-phase external clock, the processor contains 17 internal registers and built-in dynamic RAM refresh circuitry and has three modes of interrupt response.

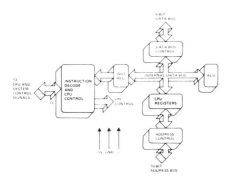

The architecture of the Z80 resembles that of the 8080A, except that there is a second bank of eight 8-bit registers that mirrors the eight registers in the 8080A. All timing generation is on the processor chip except the oscillator, and the Address bus is structured so that refresh addresses appear on the lower half of the bus to refresh dynamic RAMs. A minimal system consists of the processor, a clock source and some memory.

Specifications

Data word size:	8 bits
Address bus size:	16 bits
Direct addressing range:	65,536 words
Instruction word size:	One to three bytes
Number of basic instructions:	158
Shortest instruction/time (Load register to register):	1 μs
Longest instruction/time (Set bit at address IX+d):	5.75 μs
Clock frequency (min/max):	5 kHz/4.5 MHz
Clock phases/voltage swing:	1/5 V
Dedicated I/O control lines:	5
Package:	40-pin DIP
Power requirements:	5 V/90 mA (Z80A)
	5 V/60 mA (Z80)

Comments

The instruction set of the Z80 contains all 78 op codes of the 8080A's instruction set as well as another 80 codes. Of the 158 total instructions, there are 21 8-bit Load commands, 20 16-bit Load commands, 14 Exchange, Block transfer and Search instructions, 17 Arithmetic and Logic commands for 8-bit operations, 11 instructions for 16-bit arithmetic and logic operations, 12 general-purpose arithmetic commands, 16 shift and rotate functions, nine Bit set, Reset and Test commands, 11 Jump instructions, seven Call/Return directives and 12 I/O operations.

Software support includes a macroassembler that can generate relocatable code, a linker that can link together program modules and generate a load module with absolute addresses, and several high-level languages—PL/M, PL/Z and Basic. Also available is a text editor and a file maintenance and debug routine that supports the floppy-disc based program development system.

Special features of the instruction set include the block-move operations that permit large sections of data held in memory to automatically be relocated.

Hardware

Model	Description	Price† (100 qty)
Z80	CPU (commercial)	$ 16.25
Z80	CPU (military)	N/A
Z80A	8-bit-commercial	25.00
Z80-PIO	2-port parallel I/O	8.50
Z80A-PIO	Higher speed version	12.40
Z80-CTC	Quad counter/timer	8.50
Z80A-CTC	Higher speed version	12.50
Z80-DMA	Two port direct memory access	36.00*
Z80A-DMA	Higher speed version	N/A
Z80-SIO	Dual full-duplex serial I/O channels	52.00
Z80A-SIO	Higher speed version	68.00
MK3886	RAM/timer & I/O (Mostek proprietary)	N/A

† Plastic packages * Ceramic only

Hardware support provided for the Z80 includes a development system with in-circuit emulation capability, real-time debug and program storage modules. The system has a dual floppy-disc operating system and can be expanded to handle up to 64 kbytes of RAM and many interface options for terminals and printers.

8-bit microprocessor, NMOS

MC6809, 6809E, also A and B versions

Alternate sources: None

Motorola, Inc.
Semiconductor Group
3501 Ed Bluestein Blvd.
Austin, TX 78721
(512) 928-6000

Although presenting an 8-bit data bus to the outside world, the MC6809 family of processors can perform full 16-bit operations internally. The 6809, 68A09 and the 68B09 (1, 1.5 and 2-MHz clock rates) have on-chip clock oscillators while the E-suffix versions do not. Otherwise they perform identically. The instruction set has been enhanced beyond that of the MC6800 family of parts, and includes many 16-bit operations and many new register operations.

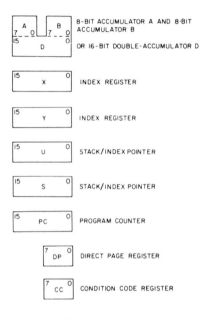

8-BIT ACCUMULATOR A AND 8-BIT ACCUMULATOR B

OR 16-BIT DOUBLE-ACCUMULATOR D

INDEX REGISTER

INDEX REGISTER

STACK/INDEX POINTER

STACK/INDEX POINTER

PROGRAM COUNTER

DIRECT PAGE REGISTER

CONDITION CODE REGISTER

Specifications

Data word size	8/16 bits
Address bus size	16 bits
Direct addressing range	64 kbytes
Instruction word size	1 to 4 bytes
Number of basic instructions	59
Shortest instruction/time (many)	2 μs*
Longest instruction/time (software interrupt)	6 μs*
Clock frequency (min/max)	100 kHz/2 MHz
Clock phases/voltage swing	Internal or 1/TTL
Dedicated I/O control lines	3
Package	40-pin DIP
Power requirements	5 V/250 mA

*2 MHz

Hardware

Model	Description	Price (25 to 99)
MC6809P	Pseudo 16-bit μP	$36.00
MC6809L	Ceramic CPU	28.00
MC6821	Peripheral interface adapter	4.20
MC6840P	Programmable timer	13.00
MC6843C	Floppy-disk controller	29.95
MC6844C	DMA controller	29.95
MC6845P	CRT controller	26.50
MC6846P	Combined ROM/timer	Contact factory
MC6847P	Video display generator	15.70
MC6850P	Asynchronous communications adapter	3.95
MC6851P	UCIA	N/A
MC6852P	Sync. serial data adapter	4.40
MC6854P	Data link controller	19.80
MC6860P	600-bps modem	8.00
MC6862P	2400-bps demodulator	10.60
MC68488P	GPIB adapter	19.00

Comments

The instruction set has fewer instructions than that of the older 6800; however, the 6809 has several more powerful commands that can replace multiple instructions of the older processor. The 59 instructions have all the addressing modes of the 6800 plus PC relative, extended indirect, indexed indirect, and PC relative indirect.

Software support for the 6809 family consists of all 6800 family programs since most programs will be source compatible. A translator program will also be available for the user to convert 6800 program listings into 6809 code. Program development can be done on the EXORciser development system.

Software features of the 6809 include an enhanced 6800 instruction set that includes 16-bit arithmetic, extended range branches, an 8 × 8 bit multiply, enhanced pointer register manipulation, equal-size register exchanges, and auto-increment/decrement operations with any of four pointer registers. The processor architecture supports high-level languages and the multiple addressing modes provide many programming shortcuts.

Hardware support consists of the micromodule family of microprocessor cards and the EXORciser development system. All 6800 family peripheral support circuits are also bus compatible with the 6809 family, thus providing a full family for the designer.

8-bit microprocessor, CMOS

NSC800

Alternate sources: None for CMOS; several for NMOS Z80

National Semiconductor
2900 Semiconductor Dr.
Santa Clara, CA 95051
(408) 737-5000

The NSC800 is a software-compatible equivalent to the Z80 NMOS microprocessor, but fabricated in CMOS low-power technology using a new P^2 CMOS process. Capable of operating at 4 MHz (at 5 V) with a power dissipation of less than 125 mW for a three-clip all-CMOS system, the NSC800 components take advantage of existing Z80 software. The bus matches that of the 8085 and the internal architecture resembles that of the Z80.

Comments

The instruction set duplicates that of the Z80 microprocessor, which has 158 commands; 78 of these are the same as those of the 8080A. The 158 commands include 8 and 16-bit load instructions (41); exchange, block transfer and search operations (14); arithmetic commands (41); shift and rotate functions (16); bit and I/O instructions (21); and jump operations (11).

Software features include the block move operations that permit large sections of data held in memory to be relocated automatically.

Software support includes the Starplex development system and its operating system software and high-level languages. Also, a wide base of already-existing Z80 software can be accessed from many sources.

Hardware support consists of the special circuits listed in the table, a full line of P^2 CMOS MSI and SSI circuits, and all existing Z80-compatible support circuits and microcomputer equipment.

Specifications

Data word size	8 bits
Address bus size	16 bits
Direct addressing range	64 kbytes
Instrument word size	8, 16, 24 bits
Number of basic instructions	158
Shortest instruction time (load register to register)	1 μs (4 MHz)
Longest instruction time (set bit at address Ix+d)	5.75 μs (4 MHz)
Clock frequency (min/max)	4 MHz (5 V)/ 8 MHz (12 V)
Clock phases/voltage swing	1/supply dependent
Dedicated I/O control lines	9
Package size	40
Power requirements (4 MHz)	5 V/10 mA

Hardware

Model	Description	Price (100 qty)
NSC800	CMOS 4-MHz CPU	N/A
NSC810	RAM-I/O-timer	N/A
NSC830	ROM-I/O	N/A
NMC6504	4-k × 1 static CMOS RAM	N/A
NMC6514	1-k × 4 static CMOS RAM	N/A

16-bit microprocessor, NMOS (HMOS)

MCS-86 (8086, 8088)

Alternate sources: None

Intel Corp.
3065 Bowers Ave.
Santa Clara, CA 95051
(408) 987-8080

The 8086 is a 16-bit processor capable of performing bit, byte, word and block operations including 8 and 16-bit signed and unsigned arithmetic in binary and decimal formats. Arithmetic operations include multiply and divide. Through the use of a memory segmentation technique, the 8086 can directly address up to 1 Mbyte of memory using 24 operand addressing modes. However, the 8086 is also upward compatible with assembly language program listings from the 8080 and 8085 processors. Also available is the 8088 CPU. This processor has an 8-bit external data bus and a full 16-bit internal bus, compatible with the 8086. All software is object-code compatible between the 8086 and 8088.

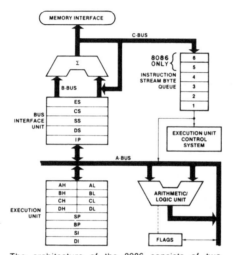

The architecture of the 8086 consists of two asynchronous processors, one to control the basic processor operations and bus and the other to prepare and manipulate the data. No I/O lines are dedicated on the CPU, but the bus can provide all the necessary control lines to the various peripheral circuits. Capable of supporting multiprocessor configurations, the 8086 uses its LOCK signal to support a read/modify/write sequence and a TEST signal for external processor synchronization.

Specifications

Data word size	16 bits
Address bus size	20 bits
Direct addressing range	1,048,576 bytes
Instruction word size	1 to 6 bytes
Number of basic instructions	97
Shortest instruction/time (many)	400 ns
Longest instruction/time (16-bit signed-integer div.)	37.8 μs
Clock frequency (min/max)	0.5/5 MHz
Clock phases/voltage swing	1/TTL
Dedicated I/O control lines	3
Package	40-pin DIP
Power requirements	5 V/275 mA

Hardware

Model	Description	Price (100 qty)
D8086	CPU, commercial	$ 86.65
D8086-2	8-MHz version	200.00
D8088	CPU, commercial	78.00
P8237-2	5 MHz DMA controller	25.00
P8155-2	RAM-I/O-timer	21.00
P8156-2	Active-H version	21.00
P8289	Bus arbiter	38.00

Comments

The instruction set of the 8086 16-bit microprocessor handles bit, byte, word and block operations with 24 different operand addressing modes. The 97 basic types of instructions can be grouped in six functional areas: data transfer (16), arithmetic (20), logic (12), string manipulation (11), control transfer (26) and processor control (12).

Software support is available on the Intellec microcomputer development system and includes PL/M-86, ASM-86 (assembly), CONV-86 (8080/8085 source to 89086 source converter), utility programs, libraries, link and locate capabilities, and a soon to be announced in-circuit emulation capability. The users library, insite is also accessible.

Software features of the 8086 include efficient block operations that can be performed using single-byte primitive instructions with a repeat prefix. The instruction group includes move, compare, scan, load and store operations on words or bytes. Arithmetic capability includes 8 and 16-bit signed and unsigned multiply and divide.

Hardware support currently consists of the SDK-86 system design kit that provides the user with a prelaid-out circuit board, keyboard and LED hex display. A system monitor provides general software utilities and system diagnostic programs. The SDK-86 can also be interfaced to the Intellec system for use as a circuit test bed.

16-bit microprocessor, NMOS

MC68000

Alternate sources: None

Motorola Inc.
Semiconductor Group
3501 Ed Bluestein Blvd.
Austin, TX 78721
(512) 928-6000

The most advanced microprocessor made by Motorola, the MC68000 performs operations on bit, BCD, byte, 16-bit word and double-word data. The 16-bit processor has full 32-bit-wide registers. The processor can directly address 16,777,216 bytes of memory and is organized so that it has a separate data and address bus—a 16-line data bus and a 23-line address bus. Housed in a 64-pin DIP, the processor can even mate with existing 6800-family peripheral products.

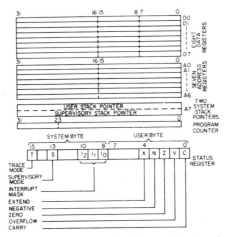

The architecture of the MC68000 resembles that of a mainframe computer—all internal registers are 32-bits wide. The program counter is a full 24 bits, of which 23 go directly to the address bus. The 24th bit generates special strobe signals that can be externally recombined to form the 24th address bit. Just an external clock, memory and I/O circuits are needed for operation.

Comments

The instruction set of the MC68000 contains just 56 basic commands, but almost all can take advantage of the 14 types of addressing modes. Commands include signed and unsigned multiply and divide operations, special Trap instructions, powerful subroutine call and return functions and multiple-function instructions.

Software features of the instruction set include a structure that supports high-level languages such as Pascal, Basic, Cobol and Fortran. Each instruction, with few exceptions, operates on bytes, words and double words, and can use any of the 14 addressing modes. The large addressing range and the powerful subroutine link and unlink instructions permit re-entrant code to be generated easily. Special Trap instructions make the code easier to test and there are 16 trap vectors available to the programmer.

Software support for the MC68000 includes a dual-disk operating system, debug aids, assemblers, and high-level languages—Pascal, Basic, Fortran and

Specifications

Data word size	16 bits
Address bus size	23 bits*
Direct addressing range	16,777,216 bytes
Instruction word size	2 to 10 bytes
Number of basic instructions	56
Shortest instruction/time (move byte to regis)	0.5 μs
Longest instruction/time (unsigned divide)	N/A
Clock frequency (min/max)	1MHz
Clock phases/voltage swing	1/TTL
Dedicated I/O control lines	6
Package	64-pin DIP
Power requirements	5 V/300 mA

* The 24th bit is generated external to the processor by gating two strobe lines.

Hardware

Model	Description	Price (unit qty)
MC68000	16-bit microprocessor	$249.00
DMAC	DMA controller	N/A
MMU	Memory manager unit	N/A
BAM	Bus arbitration module	N/A
	All 6800 peripherals	
MEX68KDM	Design Module	1795.00
M68KOXASMBL2	370 version of cross macro assembler	1500.00
M68KOXASMBL3	PDP-11 version	1500.00
M68KOXASMBL0	Exorciser version (MC6800 CPU)	990.00
M68KOXASMBL1	Exorciser version (MC6809 CPU)	990.00

Cobol—as well as MPL. For current MC6800 users, a translator program that converts 6800 assembly-language programs into 68000 code is also available. Cross software that can run on EXORciser systems is under development. It will include a cross-assembler, a simulator and MPL.

Hardware support for the processor includes all of the MC6800 family peripheral chips—parallel and serial interfaces, baud-rate generators, interrupt controllers, IEEE-488 interfaces, video controllers, and more. Also, three specialized support chips—a DMA controller, a bus arbitrator, and a memory manager—are under development.

16-bit microprocessor, NMOS
Z8000

Zilog Inc.
10460 Bubb Rd.
Cupertino, CA 95014
(408) 446-4666

Alternate sources: Advanced Micro Devices

The Z8000 16-bit microprocessor comes in two versions—a nonsegmented version that can address 64 kbytes of memory in any of six address spaces, and a segmented version that can address up to 8 Mbytes in each space. The nonsegmented version comes in a 40-pin DIP and the segmented unit in a 48-pin DIP. The CPU contains numerous registers, can handle bit, BCD, byte, word, double word, byte string and word string data. The six different address spaces of the processor include code, data and stack for both system and normal modes.

Specifications

Data word size	16 bits
Address bus size	23 bits/16 bits
Direct addressing range	8 Mbytes/64 kbytes
Instruction word size	2 to 6 bytes
Number of basic instructions	110+
Shortest instruction/time (many)	(4 MHz clock) 750 ns
Longest instruction/time (divide, signed)	90 μs
Clock frequency (min/max)	8 MHz
Clock phases/voltage swing	1/TTL
Dedicated I/O control lines	3
Package	40 or 48-pin DIP
Power requirements	5 V/300 mA

The architecture of the Z8000 is a regular register structure that permits efficient compiler-generated code to be run. There are 16 general-purpose registers in addition to the special system registers. All 16 can serve as accumulators and all but one can serve as index registers. The architecture can also support multiprocessing via two control lines.

Comments

The instruction set contains more than 110 types of instructions; and with few exceptions, byte, word and double-word data elements can be processed by all instructions. Again with few exceptions, each instruction can use any of the five main addressing modes. There are, though, eight different addressing modes—register, indirect register, direct address, indexed, immediate, base address, base indexed and relative address with auto increment/decrement.

Software features of the Z8000 include the advanced 16 and 32-bit math operations—signed and unsigned multiply and divide—as well as the advanced bit, nibble, byte and word operations. Also, special commands that permit incrementing registers by 1 to 16 (decrementing, too) are very handy.

Hardware

Model	Description	Price (100 qty)
Z8001	Segmented 16-bit CPU	$139.30
Z8002	Nonsegmented 16-bit CPU	107.10
Z8010	Memory management unit	N/A
Z8016	DMA controller	N/A
Z8030	Serial I/O controller	N/A
Z8034	Universal peripheral controller	N/A
Z8036	Counter and I/O	N/A
Z8038	FIO interface unit	N/A
Z8052	CRT controller	N/A
Z8060	FIFO register	N/A
Z8065	Burst error processor	N/A
Z6132	4-k × 8 quasi-static RAM	57.65
Z8	Single-chip processor	Contact factory

Software support will consist of an assembler and editor for assembly language program development and high-level languages for advanced program development.

Hardware support consists of a complete family of peripheral support chips, as well as smart controllers, built around the Z8 microcomputer. Extensions to the Z80 development system and new hardware will make both hardware and software development possible. Both Zilog and its alternate source, AMD, will be introducing the support circuits during late 1979 and 1980.

Appendix 3 All-in-one processors

All-in-one processors

Word size in bits (data/inst.)	Original Source Manufacturer	Device	Process technology	On-chip RAM size	On-chip ROM/ PROM size (words)	Off-chip memory expansion	Number of basic instructions	Maximum clock frequency (kHz)	On-chip clock	Instruction time (shortest/longest) μs	TTL compatible	BCD arithmetic	On-chip interrupts/levels
4/8	AMI	S2000	NMOS	64×4	1024×8	Yes	51	900	Yes	4.5/9	Yes	Yes	No
4/8		S2000A	NMOS	64×4	1024×8	Yes	51	900	Yes	4.5/9	Yes	Yes	No
4/8		S2150	NMOS	64×4	1536×8	Yes	51	1800	Yes	4.5/9	Yes	Yes	No
4/8		S2150A	NMOS	64×4	1536×8	Yes	51	1800	Yes	4.5/9	Yes	Yes	No
4/8		S2205	NMOS	32×4	512×8	Yes	63	3600	Yes	4.5/9	Yes	Yes	Yes/2
4/8		SA2205	NMOS	32×4	512×8	Yes	63	3600	Yes	4.5/9	Yes	Yes	Yes/2
4/8		S2210	NMOS	64×4	1024×8	Yes	63	3600	Yes	4.5/9	Yes	Yes	Yes/2
4/8		SA2210	NMOS	64×4	1024×8	Yes	63	3600	Yes	4.5/9	Yes	Yes	Yes/2
4/8		S2215	NMOS	96×4	1536×8	Yes	63	3600	Yes	4.5/9	Yes	Yes	Yes/2
4/8		SA2215	NMOS	96×4	1536×8	Yes	63	3600	Yes	4.5/9	Yes	Yes	Yes/2
4/8		S2220	NMOS	128×4	2048×8	Yes	63	3600	Yes	4.5/9	Yes	Yes	Yes/2
4/8		SA2220	NMOS	128×4	2048×8	Yes	63	3600	Yes	4.5/9	Yes	Yes	Yes/2
4/8		S2305	NMOS	32×4	512×8	Yes	63	3600	Yes	4.5/9	Yes	Yes	Yes/2
4/8		SA2305	NMOS	32×4	512×8	Yes	63	3600	Yes	4.5/9	Yes	Yes	Yes/2
4/8		S2310	NMOS	64×4	1024×8	Yes	63	3600	Yes	4.5/9	Yes	Yes	Yes/2
4/8		SA2310	NMOS	64×4	1024×8	Yes	63	3600	Yes	4.5/9	Yes	Yes	Yes/2
4/8		S2315	NMOS	96×4	1536×8	Yes	63	3600	Yes	4.5/9	Yes	Yes	Yes/2
4/8		SA2315	NMOS	96×4	1536×8	Yes	63	3600	Yes	4.5/9	Yes	Yes	Yes/2
4/8		S2320	NMOS	128×4	2048×8	Yes	63	3600	Yes	4.5/9	Yes	Yes	Yes/2
4/8		SA2320	NMOS	128×4	2048×8	Yes	63	3600	Yes	4.5/9	Yes	Yes	Yes/2
4/8		S2400	NMOS	128×4	4096×8	Yes	63	3600	Yes	4.5/9	Yes	Yes	Yes/2
4/8	Fujitsu	MB8851	CMOS	128×4	2048×8	No	70	2000	Yes	2/4	Yes	Yes	Yes/2
4/8		MB8853	CMOS	64×4	1024×8	No	70	2000	Yes	2/4	Yes	Yes	Yes/2
4/8	Motorola	MC141000	CMOS	64×4	1024×8	No	43	600	Yes	10/10	Yes	Yes	No
4/8	National	MM57109	PMOS	5×32	NA[1]	Yes	70	400	No	1220/1 S	Yes	Yes	Yes/1
4/8	Semiconductor	COP410L	NMOS	32×4	512×8	Yes	40	250	Yes	16/32	Yes	Yes	No
4/8		COP411L	NMOS	32×4	512×8	Yes	40	250	Yes	16/32	Yes	Yes	No
4/8		COP420	NMOS	64×4	1024×8	Yes	49	1000	Yes	4/8	Yes	Yes	Yes/1
4/8		COP420L	NMOS	64×4	1024×8	Yes	49	250	Yes	16/32	Yes	Yes	Yes/1
4/8		COP420C	CMOS	64×4	1024×8	Yes	49	250	Yes	16/32	Yes	Yes	Yes/1
4/8		COP421	NMOS	64×4	1024×8	Yes	49	1000	Yes	4/8	Yes	Yes	No
4/8		COP421L	NMOS	64×4	1024×8	Yes	49	250	Yes	16/32	Yes	Yes	No
4/8		COP421C	CMOS	64×4	1024×8	Yes	49	250	Yes	16/32	Yes	Yes	No
4/8		COP440	NMOS	128×4	2048×8	Yes	49	1000	Yes	4/8	Yes	Yes	Yes/1
4/8		COP444L	NMOS	128×4	2048×8	Yes	49	250	Yes	16/32	Yes	Yes	Yes/1
4/8		COP445L	NMOS	128×4	2048×8	Yes	49	250	Yes	16/32	Yes	Yes	Yes/1
4/8		COP320C	CMOS	64×4	1048×8	Yes	49	250	Yes	16/32	Yes	Yes	No
4/8		COP321C	CMOS	64×4	1048×8	Yes	49	1000	Yes	4/8	Yes	Yes	No
4/10	NEC Microcomputers	μPD548	PMOS	96×4	1920×10	Yes	72	200	No	10/20	Yes	Yes	Yes/2
4/8		μPD546	PMOS	96×4	2000×8	No	80	440	Yes	4.5/9	Yes	Yes	Yes/1
4/8		μPD553	PMOS	96×4	2000×8	No	80	440	Yes	4.5/9	Yes	Yes	Yes/1
4/8		μPD557L	PMOS	96×4	2000×8	No	80	180	Yes	11/22	Yes	Yes	Yes/1
4/8		μPD650	CMOS	96×4	2000×8	No	80	440	Yes	4.5/9	Yes	Yes	Yes/1

1. Not applicable   2. External 8 bits, internally 16 bits   3. User defined   4. Q = quad in-line
5. FP = flat pack   ? Not available   * Program   ** Pattern   † Display   †† Data

Subroutine nesting levels	General-purpose internal registers	Number of I/O lines	Additional special support circuits	Package size (DIP pins)	Voltages required (V)	Prototyping system avail.	Assembly language programming system	High-level language programming system	Time-sharing cross software	Comments
3	RAM	30	No	40	9	Yes	Yes	Yes	Yes	Includes zero-crossing detector, keyboard decode and LED drivers
3	RAM	30	No	40	9/33	Yes	Yes	Yes	Yes	Same but drivers handle vacuum fluorescent displays
3	RAM	30	No	40	9	Yes	Yes	Yes	Yes	Same extras as S2000 and LED drivers
3	RAM	30	No	40	9/33	Yes	Yes	Yes	Yes	Same extras as S2150 but v-f drivers
5	RAM	30	No	40	5	Yes	Yes	Yes	Yes	Includes zero-crossing detector and keyboard decoder
5	RAM	30	No	40	5	Yes	Yes	Yes	Yes	Same as S2205 but includes an 8-bit a/d converter
5	RAM	30	No	40	5	Yes	Yes	Yes	Yes	Same extras as S2000
5	RAM	30	No	40	5	Yes	Yes	Yes	Yes	Same as S2210 but includes an 8-bit a/d converter
5	RAM	30	No	40	5	Yes	Yes	Yes	Yes	Same extras as S2000
5	RAM	30	No	40	5	Yes	Yes	Yes	Yes	Same as S2215 but includes an 8-bit a/d converter
5	RAM	30	No	40	5	Yes	Yes	Yes	Yes	Same extras as S2000
5	RAM	30	No	40	5	Yes	Yes	Yes	Yes	Same as S2220 but includes an 8-bit a/d converter
5	RAM	30	No	40	5	Yes	Yes	Yes	Yes	Same as S2205 but has MPU bus-compatible interface
5	RAM	30	No	40	5	Yes	Yes	Yes	Yes	Same as SA2205 but has MPU bus-compatible interface
5	RAM	30	No	40	5	Yes	Yes	Yes	Yes	Same as S2210 but has MPU bus-compatible interface
5	RAM	30	No	40	5	Yes	Yes	Yes	Yes	Same as SA2210 but has MPU bus-compatible interface
5	RAM	30	No	40	5	Yes	Yes	Yes	Yes	Same as S2215 but has MPU bus-compatible interface
5	RAM	30	No	40	5	Yes	Yes	Yes	Yes	Same as SA2215 but has MPU bus-compatible interface
5	RAM	30	No	40	5	Yes	Yes	Yes	Yes	Same as S2220 but has MPU bus-compatible interface
5	RAM	30	No	40	5	Yes	Yes	Yes	Yes	Same as SA2220 but has MPU bus-compatible interface
5	RAM	30	No	40	5	Yes	Yes	Yes	Yes	Same extras as S2205
4	RAM	37	No	42	5	Yes	Yes	Yes	Yes	Has 8-bit counter/timer and serial I/O port
4	RAM	37	No	42	5	Yes	Yes	Yes	Yes	Version of 8851 with smaller RAM and ROM
1	2+RAM	23	Yes	28	3 to 6	Yes	Yes	No	Yes	Exact CMOS equivalent to TMS 1000 not the enhanced 1000C; MC141200 also available
4	1	11	Yes	28	9	No	No	No	No	Has scientific calculation ability
2	RAM	16	Yes	24	4.5 to 9.5	Yes	Yes	No	Yes	All COPs processors include serial I/O and event counting capability. Major differences between models include the I/O arrangements—input only, bidirectional, output only, etc. I/O options include LED direct segment drive. LED direct digit drive, three-state push-pull, push pull, open drain, and standard (active device to ground and a pull-up to V_{CC}).
2	RAM	15	Yes	20	4.5 to 9.5	Yes	Yes	No	Yes	
3	RAM	20	Yes	28	4.5 to 6.3	Yes	Yes	No	Yes	
3	RAM	20	Yes	28	4.5 to 9.5	Yes	Yes	No	Yes	
3	RAM	23	Yes	28	2.4 to 6.3	Yes	Yes	No	Yes	
3	RAM	16	Yes	24	4.5 to 6.3	Yes	Yes	No	Yes	
3	RAM	16	Yes	24	4.5 to 9.5	Yes	Yes	No	Yes	
3	RAM	19	Yes	24	2.4 to 6.3	Yes	Yes	No	Yes	
3	RAM	32	Yes	40	4.5 to 6.3	Yes	Yes	No	Yes	
3	RAM	23	Yes	28	4.5 to 9.5	Yes	Yes	No	Yes	
3	RAM	19	Yes	24	4.5 to 9	Yes	Yes	No	Yes	Reduced I/O version of COP444L; narrower voltage range (4.5 to 6.3 V) also available
3	RAM	23	Yes	28	2.4 to 6	Yes	Yes	No	Yes	Extended temperature (−40 to +85°C) version of 420C
3	RAM	19	Yes	24	2.4 to 6	Yes	Yes	No	Yes	Extended temperature (−40 to +88°C) version of 421C
4	RAM	35	No	42	−10	Yes	Yes	No	Yes	Well suited for POS and ECR applications
3	RAM	35	No	42	−10	Yes	Yes	No	Yes	TTL-compatible I/O lines
3	RAM	35	No	42	−10	Yes	Yes	No	Yes	I/O handles −35-V vacuum fluorescent drive
1	RAM	21	No	28	−8	Yes	Yes	No	Yes	Reduced I/O and low-power version of 553
3	RAM	35	No	42	+5	Yes	Yes	No	Yes	CMOS version of 546 (4% of the power)

All-in-one processors *(continued)*

Word size in bits (data/inst.)	Original Source Manufacturer	Device	Process technology	On-chip RAM size	On-chip ROM/ PROM size (words)	Off-chip memory expansion	Number of basic instructions	Maximum clock frequency (kHz)	On-chip clock	Instruction time (shortest/longest) μs	TTL compatible	BCD arithmetic	On-chip interrupts/levels
4/8	NEC Microcomputers	μPD547	PMOS	64×4	1000×8	Yes	58	440	Yes	4.5/9	Yes	Yes	Yes/1
4/8		μPD547L	PMOS	64×4	1000×8	Yes	58	180	Yes	11/22	Yes	Yes	Yes/1
4/8		μPD552	PMOS	64×4	1000×8	No	58	440	Yes	4.5/9	Yes	Yes	Yes/1
4/8		μPD651	CMOS	64×4	1000×8	Yes	58	440	Yes	4.5/9	Yes	Yes	Yes/1
4/8		μPD550	PMOS	32×4	640×8	No	58	440	Yes	4.5/9	Yes	Yes	Yes/1
4/8		μPD550L	PMOS	32×4	640×8	No	58	180	Yes	11/22	Yes	Yes	Yes/1
4/8		μPD554	PMOS	32×4	1000×8	No	58	440	Yes	4.5/9	Yes	Yes	Yes/1
4/8		μPD554L	PMOS	32×4	1000×8	No	58	180	Yes	11/22	Yes	Yes	Yes/1
4/8		μPD652	CMOS	32×4	1000×8	No	58	440	Yes	4.5/9	Yes	Yes	Yes/1
4/8		μPD551	PMOS	64×4	1000×8	Yes	58	440	Yes	4.5/9	Yes	Yes	Yes/1
4/8		μPD7520	PMOS	48×4	768×8	No	47	300	Yes	20/40	Yes	No	No
4/8	OKI	MSM5840RS	CMOS	128×4	2048×8	Yes	98	2000	Yes	16/32	Yes	Yes	Yes/2
4/8		MSM5842RS	CMOS	32×4	768×8	Yes	52	4000	Yes	8/16	Yes	Yes	No
4/8		MSM5845RS	CMOS	64×4	1280×8	Yes	49	4000	Yes	8/16	Yes	Yes	Yes/1
4/8		MSM58421RS	CMOS	40×4	1536×8	Yes	52	4000	Yes	8/16	Yes	Yes	No
4/8		MSM58423RS	CMOS	32×4	1280×8	Yes	52	4000	Yes	8/16	Yes	Yes	No
4/8	Panasonic	MN1400	NMOS	64×4	1024×8	No	75	300	Yes	10/20	Yes	Yes	Yes/1
4/8		MN1402	NMOS	32×4	768×8	No	57	300	Yes	10/20	Yes	Yes	Yes/1
4/8		MN1403	NMOS	16×4	512×8	No	50	300	Yes	10/20	Yes	No	Yes/1
4/8		MN1404	NMOS	16×4	512×8	No	48	300	Yes	10/20	Yes	Yes	Yes/1
4/8		MN1405	NMOS	128×4	2048×8	No	75	300	Yes	10/20	Yes	Yes	Yes/2
4/8		MN1430	PMOS	64×4	1024×8	No	75	200	Yes	15/30	No	Yes	Yes/1
4/8		MN1432	PMOS	32×4	768×8	No	57	200	Yes	15/30	No	Yes	Yes/1
4/8		MN1435	PMOS	128×4	2048×8	No	75	200	Yes	15/30	No	Yes	Yes/2
4/8		MN1450	CMOS	64×4	1024×8	No	75	500	Yes	10/20	Yes	Yes	Yes/1
4/8		MN1453	CMOS	16×4	512×8	No	50	500	Yes	10/20	Yes	Yes	Yes/1
4/8		MN1454	CMOS	16×4	512×8	No	48	500	Yes	10/20	Yes	Yes	Yes/1
4/8		MN1455	CMOS	128×4	2048×8	No	75	500	Yes	10/20	Yes	Yes	Yes/2
4/8		MN1455	CMOS	128×4	2048×8	No	75	500	Yes	6/12	Yes	No	Yes/2
4/8		MN1542	NMOS	152×4	2048×8	Yes	124	1000	Yes	2/4	Yes	Yes	Yes/4
4/8		MN1544	NMOS	256×4	4096×8	Yes	124	1000	Yes	2/4	Yes	Yes	Yes/4
4/8		MN1562	NMOS	152×4	2048×8	Yes	124	1000	Yes	2/4	Yes	Yes	Yes/4
4/8		MN1564	NMOS	256×4	4096×8	Yes	124	1000	Yes	2/4	Yes	Yes	Yes/4
4/8	Rockwell	PPS-4	PMOS	0	0	Yes	50	200/400 Two clocks	No	5/15	No	Yes	Yes/1
4/8		PPS 4/2	PMOS	0	0	Yes	50	200/400	Yes	5/15	No	Yes	No
4/8	PPS-4/1	MM77/MM77L	PMOS	96×4	1344×8	RAM only	50	100/4	Yes	10/40	Yes	Yes	Yes/1
4/8		MM78/MM78L	PMOS	128×4	2048×8	RAM only	50	100/4	Yes	10/40	Yes	Yes	Yes/1
4/8		MM78LA	PMOS	128×4	2048×8	RAM only	50	100/4	Yes	10/40	Yes	Yes	Yes/1
4/8		MM76/E	PMOS	48×4	1024×8	RAM only	50	100/4	Yes	10/30	Yes	Yes	Yes/1
4/8		MM76/EL	PMOS	48×4	640×8	RAM only	50	100/4	Yes	10/30	Yes	Yes	Yes/1
4/8		MM75	PMOS	48×4	670×8	RAM only	50	100/4	Yes	10/40	Yes	Yes	Yes/1

1. Not applicable   2. External 8 bits, internally 16 bits   3. User defined   4. Q = quad in-line
5. FP = flat pack   ? Not available   * Program   ** Pattern   . † Display   †† Data

Subroutine nesting levels	General-purpose internal registers	Number of I/O lines	Additional special support circuits	Package size (DIP pins)	Voltages required (V)	Prototyping system avail.	Assembly language programming system	High-level language programming system	Time-sharing cross software	Comments
1	RAM	35	No	42	−10	Yes	Yes	No	Yes	TTL-compatible I/O lines
1	RAM	35	No	42	−8	Yes	Yes	No	Yes	Low power version of 547 (half the current)
1	RAM	35	No	42	−10	Yes	Yes	No	Yes	I/O handles −35-V vacuum fluorescent drive
1	RAM	35	No	42	+5	Yes	Yes	No	Yes	CMOS version of 547 (4% of the power)
1	RAM	21	No	28	−10	Yes	Yes	No	Yes	I/O handles −35-V vacuum fluorescent drive
1	RAM	21	No	28	−8	Yes	Yes	No	Yes	Low-power version of 550 (half the current)
1	RAM	21	No	28	−10	Yes	Yes	No	Yes	I/O handles −35-V vacuum fluorescent drive
1	RAM	21	No	28	−8	Yes	Yes	No	Yes	Low-power version of 554 (half the current)
1	RAM	21	No	42	+5	Yes	Yes	No	Yes	CMOS version of 550 (5% of the power)
2	RAM	28	No	40	−10	Yes	Yes	No	Yes	Includes a-d converter with 2% resolution, 4% accuracy
2	RAM	24	Yes	28	−6 to −10	Yes	Yes	No	Yes	Output ports designed for LED driving; built-in programmable display controller
4	RAM	30	Yes	42	5	Yes	Yes	No	Yes	Includes 8-bit timer/counter; ROM-less evaluation chip available
1	RAM	21	Yes	28	5	Yes	Yes	No	Yes	Includes 8-bit timer/counter
2	RAM	30	Yes	42	5	Yes	Yes	No	Yes	Includes 8-bit timer/counter
1	RAM	53	Yes	60FP	5	Yes	Yes	No	Yes	Includes 12-bit timer/counter and LCD direct drive outputs
1	RAM	53	Yes	60FP	5	Yes	Yes	No	Yes	Includes 12-bit timer/counter and vacuum fluorescent direct drive outputs
2	2+RAM	34	No	40	5	No	Yes	Yes	Yes	Complete all-in-one controller
2	RAM	19	No	28	5	No	Yes	Yes	Yes	Smaller I/O version of 1400
2	RAM	13	Yes	18	5	Yes	Yes	No	Yes	All the processors in the MN1400 family are available in at least one other technology. The 18 and 16-pin versions are about the smallest μCs available, although most versions still retain at least 2/3 of the instructions available on the 1405. The CMOS versions can also be ordered with operating voltages of up to 10 V, and all models include 8-bit counter/timer with 7-bit prescaler.
2	RAM	10	Yes	16	5	Yes	Yes	No	Yes	
2	2+RAM	34	No	40	5	Yes	Yes	No	Yes	
2	2+RAM	34	No	40	−15	Yes	Yes	No	Yes	
2	RAM	19	No	28	−15	Yes	Yes	No	Yes	
2	2+RAM	34	No	40	−15	Yes	Yes	No	Yes	
2	2+RAM	34	Yes	40	4.25 to 6	Yes	Yes	No	Yes	
2	RAM	13	Yes	18	4.25 to 6	Yes	Yes	No	Yes	
2	RAM	10	Yes	16	4.25 to 6	Yes	Yes	No	Yes	
2	2+RAM	34	Yes	40	4.25 to 6	Yes	Yes	No	Yes	CMOS version of 1405/1435
2	2+RAM	34	Yes	40	4.25 to 6	Yes	Yes	No	Yes	
16	4+RAM	24	Yes	40	5	Yes	Yes	No	Yes	All MN1500 family processors include an 8-bit counter/timer and an 8-bit serial shift register; All I/O lines are bidirectional and the chips also have a power-down made to minimize power dissipation
16	4+RAM	24	Yes	40	5	Yes	Yes	No	Yes	
16	4+RAM	48	Yes	64	5	Yes	Yes	No	Yes	
16	4+RAM	48	Yes	64	5	Yes	Yes	No	Yes	
2	1	12+	Yes	42	−17/+5, −12	Yes	Yes	No	Yes	Combination ROM/RAM/I/O available
2	1	12+	Yes	42	−17/+5, −12	Yes	Yes	No	Yes	Same as PPS-4 but has internal clock
2	2+RAM	31	Yes	42	−15/+5, −10	Yes	Yes	No	Yes	I/O includes serial channel
2	2+RAM	31	Yes	42	−15/+5, −10	Yes	Yes	No	Yes	Software compatible with 77
2	2+RAM	31	Yes	42	−15/+5, −10	Yes	Yes	No	Yes	Similar to MM78/L but can drive LED or v-f 14-segment displays; offers tone generator and push-pull speaker drive outputs
1	1+RAM	31	Yes	42	−15/+5, −10	Yes	Yes	No	Yes	Larger ROM than MM76
1	1+RAM	31	Yes	42	−15/+5, −10	Yes	Yes	No	Yes	Expanded ROM version
1	1+RAM	22	Yes	28	−15/+5, −10	Yes	Yes	No	Yes	Reduced I/O version of 76

All-in-one processors *(continued)*

Word size in bits (data/inst.)	Original Source Manufacturer	Device	Process technology	On-chip RAM size	On-chip ROM/ PROM size (words)	Off-chip memory expansion	Number of basic instructions	Maximum clock frequency (kHz)	On-chip clock	Instruction time (shortest/longest) μs	TTL compatible	BCD arithmetic	On-chip interrupts/levels
4/8	Texas Instruments	TMS1000	PMOS	64×4	1024×8	No	43	400	Yes	15/15	Yes	Yes	No
4/8		TMS1000C	CMOS	64×4	1024×8	No	43	1000	Yes	6/6	Yes	Yes	No
4/8		TMS1070	PMOS	64×4	1024×8	No	43	400	Yes	15/15	Yes	Yes	No
4/8		TMS1070C	CMOS	64×4	1024×8	No	43	1000	Yes	6/6	Yes	Yes	No
4/8		TMS1100	PMOS	128×4	2048×8	No	40	400	Yes	15/15	Yes	Yes	No
4/8		TMS1100C	CMOS	128×4	2048×8	No	40	1000	Yes	6/6	Yes	Yes	No
4/8		TMS1170	PMOS	128×4	2048×8	No	40	400	Yes	15/15	Yes	Yes	No
4/8		TMS1170C	CMOS	128×4	2048×8	No	40	1000	Yes	6/6	Yes	Yes	No
4/8		TMS1200	PMOS	64×4	1024×8	No	43	400	Yes	15/15	Yes	Yes	No
4/8		TMS1200C	CMOS	64×4	1024×8	No	43	1000	Yes	6/6	Yes	Yes	No
4/8		TMS1270	PMOS	64×4	1024×8	No	43	400	Yes	15/15	Yes	Yes	No
4/8		TMS1270C	CMOS	64×4	1024×8	No	43	1000	Yes	6/6	Yes	Yes	No
4/8		TMS1300	PMOS	128×4	2048×8	No	40	400	Yes	15/15	Yes	Yes	No
4/8		TMS1300C	CMOS	128×4	2048×8	No	40	1000	Yes	6/6	Yes	Yes	No
4/8		TMS1370	PMOS	128×4	2048×8	No	40	400	Yes	15/15	Yes	Yes	No
4/8		TMS1370C	CMOS	128×4	2048×8	No	40	1000	Yes	6/6	Yes	Yes	No
4/8		TMS1400	PMOS	128×4	4096×8	No	41	550	Yes	11/11	Yes	Yes	No
4/8		TMS1470	PMOS	128×4	4096×8	No	41	550	Yes	11/11	Yes	Yes	No
4/8		TMS1600	PMOS	64×4	512×8	No	41	550	Yes	11/11	Yes	Yes	No
4/8		TMS1670	PMOS	64×4	512×8	No	41	550	Yes	11/11	Yes	Yes	No
4/8		TMS1700	PMOS	64×4	512×8	No	43	400	Yes	15/15	Yes	Yes	No
4/8		TMS2100	PMOS	128×4	2048×8	No	45	550	Yes	11/11	Yes	Yes	Yes/1
4/8		TMS2170	PMOS	128×4	2048×8	No	45	550	Yes	11/11	Yes	Yes	Yes/1
4/8		TMS2300	PMOS	128×4	2048×8	No	45	550	Yes	11/11	Yes	Yes	Yes/1
4/8		TMS2370	PMOS	128×4	2048×8	No	45	550	Yes	11/11	Yes	Yes	Yes/1
4/8		TMS1018	PMOS	64×4	1024×8	No	43	400	Yes	15/15	Yes	Yes	No
4/8		TMS1022	PMOS	64×4	2048×8	No	43	400	Yes	15/15	Yes	Yes	No
4/8		TMS1117	PMOS	128×4	2048×8	No	43	400	Yes	15/15	Yes	Yes	No
4/8		TMS1121	PMOS	128×4	2048×8	No	42	400	Yes	15/15	Yes	Yes	No
4/8	Toshiba	T3444	NMOS	16×8	256×24	Yes	3	800	Yes	3	Yes	3	Yes/1
4/8		TMP4310AP	NMOS	16×4	256×24	Yes	67	1000	Yes	33/360	Yes	Yes	Yes/2
4/8		TMP4310APL	NMOS	48×4	1024×8	Yes	67	1000	Yes	33/360	Yes	Yes	Yes/2
4/8		TMP4315BP	NMOS	64×4	1536×8	Yes	67	1000	Yes	33/360	Yes	Yes	Yes/2
4/8		TMP4320AP	NMOS	64×4	2048×8	Yes	67	1000	Yes	33/360	Yes	Yes	Yes/2
4/8		TCP4620AP	CMOS	96×4	2048×8	Yes	52	100*	Yes	20/40	Yes	No	Yes/2
4/8		TCP4630AP	CMOS	160×4	3072×8	Yes	52	100*	Yes	20/40	Yes	No	Yes/2
4/9	Applied Microcircuits	AMCC1259	CMOS	32×4	PLA-136 step	Yes	8	32.768	Yes	30/60	No	No	No
4/10	Hitachi	HMCS42	PMOS	32×4	512×10* 32×10**	No	51	500	Yes	10/20	No	Yes	No

1. Not applicable   2. External 8 bits, internally 16 bits   3. User defined   4. Q = quad in-line
5. FP = flat pack   ? Not available   * Program   ** Pattern   † Display   †† Data

Subroutine nesting levels	General-purpose internal registers	Number of I/O lines	Additional special support circuits	Package size (DIP pins)	Voltages required (V)	Prototyping system avail.	Assembly language programming system	High-level language programming system	Time-sharing cross software	Comments
1	2+RAM	23	Yes	28	−9 or −15	Yes	Yes	No	Yes	Two versions available; one for −9-V operation, the other for −15-V operation
3	2+RAM	22	Yes	28	3 to 6	Yes	Yes	No	Yes	Enhanced CMOS version of 7MS1000
1	2+RAM	22	Yes	28	−9 or −15	Yes	Yes	No	Yes	V-F drive (−35 V) capability on outputs; otherwise same as TMS1000
3	2+RAM	21	Yes	28	3 to 6	Yes	Yes	No	Yes	V-F drive (−35 V) capability on outputs; otherwise same as TMS1000
1	2+RAM	23	Yes	28	−9 or −15	Yes	Yes	No	Yes	Double memory version of TMS1000
3	2+RAM	22	Yes	28	3 to 6	Yes	Yes	No	Yes	CMOS version of TMS1100
1	2+RAM	23	Yes	28	−9 to −15	Yes	Yes	No	Yes	V-f drive version of TMS1100
3	2+RAM	22	Yes	28	3 to 6	Yes	Yes	No	Yes	V-f drive version of TMS1100C
1	2+RAM	25	Yes	40	−9 or −15	Yes	Yes	No	Yes	Expanded I/O version of TMS1000
3	2+RAM	32	Yes	40	3 to 6	Yes	Yes	No	Yes	Expanded I/O version of TMS1000C
1	2+RAM	24	Yes	40	−9 or −15	Yes	Yes	No	Yes	Expanded I/O version of TMS1070 with V-F drive
3	2+RAM	31	Yes	40	3 to 6	Yes	Yes	No	Yes	Expanded I/O version of TMS1070C with V-F drive
1	2+RAM	28	Yes	40	−9 or −15	Yes	Yes	No	Yes	Expanded I/O version of TMS1100
3	2+RAM	28	Yes	40	3 to 6	Yes	Yes	No	Yes	Expanded I/O version of TMS1100C
1	2+RAM	27	Yes	40	−9 or −15	Yes	Yes	No	Yes	Expanded I/O version of TMS1170 with V-F drive
3	2+RAM	27	Yes	40	3 to 6	Yes	Yes	No	Yes	Expanded I/O version of TMS1170C with V-F drive
3	2+RAM	19	Yes	28	−9 or −15	Yes	Yes	No	Yes	Expanded memory version of TMS1100
3	2+RAM	19	Yes	28	−9 or −15	Yes	Yes	No	Yes	V-f drive version of TMS1400
3	2+RAM	32	Yes	40	−9 or −15	Yes	Yes	No	Yes	Reduced ROM but enhanced I/O version of TMS1000
3	2+RAM	31	Yes	40	−9 or −15	Yes	Yes	No	Yes	V-f drive version of TMS1600
3	2+RAM	21	Yes	28	−9 or −15	Yes	Yes	No	Yes	Reduced ROM and I/O version of TMS1000
4	2+RAM	20	Yes	28	−9	Yes	Yes	No	Yes	Includes 8-bit a-d converter, interval timer, zero-crossing detector; handles up to −15 V on outputs
4	2+RAM	19	Yes	28	−9	Yes	Yes	No	Yes	Same as 2100 but one less I/O line and handles up to −35 V on outputs
4	2+RAM	31	Yes	40	−9	Yes	Yes	No	Yes	Expanded 2100 with timer/event counter and two a-d input channels
4	2+RAM	30	Yes	40	−9	Yes	Yes	No	Yes	Same as 2300 but one less I/O line and handles up to −35 V on outputs
N/A[1]	N/A[1]	N/A[1]	N/A[1]	28	15	N/A[1]	N/A[1]	N/A[1]	N/A[1]	Dedicated number cruncher
N/A[1]	N/A[1]	N/A[1]	N/A[1]	28	15	N/A[1]	N/A[1]	N/A[1]	N/A[1]	Dedicated CB PLL controller
N/A[1]	N/A[1]	N/A[1]	N/A[1]	28	15	N/A[1]	N/A[1]	N/A[1]	N/A[1]	Dedicated microwave oven controller
N/A[1]	N/A[1]	N/A[1]	N/A[1]	40	15	N/A[1]	N/A[1]	N/A[1]	N/A[1]	Dedicated appliance timer/controller
8	RAM	16	No	40	5	Yes	Yes	No	Yes	Intended for dedicated controllers
8	RAM	16	Yes	42	5	Yes	Yes	No	Yes	Designed for keyboard/display interfacing
8	4+RAM	16	Yes	42	5	Yes	Yes	No	Yes	Low-power version of 4310AP
8	4+RAM	16	Yes	42	5	Yes	Yes	No	Yes	Expanded-memory version of 4310
8	4+RAM	16	Yes	42	5	Yes	Yes	No	Yes	Expanded ROM version of 4320
2	2+RAM	28	No	42	5	Yes	Yes	No	Yes	On-chip 8-bit counter/timer; direct drive for LCD up to 5 digits
2	2+RAM	28	No	42	5	Yes	Yes	No	Yes	Larger memory size version of 4620
0	RAM	54	No	None	1.5	No	No	No	No	Uses two PLAs for microprogram and display-mode controls; includes direct LCD drive on 48 lines
2	RAM	22	No	28	−10	Yes	Yes	No	Yes	ROM-less evaluation chip available

All-in-one processors *(continued)*

Word size in bits (data/inst.)	Original Source Manufacturer	Device	Process technology	On-chip RAM size	On-chip ROM/ PROM size (words)	Off-chip memory expansion	Number of basic instructions	Maximum clock frequency (kHz)	On-chip clock	Instruction time (shortest/longest) μs	TTL compatible	BCD arithmetic	On-chip interrupts/levels
4/10	Hitachi	HMCS42C	CMOS	32×4	512×10* 32×10**	No	51	500	Yes	10/20	Yes	Yes	No
4/10		HMCS43	PMOS	80×4	1024×10* 64×10	No	71	500	Yes	10/20	No	Yes	Yes/2
4/10		HMCS43C	CMOS	80×4	1024×10* 64×10**	No	71	500	Yes	10/20	Yes	Yes	Yes/2
4/10		HMCS44A	PMOS	160×4	2048×10* 128×10**	No	71	500	Yes	10/20	No	Yes	Yes/2
4/10		HMCS44C	CMOS	160×4	2048×10 128×10	No	71	500	Yes	10/20	Yes	Yes	Yes/2
4/10		HMCS45A	PMOS	160×4	2048×10 128×10	No	71	500	Yes	10/20	No	Yes	Yes/2
4/10		HMCS45C	CMOS	160×4	2048×i0 128×10	No	71	500	Yes	10/20	Yes	Yes	Yes/2
4/10		HMCS46C	CMOS	160×4	4096×10	No	71	500	Yes	10/20	Yes	Yes	Yes/2
4/10		HMCS47C	CMOS	160×4	4096×10	No	71	500	Yes	10/20	Yes	Yes	Yes/2
4/10		HD44770 (LCD I)	CMOS	88×4†† 168×4†	2048×10* 128×10†	No	71	500	Yes	10	Yes	Yes	No
4/10		HD44790 (LCD III)	CMOS	128×4†† 32×4†	2048×10* 128×10†	No	71	500	Yes	10	Yes	Yes	Yes/2
4/10	Western Digital	1872	PMOS	32×4	512×10	No	37	150	Yes	6.25/12.5	Yes	Yes	Yes/1
8/8	Fairchild	F38E70	NMOS	64×8	2048×8	Yes	70+	4000	Yes	1/6.5	Yes	Yes	Yes/4
8/8		F3878	NMOS	64×8	4096×8	Yes	70+	4000	Yes	1/6.5	Yes	Yes	Yes/4
8/12	General Instrument	1650A	NMOS	32×8	512×12	No	30	1000	Yes	4/8	Yes	Yes	Yes/1
8/12		1655A/56	NMOS	32×8	512×12	No	30	1000	Yes	4/8	Yes	Yes	Yes/1
8/12		1670	NMOS	48×8	1024×13	No	40	2000	Yes	4/8	Yes	Yes	Yes/1
8/8	Hitachi	HD6801S	NMOS	128×8	4096×8	Yes	82	3580	Yes	2/12	Yes	Yes	Yes/1
8/8		HD6805V	NMOS	64×8	4096×8	Yes	61	3580	Yes	2/4	Yes	Yes	Yes/1
8/8		HD6301	CMOS	128×8	2048×8	Yes	82	3580	Yes	2/12	Yes	Yes	Yes/1
8/8		HD6305	CMOS	64×8	2048×8	Yes	61	3580	Yes	2/4	Yes	Yes	Yes/1
8/8	Intel	8021	NMOS	64×8	1024×8	No	70	3000	Yes	10/20	Yes	Yes	Yes/1
8/8		8022	NMOS	64×8	2048×8	No	70	3000	Yes	10/20	Yes	Yes	Yes/1
8/8		8041/8741	NMOS	64×8	1024×8	Yes	90	6000	Yes	2.5/5	Yes	Yes	Yes/1
8/8		8048/8748	NMOS	64×8	1024×8	Yes	96	6000	Yes	2.5/5	Yes	Yes	Yes/1
8/8		8049H-I	NMOS	128×8	2048×8	Yes	96	11000	Yes	1.4/2.8	Yes	Yes	Yes/1
8/8		i8049C	CMOS	128×8	2048×8	Yes	96	?	Yes	?	Yes	Yes	Yes/1
8/8		i8051/8751	NMOS	128×8	4096×8	Yes	111	12,000	Yes	1/4	Yes	Yes	Yes/2
8/8		i8051C	CMOS	128×8	4096×8	Yes	111	?	Yes	?	Yes	Yes	Yes/2
8/8	Intersil	80C48	CMOS	64×8	1024×8	Yes	96	6000 (5V)	Yes	2.5/5	Yes	Yes	Yes/1
8/8	Mostek	MK3870/10	NMOS	—	1024×8	Yes	70+	4000	Yes	1/6.5	Yes	Yes	Yes/4
8/8		MK3870/12	NMOS	64×8	1024×8	Yes	70+	4000	Yes	1/6.5	Yes	Yes	Yes/4
8/8		MK3870/20	NMOS	0	2048×8	Yes	70+	4000	Yes	1/6.5	Yes	Yes	Yes/4
8/8		MK3870/22	NMOS	64×8	2048×8	Yes	70+	4000	Yes	1/6.5	Yes	Yes	Yes/4
8/8		MK3870/30	NMOS	0	3072×8	Yes	70+	4000	Yes	1/6.5	Yes	Yes	Yes/4

1. Not applicable   2. External 8 bits, internally 16 bits   3. User defined   4. Q=quad in-line
5. FP=flat pack   ? Not available   * Program   ** Pattern   † Display   †† Data

Subroutine nesting levels	General-purpose internal registers	Number of I/O lines	Additional special support circuits	Package size (DIP pins)	Voltages required (V)	Prototyping system avail.	Assembly language programming system	High-level language programming system	Time-sharing cross software	Comments
2	RAM	22	No	28	5	Yes	Yes	No	Yes	ROM-less evaluation chip available; operation can halt; dissipates just 1.5 mW
3	RAM	32	No	42	−10	Yes	Yes	No	Yes	Has on-chip timer/counter and RAM-hold capability for battery back up
3	RAM	32	No	42	5	Yes	Yes	No	Yes	Same as 43 but dissipates 1/50 the power
4	RAM	32	No	42	−10	Yes	Yes	No	Yes	Includes on-chip timer/counter
4	RAM	32	No	42	5	Yes	Yes	No	Yes	Same as 44A but dissipates 1/75 the power
4	RAM	44	No	54FP	−10	Yes	Yes	No	Yes	Includes on-chip timer/counter; comes in flat package
4	RAM	44	No	54FP	5	Yes	Yes	No	Yes	Same as 45A but dissipates 1/75 the power
RAM	RAM	32	No	42	5	Yes	Yes	No	Yes	Enlarged ROM version of HMCS43C; all but 2 instructions are single-cycle
RAM	RAM	44	No	54FP	5	Yes	Yes	No	Yes	Enhanced I/O version of HMCS46C; all but 2 instructions are single-cycle
2	RAM	11	Yes	80FP	5	Yes	Yes	No	Yes	Directly drives dot matrix LCDs; has two 5-bit a-d converter channels
4	RAM	32*	Yes	80FP	5	Yes	Yes	No	Yes	Directly drives seven-segment LCDs; has counter/timer on chip
1	RAM	27	No	40	12	Yes	Yes	Yes	Yes	RAM holds BCD numbers
RAM	RAM	32	Yes	40	5	Yes	Yes	Yes	Yes	On-chip UV EPROM instead of mask ROM version of 3870
RAM	RAM	32	Yes	40	5	Yes	Yes	Yes	Yes	Similar to Mostek 3875/12 but has no standby RAM
2	RAM	32	Yes	40	5	Yes	Yes	Yes	No	32 programmable I/O lines
2	RAM	20	Yes	28	5	Yes	Yes	Yes	No	Reduced I/O version of 1650A; 1656 has 3-level stack and internal and external interrupts
6	RAM	32	Yes	40	5	Yes	Yes	Yes	No	Includes 16-bit counter/timer
RAM	RAM	31	Yes	40	5	Yes	Yes	Yes	Yes	In development; samples mid-1981; expanded ROM 6801
RAM	RAM	20	Yes	28	5	Yes	Yes	Yes	Yes	In development; samples early 1981; expanded ROM 6805
RAM	RAM	31	Yes	40	5	Yes	Yes	Yes	Yes	In development; samples mid 1981; CMOS version of 6801
RAM	RAM	20	Yes	28	5	Yes	Yes	Yes	Yes	In development; samples late 1981; CMOS 6805 with 2-k ROM
RAM	RAM	21	No	28	5	Yes	Yes	Yes	Yes	Minimal I/O CPU version
RAM	RAM	27	No	40	5	Yes	Yes	Yes	Yes	Contains two a-d converter channels
RAM	RAM	18	Yes	40	5	Yes	Yes	Yes	Yes	8041 has a ROM and 8741 a UV EPROM
8	RAM	27	Yes	40	5	Yes	Yes	Yes	Yes	8748 has UV EPROM
8	RAM	27	Yes	40	5	Yes	Yes	Yes	Yes	Enlarged memory version of 8048
8	RAM	27	Yes	40	5	Yes	Yes	Yes	Yes	CMOS equivalent to 8049 (in development)
RAM	RAM	32	Yes	40	5	Yes	Yes	Yes	Yes	Includes two 16-bit counter/timers, a full duplex serial port and Boolean logic capability; 8051 has ROM, 8751 µV EPROM
RAM	RAM	32	Yes	40	5	Yes	Yes	Yes	Yes	CMOS equivalent to 8051 (in development)
8	RAM	27	Yes	40	5 to 10	Yes	Yes	Yes	Yes	CMOS equivalent to Intel 8048; dissipates 50 mW
RAM	RAM	32	Yes	40	5	Yes	Yes	Yes	Yes	All devices in the MK3870 family use an improved architecture that divides internal RAM into 64 bytes of scratchpad registers and either 0 to 64 additional bytes of executable RAM; all units contain an 8-bit counter/timer with 7-bit prescaler
RAM	RAM	32	Yes	40	5	Yes	Yes	Yes	Yes	
RAM	RAM	32	Yes	40	5	Yes	Yes	Yes	Yes	
RAM	RAM	32	Yes	40	5	Yes	Yes	Yes	Yes	
RAM	RAM	32	Yes	40	5	Yes	Yes	Yes	Yes	

All-in-one processors *(continued)*

Word size in bits (data/inst.)	Original Source Manufacturer	Device	Process technology	On-chip RAM size	On-chip ROM/ PROM size (words)	Off-chip memory expansion	Number of basic instructions	Maximum clock frequency (kHz)	On-chip clock	Instruction time (shortest/longest) μs	TTL compatible	BCD arithmetic	On-chip interrupts/levels
8/8	Mostek	MK3870/32	NMOS	64×8	3072×8	Yes	70+	4000	Yes	1/6.5	Yes	Yes	Yes/4
8/8		MK3870/40	NMOS	0	4032×8	Yes	70+	4000	Yes	1/6.5	Yes	Yes	Yes/4
8/8		MK3870/42	NMOS	64×8	4032×8	Yes	70+	4000	Yes	1/6.5	Yes	Yes	Yes/4
8/8		MK3873/10	NMOS	0	1024×8	Yes	70+	4000	Yes	1/6.5	Yes	Yes	Yes/4
8/8		MK3873/12	NMOS	64×8	1024×8	Yes	70+	4000	Yes	1/6.5	Yes	Yes	Yes/4
8/8		MK3873/20	NMOS	64×8	2048×8	Yes	70+	4000	Yes	1/6.5	Yes	Yes	Yes/4
8/8		MK3873/22	NMOS	64×8	2048×8	Yes	70+	4000	Yes	1/6.5	Yes	Yes	Yes/4
8/8		MK3875/22	NMOS	64×8	2048×8	Yes	70+	4000	Yes	1/6.5	Yes	Yes	Yes/4
8/8		MK3875/42	NMOS	64×8	4096×8	Yes	70+	4000	Yes	1/6.5	Yes	Yes	Yes/4
8/8	Motorola	6801/68701	NMOS	128×8	2048×8	Yes	82	3580	Yes	2/12	Yes	Yes	Yes/1
8/8		MC6805P2	NMOS	64×8	1100×8	Yes	61	5000	Yes	2/4	Yes	Yes	Yes/1
8/8		MC6805U2	NMOS	64×8	2048×8	Yes	61	5000	Yes	2/4	Yes	Yes	Yes/1
8/8		MC6805R2	NMOS	64×8	2048×8	Yes	61	5000	Yes	2/4	Yes	Yes	Yes/1
8/8		MC68705P3	NMOS	112×8	1804×8	Yes	61	5000	Yes	2/4	Yes	Yes	Yes/1
8/8		MC146805G2	CMOS	112×8	2048×8	Yes	61	5000	Yes	2/4	Yes	Yes	Yes/1
8/8	National Semiconductor	INS8050	NMOS	256×8	4096×8	Yes	96	11000	Yes	1.4/2.8	Yes	Yes	Yes/1
8/8		INS8072	NMOS	64×8	2560×8	Yes	74	4k	Yes	3/1000	Yes	Yes	Yes/2
8/8	NEC Microcomputers	μPD7801	NMOS	128×8	4096×8	Yes	125	1000	Yes	2/4	Yes	Yes	Yes/5
8/8		μPD7802	NMOS	128×8	6144×8	Yes	140	1000	Yes	2/4	Yes	Yes	Yes/5
8/8		μCOM-87AD	NMOS	128×8	4096×8	Yes	160	1000	Yes	2/4	Yes	Yes	Yes/5
8/8		μCOM-87LC	CMOS	128×8	4096×8	Yes	101	4000	Yes	6/12	Yes	Yes	Yes/5
8/8		μPD80C48	CMOS	64×8	1024×8	Yes	96	6000	Yes	2.5/5	Yes	Yes	Yes/1
8/8	RCA	CDP1804	CMOS/ SOS	64×8	2048×8	Yes	113	8000	Yes	2/3	Yes	Yes	Yes/1
8/8	Rockwell	PPS-8	PMOS	0	0	Yes	100	256/4	No	4/12	No	Yes	Yes/3
8/8		PPS-8/2	PMOS	0	0	Yes	100	200/4	No	5/15	No	Yes	Yes/3
8/8		R6500/1	NMOS	64×8	2048×8	Yes	56	2000	Yes	1/3.5	Yes	Yes	Yes/1
8/8	Zilog	Z8	NMOS	144×8	2048×8	Yes	47	8000	Yes	1.5/3.75	Yes	Yes	Yes/6
16[2]	Texas Instruments	TMS 9940E/ 9940M	NMOS	128×8	2048×8	No	68	4000	Yes	2/452	Yes	Yes	Yes/4
16/17	AMI	S2811	NMOS	128×16	250×17	Yes	46	20,000	Yes	0.3	Yes	No	Yes/1
16/23	NEC Microcomputers	μPD7720	NMOS	128×16	512×23	No	48	8000	Yes	0.25	Yes	No	Yes/1
25/25	Intel	2920	NMOS	40×25	192×24	No	21	2500	Yes	0.6/0.6	Yes	N/A[1]	N/A[1]

1. Not applicable   2. External 8 bits, internally 16 bits   3. User defined   4. Q=quad in-line
5. FP=flat pack   ? Not available   * Program   ** Pattern   † Display   †† Data

Subroutine nesting levels	General-purpose internal registers	Number of I/O lines	Additional special support circuits	Package size (DIP pins)	Voltages required (V)	Prototyping system avail.	Assembly language programming system	High-level language programming system	Time-sharing cross software	Comments
RAM	RAM	32	Yes	40	5	Yes	Yes	Yes	Yes	The 3873 family includes a serial port on chip with baud-rate generator and gives up three parallel I/O lines for the
RAM	RAM	32	Yes	40	5	Yes	Yes	Yes	Yes	port. 3875 series includes provision for battery backup for
RAM	RAM	32	Yes	40	5	Yes	Yes	Yes	Yes	the on-chip RAM, thus permitting very low-power standby
RAM	RAM	29	Yes	40	5	Yes	Yes	Yes	Yes	operation
RAM	RAM	29	Yes	40	5	Yes	Yes	Yes	Yes	
RAM	RAM	29	Yes	40	5	Yes	Yes	Yes	Yes	
RAM	RAM	29	Yes	40	5	Yes	Yes	Yes	Yes	
RAM	RAM	30	Yes	40	5	Yes	Yes	Yes	Yes	
RAM	RAM	30	Yes	40	5	Yes	Yes	Yes	Yes	
RAM	RAM	31	Yes	40	5	Yes	Yes	Yes	Yes	6801 has masked ROM, 701 has UV EPROM
RAM	RAM	20	Yes	28	5	Yes	Yes	Yes	Yes	Includes 8-bit counter/timer; zero-crossing detector, self-check mode
RAM	RAM	32	Yes	40	5	Yes	Yes	Yes	Yes	Expanded I/O and ROM version of P2
RAM	RAM	32	Yes	40	5	Yes	Yes	Yes	Yes	Similar to U2 but includes 4-channel a-d converter
RAM	RAM	20	Yes	28	5	Yes	Yes	Yes	Yes	UV EPROM version of 6805P2
RAM	RAM	32	Yes	40	3 to 6	Yes	Yes	Yes	Yes	ROM version of 146805E2; dissipates <1 mW in standby, 20 mW active
8	RAM	27	Yes	40	5	Yes	Yes	Yes	Yes	Enlarged proprietary version of Intel 8049 processor with transparent improvements
RAM	RAM	0	Yes	40	5	Yes	Yes	Yes	Yes	Three-state data/address bus for user selectable I/O
RAM	16+RAM	48	Yes	64Q	5	Yes	Yes	Yes	Yes	Includes 12-bit timer/counter, serial I/O port in addition to 48 I/O lines, and is housed in 64-pin quad-in-line package
RAM	16+RAM	48	Yes	64Q[4]	5	Yes	Yes	No	Yes	7801 with 6-k ROM
RAM	16+RAM	48	Yes	64Q[4]	5	Yes	Yes	No	Yes	7801 with multiply/divide instructions, 8-channel a-d converter, 16-bit counter/timer, serial I/O
RAM	16+RAM	46	Yes	64FP[5]	5	Yes	Yes	No	Yes	CMOS 7801 with reduced instruction set, halt, and stop modes.
8	RAM	27	Yes	40	5	Yes	Yes	Yes	Yes	CMOS version of 8048 (1/30 the power)
RAM	RAM	13	Yes	40	5 to 10	Yes	Yes	Yes	Yes	Compatible with 1802 software and hardware
16	2	15	Yes	42	−17/+5, −12	Yes	Yes	No	Yes	Combination RAM/ROM/I/O support
16	2	15	Yes	42	−17/+5, −12	Yes	Yes	No	Yes	I/O chip includes clock
RAM	RAM	32	Yes	40	5	Yes	Yes	Yes	Yes	Single chip version 6502
RAM	RAM	32	Yes	40	5	Yes	Yes	Yes	Yes	Has two counter/timers and UART
64	RAM	32	No	40	5	Yes	Yes	Yes	Yes	Two versions available, one has a 2 k EPROM, the other 2 k ROM
1	8×16	8	No	28	5	Yes	Yes	No	No	Programmable digital signal processor includes 12 × 12 parallel multiplier
4	RAM	12	No	28	5	Yes	Yes	No	Yes	Includes a second data coefficient ROM (512 × 13 bits), has serial port, 16×16 bit parallel multiplier, and two accumulators
0	RAM	12	No	28	5, −5	Yes	Yes	Yes	Yes	Analog processor accepts four analog inputs and delivers up to eight digitally processed analog outputs

Appendix 4 Microcomputer data sheets

4-bit microcomputers: TMS1000 family (TMS2100, 2170, 2300, 2370)

Texas Instruments
13400 N. Central Expwy (M/S308)
Dallas, TX 75222
(214) 995-2011

Alternate sources: None

Besides an on-chip 8-bit a-d converter with 2 input channels and an 8-bit timer, the TMS2100, 2170, 2300, and 2370 also possess 2048 bytes of ROM, 128 nibbles of RAM, one level of interrupt, a clock oscillator, and two 4-bit working registers. The main differences between the circuits lie in the I/O capabilities and the output-drive voltage capability. The 2100 and 2300 can both handle up to −15 V on the output lines and offer 20 and 31 I/O lines in 28 and 40-pin DIPs, respectively. The 2170 and 2370 each have one less I/O line because of an extra high-voltage pull-down line, but can handle up to −35 V on the outputs.

Comments

The instruction set of the TMS2100/2300 µCs is basically that of the TMS1100 µC with the addition of 5 new instructions that handle the a-d converter, the decrementer, and I/O transfers.

Software features of the instruction set include the new commands that permit the processor to control the a-d converter and timer (decrementer) and to perform some port-to-accumulator and accumulator-to-accumulator transfers.

Software support for the TMS1000 family consists of an assembler, simulator, and cross-software, a high-level language compiler (TIML), and a variety of utility programs. Time-sharing software (an assembler and a simulator) is also available.

Hardware support starts with a ROM-less version of each major chip in the family, as well as a hardware evaluator and a debugging unit. The ROM-less chips permit external ROM and RAM or both to be used for program development and low-volume production. Also available are the AMPL development system, a 990-mini-based system for program development, a few direct support circuits, and a wide variety of processor types.

Specifications

Data word size	4 bits
Address bus size	9 to 12 bits (internal)
On-chip ROM size	512 to 4096 bytes
On-chip RAM size	64 or 128 × 4 bits
Number of basic instructions	45
Execution instruction time (all)	15 µs
Clock frequency (min/max)	0.55 MHz
Clock phases/voltage swing	1/PMOS (internal)
Package size	28 or 40-pin DIP
Power requirements	−9 V/−15 mA

Hardware

Model	Description	Price (100,000 qty)
TMS2100	28-pin µC, low-V output	$ 4.25
TMS2170	28-pin µC, high-V output	$ 5.00
TMS2300	40-pin µC, low-V output	$ 5.25
TMS2370	40-pin µC, high-V output	$ 6.00
TMS1000	28-pin µC, 1-k ROM	$ 2.00
TMS1000C	28-pin µC CMOS equiv.	$ 4.50
TMS1070	28-pin µC, high-V TMS1000	Consult fact.
TMS1070C	CMOS equiv. to 1070	Consult fact.
TMS1100	28-pin µC, double mem. 1000	$ 2.50
TMS1100C	CMOS version of 1100	TBA
TMS1170	High-V driver version, 1100	Consult fact.
TMS1170C	CMOS high-V version, 1170	TBA
TMS1200	40-pin µC, same mem. as 1000	$ 2.50
TMS1200C	CMOS equiv. of 1200	Consult. fact.
TMS1270	High-V drive version, 1200	Consult fact.
TMS1270C	CMOS version of 1270	Consult fact.
TMS1300	40-pin µC, same mem. as 1100	$ 2.85
TMS1300C	CMOS equiv. of 1300	TBA
TMS1370	High-V driver version, 1300	Consult fact.
TMS1370C	CMOS version of 1370	TBA
TMS1400	28-pin µC, 4-k ROM	$ 4.25
TMS1470	High-V drive version, 1400	Consult fact.
TMS1600	40-pin µC, 4-k ROM	$ 4.90
TMS1670	High-V drive 1600	Consult fact.
TMS1700	28-pin µC, 0.5-k ROM	$ 1.50
TMS1022	Dedicated CB PLL controller	Consult fact.
TMS1117	Dedicated µW oven controller	$ 16.17*
TMS1121	Dedicated appliance timer	$ 16.17*
TMS1096SJPL	ROM-less 2100/2300 µC	Consult fact.
TMS1097JLP (SE5)	ROM-less 1400 µC	$ 75.00*
TMS1098JLP (SE2)	ROM-less 1100 µC	$ 24.75*
TMS1098JLC (SE4)	CMOS version	$ 75.00*
TMS1099JLP (SE1)	ROM-less 1100 µC	$ 18.21*
TMS1099JLC (SE3)	CMOS version	$ 61.86*
TMS1024/1026	16 to 4-line multiplexer	$2.61/CF*
TMS1025/1027	28 to 4-line multiplexer	$3.21/CF*
TMS1976	Capacitive keyboard controller	$ 2.26*
TMS0117	BCD in BCD out calendar	$ 21.35*
SEB2	TMS1000 eval. board	$ 210.00
SEB3	TMS1100 eval. board	$ 240.00
SEB4	TMS1000C eval. bd.	$ 252.00
SEB5	TMS1100C eval. bd.	TBA
SEB6	TMS1400/1600 eval. board	$ 300
SEB7	TMS2100/2300 eval. board	TBA

*Unit quantity

8-bit microcomputers: M6805 family (MC6805P2, 6805U2, 6805R2, 68705P3, 146805E2, 146805G2)

Motorola, Inc.
Semiconductor Group
3501 Ed Bluestein Blvd.
Austin, TX 78721
(512) 928-6000

Alternate sources: AMI for the P2, Hitachi for the U2, R2, and a proprietary version (the HD6805V with 4-k ROM).

The M6805 family of single-chip μCs provides not only a complete system on a chip, but self-testing as well. A separate ROM on the chip provides self-check program storage for a routine that performs nearly a 95% check of the processor's functionality. The program checks the RAM, the ROM, the address/data lines, the interrupts, the timer, and the I/O lines several times a second. The 6 available versions have different features. The MC6805P2 comes in a 28-pin DIP and offers 1100 bytes of user ROM and hardware-programmable timer options. Its EPROM counterpart, the MC68705P3, has a UV EPROM instead of the mask ROM. The R2 version includes an 8-bit, 4-channel a-d converter on the chip along with 2 kbytes of ROM, and the U2 version comes in a 40-pin DIP and has 32 I/O lines. Two CMOS versions of the NMOS processors are the MCI46805E2, which is a ROM-less version of the P2 circuit, and the 146805G2, which is a CMOS brother to the 6805U2. The MC146805E2 also provides for software rather than hardware programming of the timer functions, and has 112 bytes of RAM instead of 64, as does the G2 CMOS version.

Comments

The instruction set of the M6805 family consists of 61 commands that can be loosely grouped into 5 categories: register and memory operations (16), read/modify/write instructions (11), branch commands (17), bit-manipulation operations (4), and control functions (13).

Software features include direct bit-set, clear, and test instructions; but otherwise the instruction set is similar to that of the MC6800. Modifications have been made to adjust operation to an 8-bit index register, a single accumulator, and reduced stack control.

Software support builds on the MC6800 family base by using the EXORciser development system and the available assemblers, editors, and debug routines. Although the M6805 family is not totally source or object-code compatible with the MC6800, the instructions are similar.

Hardware support depends on the application. In the stand-alone mode, no support is needed. However, in multiple-chip systems, the entire family of MC6800-compatible support circuits can be used.

Hardware		
Model	**Description**	**Price (100-qty)**
MC6805P2	28-pin μC, NMOS, 1.1-k ROM	Consult fact.
MC6805R2	28-pin μC, NMOS, 2-k ROM 4-channel a-d	Consult fact.
MC6805U2	40-pin μC, NMOS, 2-k ROM 32 I/O lines	Consult fact.
MC68705P3	28-pin μC, NMOS, UV EPROM	$50-70
MC146805E2	28-pin μP, CMOS, no ROM	$30-40
MC146805G2	28-pin μC, CMOS, 2-k ROM	Consult fact.

Specifications	
Data word size	8 bits
Address bus size	11, 12, or 13 bits
On-chip ROM size	0, 1.1, or 2 kbytes
Direct addressing range	2, 4 or 8 kbytes
On-chip RAM size	64 or 112 bytes
Instruction word size	1 or 2 bytes
Number of basic instructions	61
Shortest instruction time (single byte)	2 μs
Longest instruction time (multiple byte)	10 or 11 μs
Clock frequency (min/max)	dc/5 MHz
Clock phases/voltage swing	1/TTL (internal)
Dedicated I/O control lines	20 to 32 lines
Package size	28 or 40-pin DIP
Power requirements	5 V/80 mA (NMOS) 3 to 6 V/2 mA (CMOS)

8-bit microcomputer, NMOS, CMOS

MC6805, 68705, 146805, 6805R2

Alternate sources: None

Motorola Inc.
Semiconductor Group
3501 Ed Bluestein Blvd.
Austin, TX 78721
(512) 928-6000

The MC6805 family of single-chip microcomputers provide not only a complete system on a chip, but self-testing as well. A separate 116-byte ROM on the chip provides the self-test program storage for a routine that performs a close to 95% check of the processor's functionality. The program checks the RAM, the ROM, the address/data lines, the interrupts and the I/O lines several times a second. The four versions of the chip will have different features: The NMOS 6805 will come in a 28-pin DIP with 1100 bytes of ROM and hardware-programmable timer options. Its UV EPROM counterpart, the 68705 has a UV EPROM instead of the ROM. The 146805 CMOS version will offer no ROM, but will have additional RAM and software control of the on-chip timer. Finally, the 6805R2 is expected to include 2 kbytes of mask ROM, a four-channel a/d converter and 28 additional I/O lines.

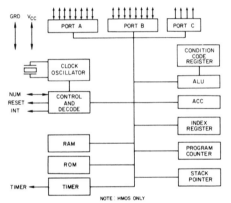

The architecture of the 6805 family follows the architecture of the basic 6800 processor. On the chip are a programmable 8-bit timer with 7-bit prescaler, clock oscillator, 1100 bytes of program ROM, 64 bytes of scratch-pad RAM and 20 I/O lines (6805), along with a reduced-instruction 6800-type CPU. All ports and the timer are addressed as memory registers—and some of the address space is reserved for future use as I/O or RAM.

Specifications

Data word size	8 bits
Address bus size	11 bits
Direct addressing range	1100 bytes
Instruction word size	8 bits
Number of basic instructions	61
Clock frequency (min/max)	dc/3.58 MHz
Clock phases/voltage swing	1/TTL
Dedicated I/O control lines	20
Package size	28
Power requirements	5 V

Hardware

Model	Description	Price (100 qty)
MC6805	28-pin μC with ROM	Consult factory
MC68705	μC with UV EPROM	
MC146805	CMOS version, no ROM	
MC6805R2	μC with a/d converter	

Comments

The instruction set of the M6805 family consists of 61 commands that can be loosely grouped into five categories: register and memory operations (16), read/modify/write instructions (11), branch commands (19), bit manipulation operations (4) and control functions (11).

Software features include the large selection of conditional branches; but otherwise the instruction set is similar to that of the 6800. Modifications have been made to adjust operation to an 8-bit index register, a single accumulation and reduced stack control.

Software support builds on the 6800-family base by using the EXORciser development system and the available assemblers and editors. Although the 6805 is not totally source or object-code compatible with the 6800, the instructions are similar.

Hardware support depends on the application. In a stand-alone mode, no support is needed. However, in multiple chip systems, the entire family of 6800-compatible support circuits can be used.

8-bit, microcomputer, NMOS

Z8

Alternate sources: Synertek

Zilog, Inc.
10460 Bubb Rd.
Cupertino, CA 95014
(408) 446-4666

The Z8 single-chip microcomputer provides the user with an on-chip ROM capacity of 2048 bytes, a RAM capacity of 144 bytes, 32 I/O lines, two counter/timers, a programmable UART and, of course, a powerful 8-bit CPU. The I/O is totally software configurable on some ports and dedicated on others—one port is set up as four-input and four-output lines, eight lines are bit programmable as input or output, another 8-bit port is programmable in four-bit sections as input or output, and the fourth port is byte programmable as input or output. Up to 62 kbytes of external program memory and 62 kbytes of data memory can be addressed by the processor. The processor also contains a special 64-byte test ROM memory that simplifies testing independent of the end application.

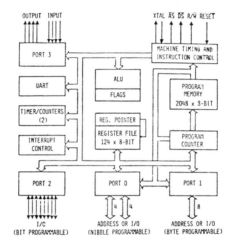

Specifications

Data word size	8 bits
Address bus size	8, 12, or 16 bits
Addressing range	126 kbytes
Instruction word size	1 to 3 bytes
Number of basic instructions	47
Shortest instruction/time (most)	1.5μs
Longest instruction/time (call)	3.75 μs
Clock frequency (min/max)	TBS*/8 MHz
Clock phases/voltage swing	1/Internal
Dedicated I/O control lines	32
Package	40-pin DIP or 64-pin QUIP
Power requirements	5 V/190 mA

* To be specified

The architecture of the Z8 uses multiple address space addressing to reach the various sections in the processor. The Z8 can access internal memory and external memory for data or instructions, and multiple register banks can rapidly be switched by use of a special pointer register. There is also a special power-down mode that permits the register file data to be retained by a separate power source.

Hardware

Model	Description	Price (1 to 9)
Z8-40 MCC	Single-chip μC	Consult factory
Z8-02MPD	ROM-less version (QUIP)	$110
PDS8000	Program dev. system	10,485 to 21,500
Z8-03	ROM-less piggyback	TBS

Comments

The instruction set of the Z8 permits the processing of bits, bytes and half bytes in 1, 2 and 3-byte instructions. There are six main addressing modes available—register, indirect register, immediate, indexed, direct address, and relative address. Other addressing modes include auto-increment, register pair, indirect register pair. The instructions are grouped into eight main areas—load, arithmetic, logic, program control, bit manipulation, rotate and shift, block transfer, and CPU control.

Software support for the Z8 consists of all the programming aids available for the Z80 microprocessor, including a Z8 cross assembler on the Z80 development system.

Software features of the Z8 processor include efficient and fast I/O transfer and bit handling instructions as well as six vectored interrupts that are maskable and prioritized. The novel register structure of the processor and the pointer register permit the CPU to switch rapidly between nine sets of 16 working registers. Software controls the I/O port configurations and the programmable UART on the chip, as well as the two 8-bit counter/timers.

Hardware support for the Z8 processor consists of all the upcoming Z8000 hardware and peripheral chips. However, the Z8 also has a ROM-less version that comes in a 64-pin QUIP, or a 40-pin piggyback DIP.

```
8080/8085 subroutine for dividing an unsigned 16-bit dividend by
an unsigned 8-bit divisor
LABEL    OPCODE OPERAND COMMENT
                        ;Divisor is in C
                        ;Dividend is originally in H,L
                        ;Quotient will be in L
                        ;Remainder will be in H
         MVI    B, 8    ;Initialise counter B with 8
LOOP:    DAD    H       ;Shift dividend and quotient left
         MOV    A, H    ;Place high part of dividend in A
         SUB    C       ;Try to subtract divisor
         MOV    H, A    ;Subtraction is possible
         INR    L       ;Add 1 to quotient
NEXT:    DCR    B       ;Decrement counter
         JNZ    LOOP    ;If not 0, continue division
         RET            ;Otherwise return
```

Appendix 5 A selection of data sheets

MOTOROLA
Semiconductors
BOX 20912 • PHOENIX, ARIZONA 85036

MC6820

PERIPHERAL INTERFACE ADAPTER (PIA)

The MC6820 Peripheral Interface Adapter provides the universal means of interfacing peripheral equipment to the MC6800 Micro-processing Unit (MPU). This device is capable of interfacing the MPU to peripherals through two 8-bit bidirectional peripheral data buses and four control lines. No external logic is required for interfacing to most peripheral devices.

The functional configuration of the PIA is programmed by the MPU during system initialization. Each of the peripheral data lines can be programmed to act as an input or output, and each of the four control/interrupt lines may be programmed for one of several control modes. This allows a high degree of flexibility in the over-all operation of the interface.

- 8-Bit Bidirectional Data Bus for Communication with the MPU
- Two Bidirectional 8-Bit Buses for Interface to Peripherals
- Two Programmable Control Registers
- Two Programmable Data Direction Registers
- Four Individually-Controlled Interrupt Input Lines; Two Usable as Peripheral Control Outputs
- Handshake Control Logic for Input and Output Peripheral Operation
- High-Impedance 3-State and Direct Transistor Drive Peripheral Lines
- Program Controlled Interrupt and Interrupt Disable Capability
- CMOS Drive Capability on Side A Peripheral Lines

MOS

(N-CHANNEL, SILICON-GATE)

PERIPHERAL INTERFACE ADAPTER

L SUFFIX
CERAMIC PACKAGE
CASE 715

NOT SHOWN: **P SUFFIX**

PLASTIC PACKAGE
CASE 711

**M6800 MICROCOMPUTER FAMILY
BLOCK DIAGRAM**

MC6800
Microprocessor

Read Only
Memory

Random
Access
Memory

MC6820
Interface
Adapter

Interface
Adapter → Modem

Address   Data
Bus   Bus

**MC6820 PERIPHERAL INTERFACE ADAPTER
BLOCK DIAGRAM**

Data Bus → Data Bus Buffers → A Buffers and Data Register → Peripheral Data

Memory Address and Control Interrupt → Selection and Control → B Buffers and Data Register → Peripheral Data

MC6820

ELECTRICAL CHARACTERISTICS (V_{CC} = 5.0 V ±5%, V_{SS} = 0, T_A = 0 to 70°C unless otherwise noted.)

Characteristic		Symbol	Min	Typ	Max	Unit
Input High Voltage	Enable	V_{IH}	V_{SS} + 2.4	–	V_{CC}	Vdc
	Other Inputs		V_{SS} + 2.0	–	V_{CC}	
Input Low Voltage	Enable	V_{IL}	V_{SS} –0.3	–	V_{SS} + 0.4	Vdc
	Other Inputs		V_{SS} –0.3	–	V_{SS} + 0.8	
Input Leakage Current R/W, $\overline{Reset}$, RS0, RS1, CS0, CS1, $\overline{CS2}$, CA1,		I_{in}	–	1.0	2.5	μAdc
(V_{in} = 0 to 5.25 Vdc) CB1, Enable						
Three-State (Off State) Input Current D0-D7, PB0-PB7, CB2		I_{TSI}	–	2.0	10	μAdc
(V_{in} = 0.4 to 2.4 Vdc)						
Input High Current PA0-PA7, CA2		I_{IH}	–100	–250	–	μAdc
(V_{IH} = 2.4 Vdc)						
Input Low Current PA0-PA7, CA2		I_{IL}	–	–1.0	–1.6	mAdc
(V_{IL} = 0.4 Vdc)						
Output High Voltage		V_{OH}				Vdc
(I_{Load} = –205 μAdc, Enable Pulse Width < 25 μs) D0-D7			V_{SS} + 2.4	–	–	
(I_{Load} = –100 μAdc, Enable Pulse Width <25 μs) Other Outputs			V_{SS} + 2.4	–	–	
Output Low Voltage		V_{OL}	–	–	V_{SS} + 0.4	Vdc
(I_{Load} = 1.6 mAdc, Enable Pulse Width < 25 μs)						
Output High Current (Sourcing)		I_{OH}				
(V_{OH} = 2.4 Vdc) D0-D7			–205	–	–	μAdc
Other Outputs			–100	–	–	μAdc
(V_O = 1.5 Vdc, the current for driving other than TTL, e.g.,						
Darlington Base) PB0-PB7, CB2			–1.0	–2.5	–10	mAdc
Output Low Current (Sinking)		I_{OL}	1.6	–	–	mAdc
(V_{OL} = 0.4 Vdc)						
Output Leakage Current (Off State) $\overline{IRQA}$, $\overline{IRQB}$		I_{LOH}	–	1.0	10	μAdc
(V_{OH} = 2.4 Vdc)						
Power Dissipation		P_D	–	–	650	mW
Input Capacitance	Enable	C_{in}	–	–	20	pF
(V_{in} = 0, T_A = 25°C, f = 1.0 MHz) D0-D7			–	–	12.5	
PA0-PA7, PB0-PB7, CA2, CB2			–	–	10	
R/W, $\overline{Reset}$, RS0, RS1, CS0, CS1, $\overline{CS2}$, CA1, CB1			–	–	7.5	
Output Capacitance $\overline{IRQA}$, $\overline{IRQB}$		C_{out}	–	–	5.0	pF
(V_{in} = 0, T_A = 25°C, f = 1.0 MHz) PB0-PB7			–	–	10	
Peripheral Data Setup Time (Figure 1)		t_{PDSU}	200	–	–	ns
Delay Time, Enable negative transition to CA2 negative transition (Figure 2, 3)		t_{CA2}	–	–	1.0	μs
Delay Time, Enable negative transition to CA2 positive transition (Figure 2)		t_{RS1}	–	–	1.0	μs
Rise and Fall Times for CA1 and CA2 input signals (Figure 3)		t_r, t_f	–	–	1.0	μs
Delay Time from CA1 active transition to CA2 positive transition (Figure 3)		t_{RS2}	–	–	2.0	μs
Delay Time, Enable negative transition to Peripheral Data valid (Figures 4, 5)		t_{PDW}	–	–	1.0	μs
Delay Time, Enable negative transition to Peripheral CMOS Data Valid (V_{CC} – 30% V_{CC}, Figure 4; Figure 12 Load C) PA0-PA7, CA2		t_{CMOS}	–	–	2.0	μs
Delay Time, Enable positive transition to CB2 negative transition (Figure 6, 7)		t_{CB2}	–	–	1.0	μs
Delay Time, Peripheral Data valid to CB2 negative transition (Figure 5)		t_{DC}	20	–	–	ns
Delay Time, Enable positive transition to CB2 positive transition (Figure 6)		t_{RS1}	–	–	1.0	μs
Rise and Fall Time for CB1 and CB2 input signals (Figure 7)		t_r, t_f	–	–	1.0	μs
Delay Time, CB1 active transition to CB2 positive transition (Figure 7)		t_{RS2}	–	–	2.0	μs
Interrupt Release Time, $\overline{IRQA}$ and $\overline{IRQB}$ (Figure 8)		t_{IR}	–	–	1.6	μs
Reset Low Time* (Figure 9)		t_{RL}	2.0	–	–	μs

*The Reset line must be high a minimum of 1.0 μs before addressing the PIA.

 MOTOROLA *Semiconductor Products Inc.*

MC6820

MAXIMUM RATINGS

Rating	Symbol	Value	Unit
Supply Voltage	V_{CC}	−0.3 to +7.0	Vdc
Input Voltage	V_{in}	−0.3 to +7.0	Vdc
Operating Temperature Range	T_A	0 to +70	°C
Storage Temperature Range	T_{stg}	−55 to +150	°C
Thermal Resistance	θ_{JA}	82.5	°C/W

This device contains circuitry to protect the inputs against damage due to high static voltages or electric fields; however, it is advised that normal precautions be taken to avoid application of any voltage higher than maximum rated voltages to this high impedance circuit.

BUS TIMING CHARACTERISTICS

READ (Figures 10 and 12)

Characteristic	Symbol	Min	Typ	Max	Unit
Enable Cycle Time	t_{cycE}	1.0	–	–	μs
Enable Pulse Width, High	PW_{EH}	0.45	–	25	μs
Enable Pulse Width, Low	PW_{EL}	0.43	–	–	μs
Setup Time, Address and R/W valid to Enable positive transition	t_{AS}	160	–	–	ns
Data Delay Time	t_{DDR}	–	–	320	ns
Data Hold Time	t_H	10	–	–	ns
Address Hold Time	t_{AH}	10	–	–	ns
Rise and Fall Time for Enable input	t_{Er}, t_{Ef}	–	–	25	ns

WRITE (Figures 11 and 12)

Characteristic	Symbol	Min	Typ	Max	Unit
Enable Cycle Time	t_{cycE}	1.0	–	–	μs
Enable Pulse Width, High	PW_{EH}	0.45	–	25	μs
Enable Pulse Width, Low	PW_{EL}	0.43	–	–	μs
Setup Time, Address and R/W valid to Enable positive transition	t_{AS}	160	–	–	ns
Data Setup Time	t_{DSW}	195	–	–	ns
Data Hold Time	t_H	10	–	–	ns
Address Hold Time	t_{AH}	10	–	–	ns
Rise and Fall Time for Enable input	t_{Er}, t_{Ef}	–	–	25	ns

FIGURE 1 – PERIPHERAL DATA SETUP TIME
(Read Mode)

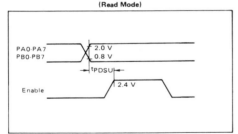

FIGURE 2 – CA2 DELAY TIME
(Read Mode; CRA-5 = CRA-3 = 1, CRA-4 = 0)

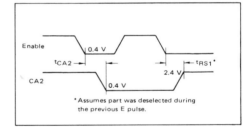

*Assumes part was deselected during the previous E pulse.

FIGURE 3 – CA2 DELAY TIME
(Read Mode; CRA-5 = 1, CRA-3 = CRA-4 = 0)

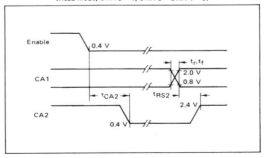

 MOTOROLA *Semiconductor Products Inc.*

MC6820

FIGURE 4 – PERIPHERAL CMOS DATA DELAY TIMES
(Write Mode; CRA-5 = CRA-3 = 1, CRA-4 = 0)

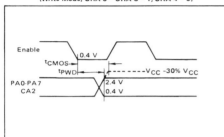

FIGURE 5 – PERIPHERAL DATA AND CB2 DELAY TIMES
(Write Mode; CRB-5 = CRB-3 = 1, CRB-4 = 0)

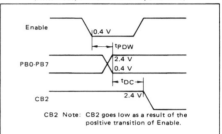

CB2 Note: CB2 goes low as a result of the positive transition of Enable.

FIGURE 6 – CB2 DELAY TIME
(Write Mode; CRB-5 = CRB-3 = 1, CRB-4 = 0)

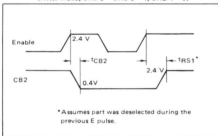

*Assumes part was deselected during the previous E pulse.

FIGURE 7 – CB2 DELAY TIME
(Write Mode; CRB-5 = 1, CRB-3 = CRB-4 = 0)

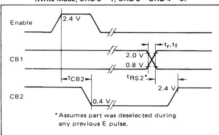

*Assumes part was deselected during any previous E pulse.

FIGURE 8 – IRQ RELEASE TIME

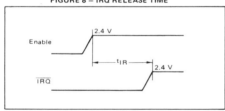

FIGURE 9 – RESET LOW TIME

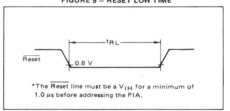

*The Reset line must be a V_{IH} for a minimum of 1.0 μs before addressing the PIA.

FIGURE 10 – BUS READ TIMING CHARACTERISTICS
(Read Information from PIA)

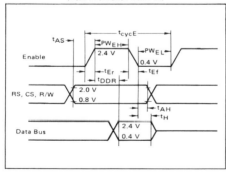

FIGURE 11 – BUS WRITE TIMING CHARACTERISTICS
(Write Information into PIA)

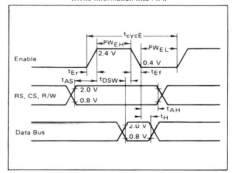

 MOTOROLA *Semiconductor Products Inc.*

MC6820

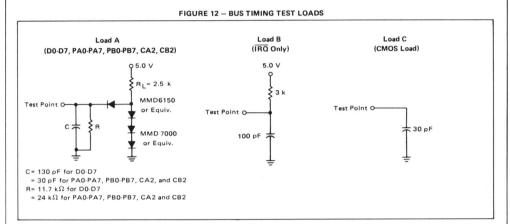

FIGURE 12 – BUS TIMING TEST LOADS

Load A
(D0-D7, PA0-PA7, PB0-PB7, CA2, CB2)

R$_L$ = 2.5 k

5.0 V

MMD6150
or Equiv.

MMD 7000
or Equiv.

Test Point

C   R

C = 130 pF for D0-D7
= 30 pF for PA0-PA7, PB0-PB7, CA2, and CB2
R = 11.7 kΩ for D0-D7
= 24 kΩ for PA0-PA7, PB0-PB7, CA2 and CB2

Load B
($\overline{IRQ}$ Only)

5.0 V

3 k

Test Point

100 pF

Load C
(CMOS Load)

Test Point

30 pF

PIA INTERFACE SIGNALS FOR MPU

The PIA interfaces to the MC6800 MPU with an eight-bit bi-directional data bus, three chip select lines, two register select lines, two interrupt request lines, read/write line, enable line and reset line. These signals, in conjunction with the MC6800 VMA output, permit the MPU to have complete control over the PIA. VMA should be utilized in conjunction with an MPU address line into a chip select of the PIA.

PIA Bi-Directional Data (D0-D7) — The bi-directional data lines (D0-D7) allow the transfer of data between the MPU and the PIA. The data bus output drivers are three-state devices that remain in the high-impedance (off) state except when the MPU performs a PIA read operation. The Read/Write line is in the Read (high) state when the PIA is selected for a Read operation.

PIA Enable (E) — The enable pulse, E, is the only timing signal that is supplied to the PIA. Timing of all other signals is referenced to the leading and trailing edges of the E pulse. This signal will normally be a derivative of the MC6800 ϕ2 Clock.

PIA Read/Write (R/W) — This signal is generated by the MPU to control the direction of data transfers on the Data Bus. A low state on the PIA Read/Write line enables the input buffers and data is transferred from the MPU to the PIA on the E signal if the device has been selected. A high on the Read/Write line sets up the PIA for a transfer of data to the bus. The PIA output buffers are enabled when the proper address and the enable pulse E are present.

Reset — The active low Reset line is used to reset all register bits in the PIA to a logical zero (low). This line can be used as a power-on reset and as a master reset during system operation.

PIA Chip Select (CS0, CS1 and $\overline{CS2}$) — These three input signals are used to select the PIA. CS0 and CS1 must be high and $\overline{CS2}$ must be low for selection of the device. Data transfers are then performed under the control of the Enable and Read/Write signals. The chip select lines must be stable for the duration of the E pulse. The device is deselected when any of the chip selects are in the inactive state.

PIA Register Select (RS0 and RS1) — The two register select lines are used to select the various registers inside the PIA. These two lines are used in conjunction with internal Control Registers to select a particular register that is to be written or read.

The register and chip select lines should be stable for the duration of the E pulse while in the read or write cycle.

Interrupt Request ($\overline{IRQA}$ and $\overline{IRQB}$) — The active low Interrupt Request lines ($\overline{IRQA}$ and $\overline{IRQB}$) act to interrupt the MPU either directly or through interrupt priority circuitry. These lines are "open drain" (no load device on the chip). This permits all interrupt request lines to be tied together in a wire-OR configuration.

Each Interrupt Request line has two internal interrupt flag bits that can cause the Interrupt Request line to go low. Each flag bit is associated with a particular peripheral interrupt line. Also four interrupt enable bits are provided in the PIA which may be used to inhibit a particular interrupt from a peripheral device.

Servicing an interrupt by the MPU may be accomplished by a software routine that, on a prioritized basis, sequentially reads and tests the two control registers in each PIA for interrupt flag bits that are set.

The interrupt flags are cleared (zeroed) as a result of an

MC6820

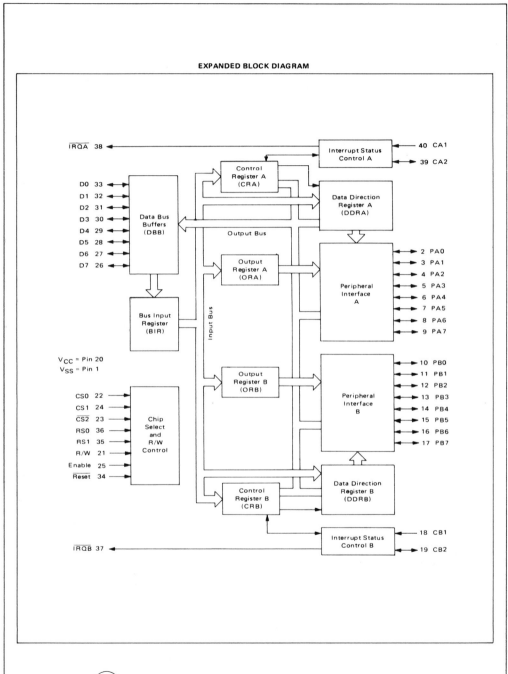

EXPANDED BLOCK DIAGRAM

MC6820

MPU Read Peripheral Data Operation of the corresponding data register. After being cleared, the interrupt flag bit cannot be enabled to be set until the PIA is deselected during an E pulse. The E pulse is used to condition the interrupt control lines (CA1, CA2, CB1, CB2). When these lines are used as interrupt inputs at least one E pulse must occur from the inactive edge to the active edge of the interrupt input signal to condition the edge sense network. If the interrupt flag has been enabled and the edge sense circuit has been properly conditioned, the interrupt flag will be set on the next active transition of the interrupt input pin.

PIA PERIPHERAL INTERFACE LINES

The PIA provides two 8-bit bi-directional data buses and four interrupt/control lines for interfacing to peripheral devices.

Section A Peripheral Data (PA0-PA7) — Each of the peripheral data lines can be programmed to act as an input or output. This is accomplished by setting a "1" in the corresponding Data Direction Register bit for those lines which are to be outputs. A "0" in a bit of the Data Direction Register causes the corresponding peripheral data line to act as an input. During an MPU Read Peripheral Data Operation, the data on peripheral lines programmed to act as inputs appears directly on the corresponding MPU Data Bus lines. In the input mode the internal pullup resistor on these lines represents a maximum of one standard TTL load.

The data in Output Register A will appear on the data lines that are programmed to be outputs. A logical "1" written into the register will cause a "high" on the corresponding data line while a "0" results in a "low". Data in Output Register A may be read by an MPU "Read Peripheral Data A" operation when the corresponding lines are programmed as outputs. This data will be read properly if the voltage on the peripheral data lines is greater than 2.0 volts for a logic "1" output and less than 0.8 volt for a logic "0" output. Loading the output lines such that the voltage on these lines does not reach full voltage causes the data transferred into the MPU on a Read operation to differ from that contained in the respective bit of Output Register A.

Section B Peripheral Data (PB0-PB7) — The peripheral data lines in the B Section of the PIA can be programmed to act as either inputs or outputs in a similar manner to PA0-PA7. However, the output buffers driving these lines differ from those driving lines PA0-PA7. They have three-state capability, allowing them to enter a high impedance state when the peripheral data line is used as an input. In addition, data on the peripheral data lines PB0-PB7 will be read properly from those lines programmed as outputs even if the voltages are below 2.0 volts for a "high". As outputs, these lines are compatible with standard TTL and may also be used as a source of up to 1 milliampere at 1.5 volts to directly drive the base of a transistor switch.

Interrupt Input (CA1 and CB1) — Peripheral Input lines CA1 and CB1 are input only lines that set the interrupt flags of the control registers. The active transition for these signals is also programmed by the two control registers.

Peripheral Control (CA2) — The peripheral control line CA2 can be programmed to act as an interrupt input or as a peripheral control output. As an output, this line is compatible with standard TTL; as an input the internal pullup resistor on this line represents one standard TTL load. The function of this signal line is programmed with Control Register A.

Peripheral Control (CB2) — Peripheral Control line CB2 may also be programmed to act as an interrupt input or peripheral control output. As an input, this line has high input impedance and is compatible with standard TTL. As an output it is compatible with standard TTL and may also be used as a source of up to 1 milliampere at 1.5 volts to directly drive the base of a transistor switch. This line is programmed by Control Register B.

NOTE: It is recommended that the control lines (CA1, CA2, CB1, CB2) should be held in a logic 1 state when $\overline{\text{Reset}}$ is active to prevent setting of corresponding interrupt flags in the control register when $\overline{\text{Reset}}$ goes to an inactive state. Subsequent to $\overline{\text{Reset}}$ going inactive, a read of the data registers may be used to clear any undesired interrupt flags.

 MOTOROLA *Semiconductor Products Inc.*

MC6820

INTERNAL CONTROLS

There are six locations within the PIA accessible to the MPU data bus: two Peripheral Registers, two Data Direction Registers, and two Control Registers. Selection of these locations is controlled by the RS0 and RS1 inputs together with bit 2 in the Control Register, as shown in Table 1.

TABLE 1 — INTERNAL ADDRESSING

RS1	RS0	Control Register Bit CRA-2	Control Register Bit CRB-2	Location Selected
0	0	1	X	Peripheral Register A
0	0	0	X	Data Direction Register A
0	1	X	X	Control Register A
1	0	X	1	Peripheral Register B
1	0	X	0	Data Direction Register B
1	1	X	X	Control Register B

X = Don't Care

INITIALIZATION

A low reset line has the effect of zeroing all PIA registers. This will set PA0-PA7, PB0-PB7, CA2 and CB2 as inputs, and all interrupts disabled. The PIA must be configured during the restart program which follows the reset.

Details of possible configurations of the Data Direction and Control Register are as follows.

DATA DIRECTION REGISTERS (DDRA and DDRB)

The two Data Direction Registers allow the MPU to control the direction of data through each corresponding peripheral data line. A Data Direction Register bit set at "0" configures the corresponding peripheral data line as an input; a "1" results in an output.

CONTROL REGISTERS (CRA and CRB)

The two Control Registers (CRA and CRB) allow the MPU to control the operation of the four peripheral control lines CA1, CA2, CB1 and CB2. In addition they allow the MPU to enable the interrupt lines and monitor the status of the interrupt flags. Bits 0 through 5 of the two registers may be written or read by the MPU when the proper chip select and register select signals are applied. Bits 6 and 7 of the two registers are read only and are modified by external interrupts occurring on control lines CA1, CA2, CB1 or CB2. The format of the control words is shown in Table 2.

TABLE 2 — CONTROL WORD FORMAT

	7	6	5	4	3	2	1	0
CRA	IRQA1	IRQA2	CA2 Control			DDRA Access	CA1 Control	

	7	6	5	4	3	2	1	0
CRB	IRQB1	IRQB2	CB2 Control			DDRB Access	CB1 Control	

Data Direction Access Control Bit (CRA-2 and CRB-2) — Bit 2 in each Control register (CRA and CRB) allows selection of either a Peripheral Interface Register or the Data Direction Register when the proper register select signals are applied to RS0 and RS1.

Interrupt Flags (CRA-6, CRA-7, CRB-6, and CRB-7) — The four interrupt flag bits are set by active transitions of signals on the four Interrupt and Peripheral Control lines when those lines are programmed to be inputs. These bits cannot be set directly from the MPU Data Bus and are reset indirectly by a Read Peripheral Data Operation on the appropriate section.

TABLE 3 — CONTROL OF INTERRUPT INPUTS CA1 AND CB1

CRA-1 (CRB-1)	CRA-0 (CRB-0)	Interrupt Input CA1 (CB1)	Interrupt Flag CRA-7 (CRB-7)	MPU Interrupt Request IRQA (IRQB)
0	0	↓ Active	Set high on ↓ of CA1 (CB1)	Disabled — IRQ remains high
0	1	↓ Active	Set high on ↓ of CA1 (CB1)	Goes low when the interrupt flag bit CRA-7 (CRB-7) goes high
1	0	↑ Active	Set high on ↑ of CA1 (CB1)	Disabled — IRQ remains high
1	1	↑ Active	Set high on ↑ of CA1 (CB1)	Goes low when the interrupt flag bit CRA-7 (CRB-7) goes high

Notes: 1. ↑ indicates positive transition (low to high)

2. ↓ indicates negative transition (high to low)

3. The Interrupt flag bit CRA-7 is cleared by an MPU Read of the A Data Register. and CRB-7 is cleared by an MPU Read of the B Data Register.

4. If CRA-0 (CRB-0) is low when an interrupt occurs (Interrupt disabled) and is later brought high, IRQA (IRQB) occurs after CRA-0 (CRB-0) is written to a "one".

 MOTOROLA *Semiconductor Products Inc.*

MC6820

Control of CA1 and CB1 Interrupt Input Lines (CRA-0, CRB-0, CRA-1, and CRB-1) — The two lowest order bits of the control registers are used to control the interrupt input lines CA1 and CB1. Bits CRA-0 and CRB-0 are used to enable the MPU interrupt signals $\overline{IRQA}$ and $\overline{IRQB}$, respectively. Bits CRA-1 and CRB-1 determine the active transition of the interrupt input signals CA1 and CB1 (Table 3).

TABLE 4 — CONTROL OF CA2 AND CB2 AS INTERRUPT INPUTS
CRA5 (CRB5) is low

CRA-5 (CRB-5)	CRA-4 (CRB-4)	CRA-3 (CRB-3)	Interrupt Input CA2 (CB2)	Interrupt Flag CRA-6 (CRB-6)	MPU Interrupt Request $\overline{IRQA}$ ($\overline{IRQB}$)
0	0	0	↓ Active	Set high on ↓ of CA2 (CB2)	Disabled — $\overline{IRQ}$ remains high
0	0	1	↓ Active	Set high on ↓ of CA2 (CB2)	Goes low when the interrupt flag bit CRA-6 (CRB-6) goes high
0	1	0	↑ Active	Set high on ↑ of CA2 (CB2)	Disabled — $\overline{IRQ}$ remains high
0	1	1	↑ Active	Set high on ↑ of CA2 (CB2)	Goes low when the interrupt flag bit CRA-6 (CRB-6) goes high

Notes: 1. ↑ indicates positive transition (low to high)

2. ↓ indicates negative transition (high to low)

3. The Interrupt flag bit CRA-6 is cleared by an MPU Read of the A Data Register and CRB-6 is cleared by an MPU Read of the B Data Register.

4. If CRA-3 (CRB-3) is low when an interrupt occurs (Interrupt disabled) and is later brought high, $\overline{IRQA}$ ($\overline{IRQB}$) occurs after CRA-3 (CRB-3) is written to a "one".

TABLE 5 — CONTROL OF CB2 AS AN OUTPUT
CRB-5 is high

CRB-5	CRB-4	CRB-3	CB2 Cleared	CB2 Set
1	0	0	Low on the positive transition of the first E pulse following an MPU Write "B" Data Register operation.	High when the interrupt flag bit CRB-7 is set by an active transition of the CB1 signal.
1	0	1	Low on the positive transition of the first E pulse after an MPU Write "B" Data Register operation.	High on the positive edge of the first "E" pulse following an "E" pulse which occurred while the part was deselected.
1	1	0	Low when CRB-3 goes low as a result of an MPU Write in Control Register "B".	Always low as long as CRB-3 is low. Will go high on an MPU Write in Control Register "B" that changes CRB-3 to "one".
1	1	1	Always high as long as CRB-3 is high. Will be cleared when an MPU Write Control Register "B" results in clearing CRB-3 to "zero".	High when CRB-3 goes high as a result of an MPU Write into Control Register "B".

 MOTOROLA *Semiconductor Products Inc.*

MC6820

Control of CA2 and CB2 Peripheral Control Lines (CRA-3, CRA-4, CRA-5, CRB-3, CRB-4, and CRB-5) — Bits 3, 4, and 5 of the two control registers are used to control the CA2 and CB2 Peripheral Control lines. These bits determine if the control lines will be an interrupt input or an output control signal. If bit CRA-5 (CRB-5) is low, CA2 (CB2) is an interrupt input line similar to CA1 (CB1) (Table 4). When CRA-5 (CRB-5) is high, CA2 (CB2) becomes an output signal that may be used to control peripheral data transfers. When in the output mode, CA2 and CB2 have slightly different characteristics (Tables 5 and 6).

TABLE 6 — CONTROL OF CA-2 AS AN OUTPUT
CRA-5 is high

CRA-5	CRA-4	CRA-3	CA2	
			Cleared	Set
1	0	0	Low on negative transition of E after an MPU Read "A" Data operation.	High when the interrupt flag bit CRA-7 is set by an active transition of the CA1 signal.
1	0	1	Low on negative transition of E after an MPU Read "A" Data operation.	High on the negative edge of the first "E" pulse which occurs during a deselect.
1	1	0	Low when CRA-3 goes low as a result of an MPU Write to Control Register "A".	Always low as long as CRA-3 is low. Will go high on an MPU Write to Control Register "A" that changes CRA-3 to "one".
1	1	1	Always high as long as CRA-3 is high. Will be cleared on an MPU Write to Control Register "A" that clears CRA-3 to a "zero".	High when CRA-3 goes high as a result of an MPU Write to Control Register "A".

PIN ASSIGNMENT

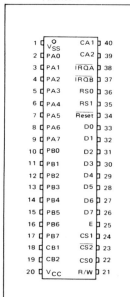

1 ▯ V$_{SS}$	CA1 ▯ 40
2 ▯ PA0	CA2 ▯ 39
3 ▯ PA1	IRQA ▯ 38
4 ▯ PA2	IRQB ▯ 37
5 ▯ PA3	RS0 ▯ 36
6 ▯ PA4	RS1 ▯ 35
7 ▯ PA5	Reset ▯ 34
8 ▯ PA6	D0 ▯ 33
9 ▯ PA7	D1 ▯ 32
10 ▯ PB0	D2 ▯ 31
11 ▯ PB1	D3 ▯ 30
12 ▯ PB2	D4 ▯ 29
13 ▯ PB3	D5 ▯ 28
14 ▯ PB4	D6 ▯ 27
15 ▯ PB5	D7 ▯ 26
16 ▯ PB6	E ▯ 25
17 ▯ PB7	CS1 ▯ 24
18 ▯ CB1	CS2 ▯ 23
19 ▯ CB2	CS0 ▯ 22
20 ▯ V$_{CC}$	R/W ▯ 21

PACKAGE DIMENSIONS

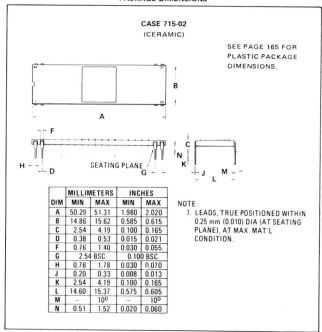

CASE 715-02
(CERAMIC)

SEE PAGE 165 FOR PLASTIC PACKAGE DIMENSIONS.

DIM	MILLIMETERS		INCHES	
	MIN	MAX	MIN	MAX
A	50.29	51.31	1.980	2.020
B	14.86	15.62	0.585	0.615
C	2.54	4.19	0.100	0.165
D	0.38	0.53	0.015	0.021
F	0.76	1.40	0.030	0.055
G	2.54 BSC		0.100 BSC	
H	0.76	1.78	0.030	0.070
J	0.20	0.33	0.008	0.013
K	2.54	4.19	0.100	0.165
L	14.60	15.37	0.575	0.605
M	–	10°	–	10°
N	0.51	1.52	0.020	0.060

NOTE:
1. LEADS, TRUE POSITIONED WITHIN 0.25 mm (0.010) DIA (AT SEATING PLANE), AT MAX. MAT'L CONDITION.

 MOTOROLA *Semiconductor Products Inc.*

8251A
PROGRAMMABLE COMMUNICATION INTERFACE

- **Synchronous and Asynchronous Operation**

  - Synchronous:
    5-8 Bit Characters
    Internal or External Character Synchronization
    Automatic Sync Insertion

  - Asynchronous:
    5-8 Bit Characters
    Clock Rate — 1, 16 or 64 Times Baud Rate
    Break Character Generation
    1, 1½, or 2 Stop Bits
    False Start Bit Detection
    Automatic Break Detect and Handling

- **Baud Rate —DC to 64k Baud**
- **Full Duplex, Double Buffered, Transmitter and Receiver**
- **Error Detection — Parity, Overrun, and Framing**
- **Fully Compatible with 8080/8085 CPU**
- **28-Pin DIP Package**
- **All Inputs and Outputs Are TTL Compatible**
- **Single 5 Volt Supply**
- **Single TTL Clock**

The 8251A is the enhanced version of the industry standard, Intel® 8251 Universal Synchronous/Asynchronous Receiver/Transmitter (USART), designed for data communications with Intel's new high performance family of microprocessors such as the 8085. The 8251A is used as a peripheral device and is programmed by the CPU to operate using virtually any serial data transmission technique presently in use (including IBM Bi-Sync). The USART accepts data characters from the CPU in parallel format and then converts them into a continuous serial data stream for transmission. Simultaneously, it can receive serial data streams and convert them into parallel data characters for the CPU. The USART will signal the CPU whenever it can accept a new character for transmission or whenever it has received a character for the CPU. The CPU can read the complete status of the USART at any time. These include data transmission errors and control signals such as SYNDET, TxEMPTY. The chip is constructed using N-channel silicon gate technology.

PIN CONFIGURATION

BLOCK DIAGRAM

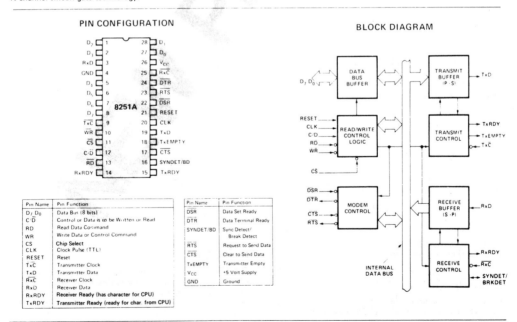

Pin Name	Pin Function
D_7/D_0	Data Bus (8 bits)
C/D	Control or Data is to be Written or Read
RD	Read Data Command
WR	Write Data or Control Command
CS	Chip Select
CLK	Clock Pulse (TTL)
RESET	Reset
TxC	Transmitter Clock
TxD	Transmitter Data
RxC	Receiver Clock
RxD	Receiver Data
RxRDY	Receiver Ready (has character for CPU)
TxRDY	Transmitter Ready (ready for char. from CPU)

Pin Name	Pin Function
DSR	Data Set Ready
DTR	Data Terminal Ready
SYNDET/BD	Sync Detect/ Break Detect
RTS	Request to Send Data
CTS	Clear to Send Data
TxEMPTY	Transmitter Empty
V_{CC}	+5 Volt Supply
GND	Ground

8251A

8251A BASIC FUNCTIONAL DESCRIPTION

General

The 8251A is a Universal Synchronous/Asynchronous Receiver/Transmitter designed specifically for the 80/85 Microcomputer Systems. Like other I/O devices in a Microcomputer System, its functional configuration is programmed by the system's software for maximum flexibility. The 8251A can support virtually any serial data technique currently in use (including IBM "bi-sync").

In a communication environment an interface device must convert parallel format system data into serial format for transmission and convert incoming serial format data into parallel system data for reception. The interface device must also delete or insert bits or characters that are functionally unique to the communication technique. In essence, the interface should appear "transparent" to the CPU, a simple input or output of byte-oriented system data.

Data Bus Buffer

This 3-state, bidirectional, 8-bit buffer is used to interface the 8251A to the system Data Bus. Data is transmitted or received by the buffer upon execution of INput or OUTput instructions of the CPU. Control words, Command words and Status information are also transferred through the Data Bus Buffer. The command status and data in, and data out are separate 8-bit registers to provide double buffering.

This functional block accepts inputs from the system Control bus and generates control signals for overall device operation. It contains the Control Word Register and Command Word Register that store the various control formats for the device functional definition.

RESET (Reset)

A "high" on this input forces the 8251A into an "Idle" mode. The device will remain at "Idle" until a new set of control words is written into the 8251A to program its functional definition. Minimum RESET pulse width is 6 t_{CY} (clock must be running).

CLK (Clock)

The CLK input is used to generate internal device timing and is normally connected to the Phase 2 (TTL) output of the 8224 Clock Generator. No external inputs or outputs are referenced to CLK but the frequency of CLK must be greater than 30 times the Receiver or Transmitter data bit rates.

$\overline{WR}$ (Write)

A "low" on this input informs the 8251A that the CPU is writing data or control words to the 8251A.

$\overline{RD}$ (Read)

A "low" on this input informs the 8251A that the CPU is reading data or status information from the 8251A.

C/$\overline{D}$ (Control/Data)

This input, in conjunction with the $\overline{WR}$ and $\overline{RD}$ inputs, informs the 8251A that the word on the Data Bus is either a data character, control word or status information.
1 = CONTROL/STATUS   0 = DATA

$\overline{CS}$ (Chip Select)

A "low" on this input selects the 8251A. No reading or writing will occur unless the device is selected. When $\overline{CS}$ is high, the Data Bus in the float state and $\overline{RD}$ and $\overline{WR}$ will have no effect on the chip.

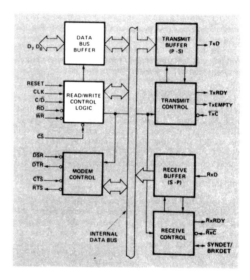

C/$\overline{D}$	$\overline{RD}$	$\overline{WR}$	$\overline{CS}$	
0	0	1	0	8251A DATA ⇒ DATA BUS
0	1	0	0	DATA BUS ⇒ 8251A DATA
1	0	1	0	STATUS ⇒ DATA BUS
1	1	0	0	DATA BUS ⇒ CONTROL
X	1	1	0	DATA BUS ⇒ 3-STATE
X	X	X	1	DATA BUS ⇒ 3-STATE

Modem Control

The 8251A has a set of control inputs and outputs that can be used to simplify the interface to almost any Modem. The Modem control signals are general purpose in nature and can be used for functions other than Modem control, if necessary.

8251A

$\overline{\text{DSR}}$ (Data Set Ready)

The $\overline{\text{DSR}}$ input signal is a general purpose, 1-bit inverting input port. Its condition can be tested by the CPU using a Status Read operation. The $\overline{\text{DSR}}$ input is normally used to test Modem conditions such as Data Set Ready.

$\overline{\text{DTR}}$ (Data Terminal Ready)

The $\overline{\text{DTR}}$ output signal is a general purpose, 1-bit inverting output port. It can be set "low" by programming the appropriate bit in the Command Instruction word. The $\overline{\text{DTR}}$ output signal is normally used for Modem control such as Data Terminal Ready or Rate Select.

$\overline{\text{RTS}}$ (Request to Send)

The $\overline{\text{RTS}}$ output signal is a general purpose, 1-bit inverting output port. It can be set "low" by programming the appropriate bit in the Command Instruction word. The $\overline{\text{RTS}}$ output signal is normally used for Modem control such as Request to Send.

$\overline{\text{CTS}}$ (Clear to Send)

A "low" on this input enables the 8251A to transmit serial data if the Tx Enable bit in the Command byte is set to a "one." If either a Tx Enable off or CTS off condition occurs while the Tx is in operation, the Tx will transmit all the data in the USART, written prior to Tx Disable command before shutting down.

Transmitter Buffer

The Transmitter Buffer accepts parallel data from the Data Bus Buffer, converts it to a serial bit stream, inserts the appropriate characters or bits (based on the communication technique) and outputs a composite serial stream of data on the TxD output pin on the falling edge of $\overline{\text{TxC}}$. The transmitter will begin transmission upon being enabled if $\overline{\text{CTS}} = 0$. The TxD line will be held in the marking state immediately upon a master Reset or when Tx Enable/$\overline{\text{CTS}}$ off or TxEMPTY.

Transmitter Control

The transmitter Control manages all activities associated with the transmission of serial data. It accepts and issues signals both externally and internally to accomplish this function.

TxRDY (Transmitter Ready)

This output signals the CPU that the transmitter is ready to accept a data character. The TxRDY output pin can be used as an interrupt to the system, since it is masked by Tx Disabled, or, for Polled operation, the CPU can check TxRDY using a Status Read operation. TxRDY is automatically reset by the leading edge of $\overline{\text{WR}}$ when a data character is loaded from the CPU.

Note that when using the Polled operation, the TxRDY status bit is *not* masked by Tx Enabled, but will only indicate the Empty/Full Status of the Tx Data Input Register.

TxE (Transmitter Empty)

When the 8251A has no characters to transmit, the TxEMPTY output will go "high". It resets automatically upon receiving a character from the CPU. TxEMPTY can be used to indicate the end of a transmission mode, so that the CPU "knows" when to "turn the line around" in the half-duplexed operational mode. TxEMPTY is independent of the Tx Enable bit in the Command instruction.

In SYNChronous mode, a "high" on this output indicates that a character has not been loaded and the SYNC character or characters are about to be or are being transmitted automatically as "fillers". TxEMPTY does not go low when the SYNC characters are being shifted out.

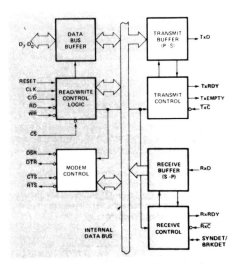

$\overline{\text{TxC}}$ (Transmitter Clock)

The Transmitter Clock controls the rate at which the character is to be transmitted. In the Synchronous transmission mode, the Baud Rate (1x) is equal to the $\overline{\text{TxC}}$ frequency. In Asynchronous transmission mode the baud rate is a fraction of the actual $\overline{\text{TxC}}$ frequency. A portion of the mode instruction selects this factor; it can be 1, 1/16 or 1/64 the $\overline{\text{TxC}}$.

For Example:

    If Baud Rate equals 110 Baud,
    $\overline{\text{TxC}}$ equals 110 Hz (1x)
    $\overline{\text{TxC}}$ equals 1.76 kHz (16x)
    $\overline{\text{TxC}}$ equals 7.04 kHz (64x).

The falling edge of $\overline{\text{TxC}}$ shifts the serial data out of the 8251A.

8251A

Receiver Buffer

The Receiver accepts serial data, converts this serial input to parallel format, checks for bits or characters that are unique to the communication technique and sends an "assembled" character to the CPU. Serial data is input to RxD pin, and is clocked in on the rising edge of $\overline{RxC}$.

Receiver Control

This functional block manages all receiver-related activities which consist of the following features:

The RxD initialization circuit prevents the 8251A from mistaking an unused input line for an active low data line in the "break condition". Before starting to receive serial characters on the RxD line, a valid "1" must first be detected after a chip master Reset. Once this has been determined, a search for a valid low (Start bit) is enabled. This feature is only active in the asynchronous mode, and is only done once for each master Reset.

The False Start bit detection circuit prevents false starts due to a transient noise spike by first detecting the falling edge and then strobing the nominal center of the Start bit (RxD = low).

The Parity Toggle F/F and Parity Error F/F circuits are used for parity error detection and set the corresponding status bit.

The Framing Error Flag F/F is set if the Stop bit is absent at the end of the data byte (asynchronous mode), and also sets the corresponding status bit.

RxRDY (Receiver Ready)

This output indicates that the 8251A contains a character that is ready to be input to the CPU. Rx RDY can be connected to the interrupt structure of the CPU or, for Polled operation, the CPU can check the condition of RxRDY using a Status Read operation.

Rx Enable off both masks and holds RxRDY in the Reset Condition. For Asynchronous mode, to set RxRDY, the Receiver must be Enabled to sense a Start Bit and a complete character must be assembled and transferred to the Data Output Register. For Synchronous mode, to set RxRDY, the Receiver must be enabled and a character must finish assembly and be transferred to the Data Output Register.

Failure to read the received character from the Rx Data Output Register prior to the assembly of the next Rx Data character will set overrun condition error and the previous character will be written over and lost. If the Rx Data is being read by the CPU when the internal transfer is occurring, overrun error will be set and the old character will be lost.

$\overline{RxC}$ (Receiver Clock)

The Receiver Clock controls the rate at which the character is to be received. In Synchronous Mode, the Baud Rate (1x) is equal to the actual frequency of $\overline{RxC}$. In Asynchronous Mode, the Baud Rate is a fraction of the actual $\overline{RxC}$ fre-

quency. A portion of the mode instruction selects this factor; 1, 1/16 or 1/64 the $\overline{RxC}$.

For Example:

Baud Rate equals 300 Baud, if
$\overline{RxC}$ equals 300 Hz (1x)
$\overline{RxC}$ equals 4800 Hz (16x)
$\overline{RxC}$ equals 19.2 kHz (64x).

Baud Rate equals 2400 Baud, if
$\overline{RxC}$ equals 2400 Hz (1x)
$\overline{RxC}$ equals 38.4 kHz (16x)
$\overline{RxC}$ equals 153.6 kHz (64x).

Data is sampled into the 8251A on the rising edge of $\overline{RxC}$.

NOTE: In most communications systems, the 8251A will be handling both the transmission and reception operations of a single link. Consequently, the Receive and Transmit Baud Rates will be the same. Both $\overline{TxC}$ and $\overline{RxC}$ will require identical frequencies for this operation and can be tied together and connected to a single frequency source ·(Baud Rate Generator) to simplify the interface.

SYNDET (SYNC Detect)/BRKDET (Break Detect)

This pin is used in SYNChronous Mode for SYNDET and may be used as either input or output, programmable through the Control Word. It is reset to output mode low upon RESET. When used as an output (internal Sync mode), the SYNDET pin will go "high" to indicate that the 8251A has located the SYNC character in the Receive mode. If the 8251A is programmed to use double Sync characters (bi-sync), then SYNDET will go "high" in the middle of the last bit of the second Sync character. SYNDET is automatically reset upon a Status Read operation.

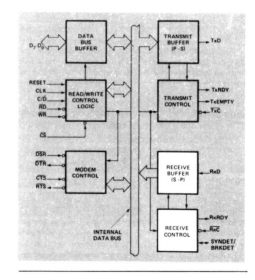

8251A

When used as an input (external SYNC detect mode), a positive going signal will cause the 8251A to start assembling data characters on the rising edge of the next $\overline{\text{RxC}}$. Once in SYNC, the "high" input signal can be removed. the period of $\overline{\text{RxC}}$. When External SYNC Detect is programmed, the Internal SYNC Detect is disabled.

Break Detect (Async Mode Only)

This output will go high whenever an all zero word of the programmed length (including start bit, data bit, parity bit, and *one* stop bit) is received. Break Detect may also be read as a Status bit. It is reset only upon a master chip Reset or Rx Data returning to a "one" state.

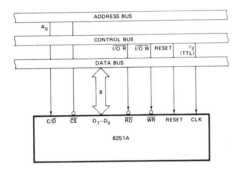

8251A Interface to 8080 Standard System Bus

DETAILED OPERATION DESCRIPTION

General

The complete functional definition of the 8251A is programmed by the system's software. A set of control words must be sent out by the CPU to initialize the 8251A to support the desired communications format. These control words will program the: BAUD RATE, CHARACTER LENGTH, NUMBER OF STOP BITS, SYNCHRONOUS or ASYNCHRONOUS OPERATION, EVEN/ODD/OFF PARITY, etc. In the Synchronous Mode, options are also provided to select either internal or external character synchronization.

Once programmed, the 8251A is ready to perform its communication functions. The TxRDY output is raised "high" to signal the CPU that the 8251A is ready to receive a data character from the CPU. This output (TxRDY) is reset automatically when the CPU writes a character into the 8251A. On the other hand, the 8251A receives serial data from the MODEM or I/O device. Upon receiving an entire character, the RxRDY output is raised "high" to signal the CPU that the 8251A has a complete character ready for the CPU to fetch. RxRDY is reset automatically upon the CPU data read operation.

The 8251A cannot begin transmission until the Tx **Enable** (Transmitter Enable) bit is set in the Command Instruction and it has received a Clear To Send ($\overline{\text{CTS}}$) input. The TxD output will be held in the marking state upon Reset.

Programming the 8251A

Prior to starting data transmission or reception, the 8251A must be loaded with a set of control words generated by the CPU. These control signals define the complete functional definition of the 8251A and must immediately follow a Reset operation (internal or external).

The control words are split into two formats:

1. Mode Instruction
2. Command Instruction

Mode Instruction

This format defines the general operational characteristics of the 8251A. It must follow a Reset operation (internal or external). Once the Mode Instruction has been written into the 8251A by the CPU, SYNC characters or Command Instructions may be inserted.

Command Instruction

This format defines a status word that is used to control the actual operation of the 8251A.

Both the Mode and Command Instructions must conform to a specified sequence for proper device operation. The Mode Instruction must be inserted immediately following a Reset operation, prior to using the 8251A for data communication.

All control words written into the 8251A after the Mode Instruction will load the Command Instruction. Command Instructions can be written into the 8251A at any time in the data block during the operation of the 8251A. To return to the Mode Instruction format, the master Reset bit in the Command Instruction word can be set to initiate an internal Reset operation which automatically places the 8251A back into the Mode Instruction format. Command Instructions must follow the Mode Instructions or Sync characters.

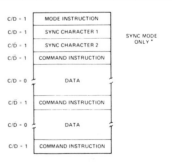

* The second SYNC character is skipped if MODE instruction has programmed the 8251A to single character Internal SYNC Mode. Both SYNC characters are skipped if MODE instruction has programmed the 8251A to ASYNC mode.

Typical Data Block

Mode Instruction Definition

The 8251A can be used for either Asynchronous or Synchronous data communication. To understand how the Mode Instruction defines the functional operation of the 8251A, the designer can best view the device as two separate components sharing the same package, one Asynchronous the other Synchronous. The format definition can be changed only after a master chip Reset. For explanation purposes the two formats will be isolated.

NOTE: When parity is enabled it is not considered as one of the data bits for the purpose of programming the word length. The actual parity bit received on the Rx Data line cannot be read on the Data Bus. In the case of a programmed character length of less than 8 bits, the least significant Data Bus bits will hold the data; unused bits are "don't care" when writing data to the 8251A, and will be "zeros" when reading the data from the 8251A.

Asynchronous Mode (Transmission)

Whenever a data character is sent by the CPU the 8251A automatically adds a Start bit (low level) followed by the data bits (least significant bit first), and the programmed number of Stop bits to each character. Also, an even or odd Parity bit is inserted prior to the Stop bit(s), as defined by the Mode Instruction. The character is then transmitted as a serial data stream on the TxD output. The serial data is shifted out on the falling edge of $\overline{TxC}$ at a rate equal to 1, 1/16, or 1/64 that of the $\overline{TxC}$, as defined by the Mode Instruction. BREAK characters can be continuously sent to the TxD if commanded to do so.

When no data characters have been loaded into the 8251A the TxD output remains "high" (marking) unless a Break (continuously low) has been programmed.

Asynchronous Mode (Receive)

The RxD line is normally high. A falling edge on this line triggers the beginning of a START bit. The validity of this START bit is checked by again strobing this bit at its nominal center (16X or 64X mode only). If a low is detected again, it is a valid START bit, and the bit counter will start counting. The bit counter thus locates the center of the data bits, the parity bit (if it exists) and the stop bits. If parity error occurs, the parity error flag is set. Data and parity bits are sampled on the RxD pin with the rising edge of $\overline{RxC}$. If a low level is detected as the STOP bit, the Framing Error flag will be set. The STOP bit signals the end of a character. Note that the *receiver* requires only *one* stop bit, regardless of the number of stop bits programmed. This character is then loaded into the parallel I/O buffer of the 8251A. The RxRDY pin is raised to signal the CPU that a character is ready to be fetched. If a previous character has not been fetched by the CPU, the present character replaces it in the I/O buffer, and the OVERRUN Error flag is raised (thus the previous character is lost). All of the error flags can be reset by an Error Reset Instruction. The occurrence of any of these errors will not affect the operation of the 8251A.

Mode Instruction Format, Asynchronous Mode

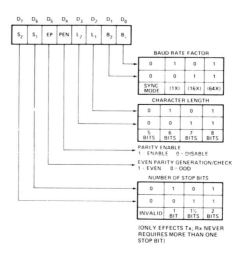

Asynchronous Mode

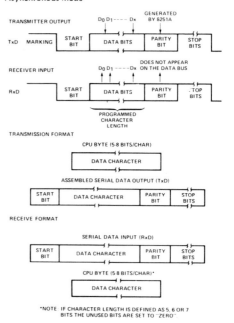

8251A

Synchronous Mode (Transmission)

The TxD output is continuously high until the CPU sends its first character to the 8251A which usually is a SYNC character. When the $\overline{CTS}$ line goes low, the first character is serially transmitted out. All characters are shifted out on the falling edge of $\overline{TxC}$. Data is shifted out at the same rate as the $\overline{TxC}$.

Once transmission has started, the data stream at the TxD output must continue at the $\overline{TxC}$ rate. If the CPU does not provide the 8251A with a data character before the 8251A Transmitter Buffers become empty, the SYNC characters (or character if in single SYNC character mode) will be automatically inserted in the TxD data stream. In this case, the TxEMPTY pin is raised high to signal that the 8251A is empty and SYNC characters are being sent out. TxEMPTY does not go low when the SYNC is being shifted out (see figure below). The TxEMPTY pin is internally reset by a data character being written into the 8251A.

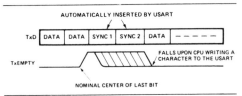

Synchronous Mode (Receive)

In this mode, character synchronization can be internally or externally achieved. If the SYNC mode has been programmed, ENTER HUNT command should be included in the first command instruction word written. Data on the RxD pin is then sampled in on the rising edge of $\overline{RxC}$. The content of the Rx buffer is compared at every bit boundary with the first SYNC character until a match occurs. If the 8251A has been programmed for two SYNC characters, the subsequent received character is also compared; when both SYNC characters have been detected, the USART ends the HUNT mode and is in character synchronization. The SYNDET pin is then set high, and is reset automatically by a STATUS READ. If parity is programmed, SYNDET will not be set until the middle of the parity bit instead of the middle of the last data bit.

In the external SYNC mode, synchronization is achieved by applying a high level on the SYNDET pin, thus forcing the 8251A out of the HUNT mode. The high level can be removed after one $\overline{RxC}$ cycle. An ENTER HUNT command has no effect in the asynchronous mode of operation.

Parity error and overrun error are both checked in the same way as in the Asynchronous Rx mode. Parity is checked when not in Hunt, regardless of whether the Receiver is enabled or not.

The CPU can command the receiver to enter the HUNT mode if synchronization is lost. This will also set all the used character bits in the buffer to a "one", thus preventing a possible false SYNDET caused by data that happens to be in the Rx Buffer at ENTER HUNT time. Note that the SYNDET F/F is reset at each Status Read, regardless of whether internal or external SYNC has been programmed. This does not cause the 8251A to return to the HUNT mode. When in SYNC mode, but not in HUNT, Sync Detection is still functional, but only occurs at the "known" word boundaries. Thus, if one Status Read indicates SYNDET and a second Status Read also indicates SYNDET, then the programmed SYNDET characters have been received since the previous Status Read. (If double character sync has been programmed, then both sync characters have been contiguously received to gate a SYNDET indication.) When external SYNDET mode is selected, internal Sync Detect is disabled, and the SYNDET F/F may be set at any bit boundary.

Mode Instruction Format

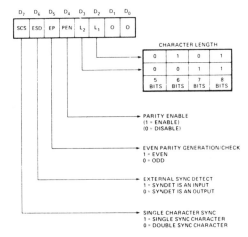

NOTE: IN EXTERNAL SYNC MODE, PROGRAMMING DOUBLE CHARACTER SYNC WILL AFFECT ONLY THE Tx.

Data Format, Synchronous Mode

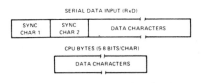

COMMAND INSTRUCTION DEFINITION

Once the functional definition of the 8251A has been programmed by the Mode Instruction and the Sync Characters are loaded (if in Sync Mode) then the device is ready to be used for data communication. The Command Instruction controls the actual operation of the selected format. Functions such as: Enable Transmit/Receive, Error Reset and Modem Controls are provided by the Command Instruction.

Once the Mode Instruction has been written into the 8251A and Sync characters inserted, if necessary, then all further "control writes" (C/$\overline{D}$ = 1) will load a Command Instruction. A Reset Operation (internal or external) will return the 8251A to the Mode Instruction format.

STATUS READ DEFINITION

In data communication systems it is often necessary to examine the "status" of the active device to ascertain if errors have occurred or other conditions that require the processor's attention. The 8251A has facilities that allow the programmer to "read" the status of the device at any time during the functional operation. (The status update is inhibited during status read).

A normal "read" command is issued by the CPU with C/$\overline{D}$ = 1 to accomplish this function.

Some of the bits in the Status Read Format have identical meanings to external output pins so that the 8251A can be used in a completely Polled environment or in an interrupt driven environment. TxRDY is an exception.

Note that status update can have a maximum delay of 28 clock periods from the actual event affecting the status.

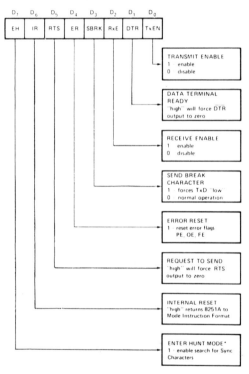

Note: Error Reset must be performed whenever RxEnable and Enter Hunt are programmed.

Command Instruction Format

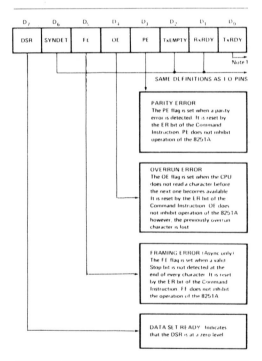

Status Read Format

Note 1: TxRDY status bit has different meanings from the TxRDY output pin. The former is not conditioned by $\overline{CTS}$ and TxEN, the latter is conditioned by both $\overline{CTS}$ and TxEN.

i.e. TxRDY status bit = DB Buffer Empty

TxRDY pin out = DB Buffer Empty · ($\overline{CTS}$ = 0) · (TxEN = 1)

8251A

APPLICATIONS OF THE 8251A

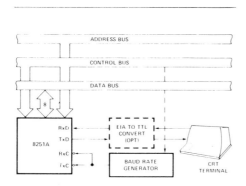

Asynchronous Serial Interface to CRT Terminal,
DC-9600 Baud

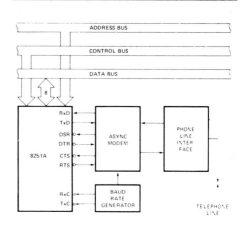

Asynchronous Interface to Telephone Lines

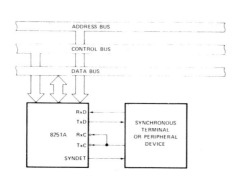

Synchronous Interface to Terminal or Peripheral Device

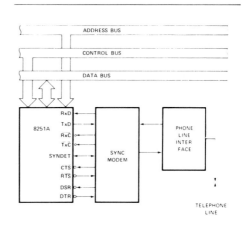

Synchronous Interface to Telephone Lines

8251A

ABSOLUTE MAXIMUM RATINGS*

Ambient Temperature Under Bias. . . . . 0°C to 70°C
Storage Temperature . . . . –65°C to +150°C
Voltage On Any Pin
    With Respect to Ground . . . . –0.5V to +7V
Power Dissipation . . . . 1 Watt

COMMENT: Stresses above those listed under "Absolute Maximum Ratings" may cause permanent damage to the device. This is a stress rating only and functional operation of the device at these or any other conditions above those indicated in the operational sections of this specification is not implied. Exposure to absolute maximum rating conditions for extended periods may affect device reliability.

D.C. CHARACTERISTICS

$T_A = 0°C$ to $70°C$; $V_{CC} = 5.0V \pm 5\%$; GND = 0V

Symbol	Parameter	Min.	Max.	Unit	Test Conditions
V_{IL}	Input Low Voltage	–0.5	0.8	V	
V_{IH}	Input High Voltage	2.0	V_{CC}	V	
V_{OL}	Output Low Voltage		0.45	V	$I_{OL} = 2.2\,mA$
V_{OH}	Output High Voltage	2.4		V	$I_{OH} = -400\,\mu A$
I_{OFL}	Output Float Leakage		±10	μA	$V_{OUT} = V_{CC}$ TO 0.45V
I_{IL}	Input Leakage		±10	μA	$V_{IN} = V_{CC}$ TO 0.45V
I_{CC}	Power Supply Current		100	mA	All Outputs = High

CAPACITANCE

$T_A = 25°C$; V_{CC} = GND = 0V

Symbol	Parameter	Min.	Max.	Unit	Test Conditions
C_{IN}	Input Capacitance		10	pF	fc = 1MHz
$C_{I/O}$	I/O Capacitance		20	pF	Unmeasured pins returned to GND

TEST LOAD CIRCUIT:

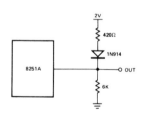

Figure 1.

TYPICAL Δ OUTPUT DELAY VS. Δ CAPACITANCE (dB)

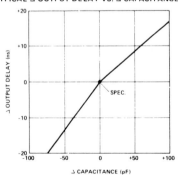

8251A

A.C. CHARACTERISTICS

T_A = 0°C to 70°C; V_{CC} = 5.0V ±5%; GND = 0V

BUS PARAMETERS: (Note 1)

READ CYCLE

SYMBOL	PARAMETER	MIN.	MAX.	UNIT	TEST CONDITIONS
t_{AR}	Address Stable Before $\overline{READ}$ ($\overline{CS}$, C/$\overline{D}$)	0		ns	Note 2
t_{RA}	Address Hold Time for $\overline{READ}$ ($\overline{CS}$, C/$\overline{D}$)	0		ns	Note 2
t_{RR}	$\overline{READ}$ Pulse Width	250		ns	
t_{RD}	Data Delay from $\overline{READ}$		200	ns	3, C_L = 150 pF
t_{DF}	$\overline{READ}$ to Data Floating	10	100	ns	

WRITE CYCLE

SYMBOL	PARAMETER	MIN.	MAX.	UNIT	TEST CONDITIONS
t_{AW}	Address Stable Before $\overline{WRITE}$	0		ns	
t_{WA}	Address Hold Time for $\overline{WRITE}$	0		ns	
t_{WW}	$\overline{WRITE}$ Pulse Width	250		ns	
t_{DW}	Data Set Up Time for $\overline{WRITE}$	150		ns	
t_{WD}	Data Hold Time for $\overline{WRITE}$	0		ns	
t_{RV}	Recovery Time Between WRITES	6		t_{CY}	Note 4

NOTES: 1. AC timings measured V_{OH} = 2.0, V_{OL} = 0.8, and with load circuit of Figure 1.
2. Chip Select ($\overline{CS}$) and Command/Data (C/$\overline{D}$) are considered as Addresses.
3. Assumes that Address is valid before $\overline{R_D}\downarrow$.
4. This recovery time is for Mode Initialization only. Write Data is allowed only when TxRDY = 1.
   Recovery Time between Writes for Asynchronous Mode is 8 t_{CY} and for Synchronous Mode is 16 t_{CY}.

INPUT waveforms for AC tests:

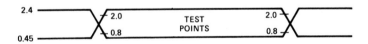

8251A

OTHER TIMINGS:

SYMBOL	PARAMETER	MIN.	MAX.	UNIT	TEST CONDITIONS
t_{CY}	Clock Period	320	1.35	μs	Notes 5, 6
t_ϕ	Clock High Pulse Width	120	t_{CY-90}	ns	
$t_{\overline{\phi}}$	Clock Low Pulse Width	90		ns	
t_R, t_F	Clock Rise and Fall Time	5	20	ns	
t_{DTx}	TxD Delay from Falling Edge of $\overline{TxC}$		1	μs	
t_{SRx}	Rx Data Set-Up Time to Sampling Pulse	2		μs	
t_{HRx}	Rx Data Hold Time to Sampling Pulse	2		μs	
f_{Tx}	Transmitter Input Clock Frequency				
	1x Baud Rate	DC	64	kHz	
	16x Baud Rate	DC	310	kHz	
	64x Baud Rate	DC	615	kHz	
t_{TPW}	Transmitter Input Clock Pulse Width				
	1x Baud Rate	12		t_{CY}	
	16x and 64x Baud Rate	1		t_{CY}	
t_{TPD}	Transmitter Input Clock Pulse Delay				
	1x Baud Rate	15		t_{CY}	
	16x and 64x Baud Rate	3		t_{CY}	
f_{Rx}	Receiver Input Clock Frequency				
	1x Baud Rate	DC	64	kHz	
	16x Baud Rate	DC	310	kHz	
	64x Baud Rate	DC	615	kHz	
t_{RPW}	Receiver Input Clock Pulse Width				
	1x Baud Rate	12		t_{CY}	
	16x and 64x Baud Rate	1		t_{CY}	
t_{RPD}	Receiver Input Clock Pulse Delay				
	1x Baud Rate	15		t_{CY}	
	16x and 64x Baud Rate	3		t_{CY}	
t_{TxRDY}	TxRDY Pin Delay from Center of last Bit		8	t_{CY}	Note 7
$t_{TxRDY\ CLEAR}$	TxRDY ↓ from Leading Edge of $\overline{WR}$		150	ns	Note 7
t_{RxRDY}	RxRDY Pin Delay from Center of last Bit		24	t_{CY}	Note 7
$t_{RxRDY\ CLEAR}$	RxRDY ↓ from Leading Edge of $\overline{RD}$		150	ns	Note 7
t_{IS}	Internal SYNDET Delay from Rising Edge of $\overline{RxC}$		24	t_{CY}	Note 7
t_{ES}	External SYNDET Set-Up Time Before Falling Edge of $\overline{RxC}$		16	t_{CY}	Note 7
$t_{TxEMPTY}$	TxEMPTY Delay from Center of Data Bit		20	t_{CY}	Note 7
t_{WC}	Control Delay from Rising Edge of WRITE (TxEn, $\overline{DTR}$, $\overline{RTS}$)		8	t_{CY}	Note 7
t_{CR}	Control to READ Set-Up Time ($\overline{DSR}$, $\overline{CTS}$)		20	t_{CY}	Note 7

5. The TxC and RxC frequencies have the following limitations with respect to CLK.
    For 1x Baud Rate , f_{Tx} or $f_{Rx} \leqslant 1/(30\ t_{CY})$
    For 16x and 64x Baud Rate, f_{Tx} or $f_{Rx} \leqslant 1/(4.5\ t_{CY})$

6. Reset Pulse Width = 6 t_{CY} minimum; System Clock must be running during Reset.

7. Status update can have a maximum delay of 28 clock periods from the event affecting the status.

8251A

SYSTEM CLOCK INPUT

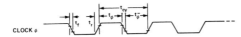

TRANSMITTER CLOCK & DATA

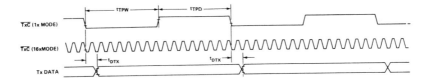

RECEIVER CLOCK & DATA

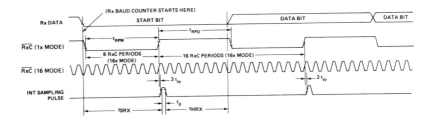

WRITE DATA CYCLE (CPU ➤ USART)

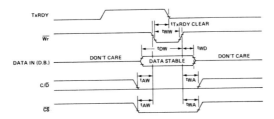

READ DATA CYCLE (CPU ◄ USART)

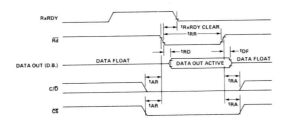

8251A

WRITE CONTROL OR OUTPUT PORT CYCLE (CPU → USART)

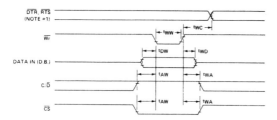

READ CONTROL OR INPUT PORT (CPU ◄— USART)

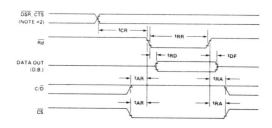

NOTE ≠1: T_WC INCLUDES THE RESPONSE TIMING OF A CONTROL BYTE.
NOTE ≠2: T_CR INCLUDES THE EFFECT OF CTS ON THE TxENBL CIRCUITRY.

TRANSMITTER CONTROL & FLAG TIMING (ASYNC MODE)

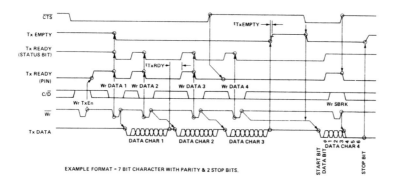

EXAMPLE FORMAT = 7 BIT CHARACTER WITH PARITY & 2 STOP BITS.

8251A

RECEIVER CONTROL & FLAG TIMING (ASYNC MODE)

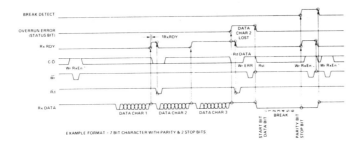

EXAMPLE FORMAT - 7 BIT CHARACTER WITH PARITY & 2 STOP BITS

TRANSMITTER CONTROL & FLAG TIMING (SYNC MODE)

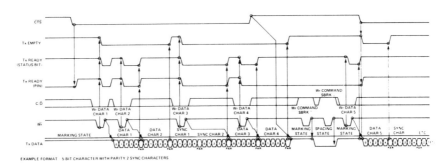

EXAMPLE FORMAT - 5 BIT CHARACTER WITH PARITY 2 SYNC CHARACTERS

RECEIVER CONTROL & FLAG TIMING (SYNC MODE)

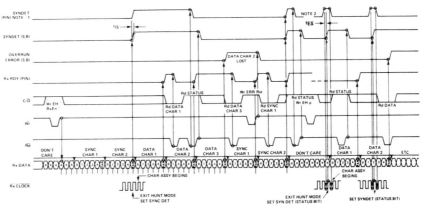

NOTE 1 INTERNAL SYNC, 2 SYNC CHARACTERS, 5 BITS, WITH PARITY
NOTE 2 EXTERNAL SYNC, 5 BITS, WITH PARITY

8155/8156
2048 BIT STATIC MOS RAM WITH I/O PORTS AND TIMER

8155 — Active Low Chip Enable ($\overline{CE}$)
8156 — Active High Chip Enable (CE)

★Directly Compatible With 8085 CPU

- 256 Word x 8 Bits
- Single +5V Power Supply
- Completely Static Operation
- Internal Address Latch
- 2 Programmable 8 Bit I/O Ports

- 1 Programmable 6 Bit I/O Port
- Programmable 14 Bit Binary Counter/Timer
- Multiplexed Address and Data Bus
- 40 Pin DIP

The 8155 and 8156 are RAM and I/O chips to be used in the MCS-85™ microcomputer system. The RAM portion is designed with 2K bit static cells organized as 256 x 8. They have a maximum access time of 400ns to permit use with no wait states in 8085 CPU.

The I/O portion consists of three general purpose I/O ports. One of the three ports can be programmed to be status pins, thus allowing the other two ports to operate in handshake mode.

A 14 bit programmable counter/timer is also included on chip to provide either a square wave or terminal count pulse for the CPU system. It operates in binary countdown mode, and its timer modes are programmable.

PIN CONFIGURATION	BLOCK DIAGRAM

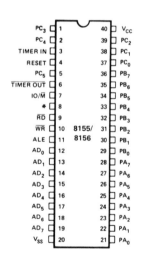

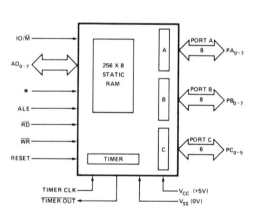

* : 8155 = $\overline{CE}$, 8156 = CE

8155/8156

8155/8156 FUNCTIONAL PIN DEFINITION

The following describes the functions of all of the 8155/8156 pins.

Symbol	Function
RESET	The Reset signal is a pulse provided by the 8085 to initialize the system. Input high on this line resets the chip and initializes the three I/O ports to input mode. The width of RESET pulse should typically be 600 nsec. (Two 8085 clock cycle times).
AD_{0-7}	These are 3-state Address/Data lines that interface with the CPU lower 8-bit Address/Data Bus. The 8-bit address is latched into the address latch on the falling edge of the ALE. The address can be either for the memory section or the I/O section depending on the polarity of the IO/$\overline{M}$ input signal. The 8-bit data is either written into the chip or Read from the chip depending on the status of $\overline{WRITE}$ or $\overline{READ}$ input signal.
CE or $\overline{CE}$	Chip Enable: On the 8155, this pin is $\overline{CE}$ and is ACTIVE LOW. On the 8156, this pin is CE and is ACTIVE HIGH.
$\overline{RD}$	Input low on this line with the Chip Enable active enables the AD_{0-7} buffers. If IO/$\overline{M}$ pin is low, the RAM content will be read out to the AD bus. Otherwise the content of the selected I/O port will be read to the AD bus.
$\overline{WR}$	Input low on this line with the Chip Enable active causes the data on the AD lines to be written to the RAM or I/O ports depending on the polarity of IO/$\overline{M}$.
ALE	Address Latch Enable: This control signal latches both the address on the AD_{0-7} lines and the state of the Chip Enable and IO/$\overline{M}$ into the chip at the falling edge of ALE.
IO/$\overline{M}$	IO/$\overline{Memory}$ Select: This line selects the memory if low and selects the IO if high.

Symbol	Function
$PA_{0-7}(8)$	These 8 pins are general purpose I/O pins. The in/out direction is selected by programming the Command/Status Register.
$PB_{0-7}(8)$	These 8 pins are general purpose I/O pins. The in/out direction is selected by programming the Command/Status Register.
$PC_{0-5}(6)$	These 6 pins can function as either input port, output port, or as control signals for PA and PB. Programming is done through the C/S Register. When PC_{0-5} are used as control signals, they will provide the following:
	PC0 — A INTR (Port A Interrupt)
	PC1 — A BF (Port A Buffer full)
	PC2 — $\overline{A\ STB}$ (Port A Strobe)
	PC3 — B INTR (Port B Interrupt)
	PC4 — B BF (Port B Buffer Full)
	PC5 — $\overline{B\ STB}$ (Port B Strobe)
TIMER IN	This is the input to the counter timer.
$\overline{TIMER\ OUT}$	This pin is the timer output. This output can be either a square wave or a pulse depending on the timer mode.
V_{CC}	+5 volt supply.
V_{SS}	Ground Reference.

8155/8156

OPERATIONAL DESCRIPTION

The 8155/8156 includes the following operational features:

- 2K Bit Static RAM organized as 256 x 8
- Two 8-bit I/O ports (PA & PB) and one 6-bit I/O port (PC)
- 14-bit binary down counter

The I/O portion contains four registers (Command/Status, PA_{0-7}, PB_{0-7}, PC_{0-5}). The IO/M (IO/Memory Select) pin selects the I/O or the memory (RAM) portion. Detailed descriptions of memory, I/O ports and timer functions will follow.

The 8-bit address on the AD lines, the Chip Enable input, and IO/$\overline{M}$ are all latched on chip at the falling edge of ALE. A low on the IO/$\overline{M}$ must be provided to select the memory section.

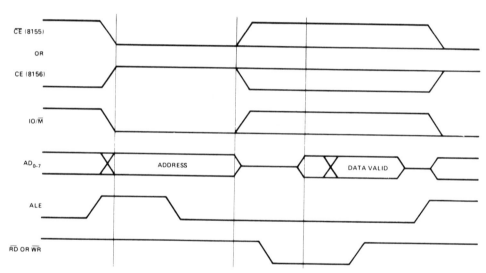

NOTE: FOR DETAILED TIMING DIAGRAM INFORMATION, SEE FIGURE 7 AND A.C. CHARACTERISTICS.

FIGURE 1. MEMORY READ/WRITE CYCLE.

8155/8156

PROGRAMMING OF THE COMMAND/ STATUS REGISTER

The command register consists of eight latches one for each bit. Four bits (0-3) define the mode of the ports, two bits (4-5) enable or disable the interrupt from port C when it acts as control port, and the last two bits (6-7) are for the timer.

The C/S register contents can be altered at any time by using the I/O address XXXXX000 during a WRITE operation. The meaning of each bit of the command byte is defined as follows:

READING THE COMMAND/STATUS REGISTER

The status register consists of seven latches one for each bit; six (0-5) for the status of the ports and one (6) for the status of the timer.

The status of the timer and the I/O section can be polled by reading the C/S Register (Address XXXXX000). Status word format is shown below:

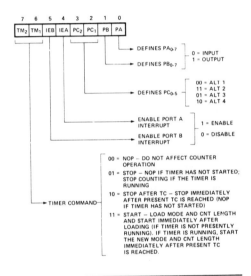

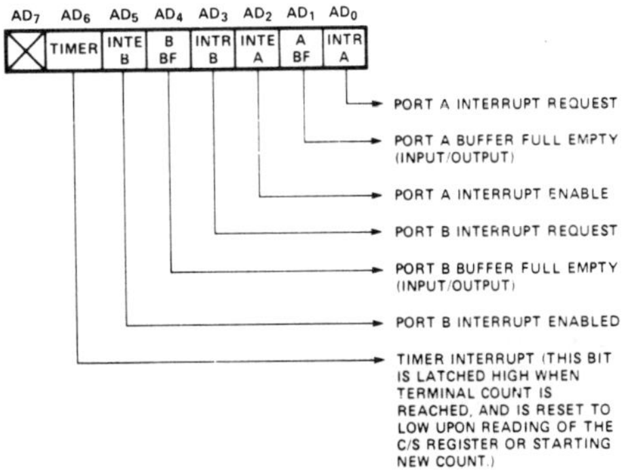

FIGURE 2. COMMAND/STATUS REGISTER BIT ASSIGNMENT.

FIGURE 3. COMMAND/STATUS REGISTER STATUS WORD FORMAT.

INPUT/OUTPUT SECTION

The I/O section of the 8155/8156 consists of four registers as described below.

- **Command/Status Register (C/S)** — This register is assigned the address XXXXX000. The C/S address serves the dual purpose.

  When the C/S register is selected during WRITE operation, a command is written into the command register. The contents of this register are *not* accessible through the pins.

  When the C/S (XXXXX000) is selected during a READ operation, the status information of the I/O ports and the timer become available on the AD_{0-7} lines.

- **PA Register** — This register can be programmed to be either input or output ports depending on the status of the contents of the C/S Register. Also depending on the command, this port can operate in either the basic mode or the strobed mode (See timing diagram). The I/O pins assigned in relation to this register are PA_{0-7}. The address of this register is XXXXX001.

- **PB Register** — This register functions the same as PA Register. The I/O pins assigned are PB_{0-7}. The address of this register is XXXXX010.

- **PC Register** — This register has the address XXXXX011 and contains only 6-bits. The 6-bits can be programmed to be either input ports, output ports or as control signals for PA and PB by properly programming the AD_2 and AD_3 bits of the C/S register.

  When PC_{0-5} is used as a control port, 3-bits are assigned for Port A and 3 for Port B. The first bit is an interrupt that the 8155 sends out. The second is an output signal indicating whether the buffer is full or empty, and the third is an input pin to accept a strobe for the strobed input mode. See Table 1.

When the 'C' port is programmed to either ALT3 or ALT4, the control signals for PA and PB are initialized as follows:

CONTROL	INPUT MODE	OUTPUT MODE
BF	Low	Low
INTR	Low	High
STB	Input Control	Input Control

TABLE 1. TABLE OF PORT CONTROL ASSIGNMENT.

The following diagram shows how I/O PORTS A and B are structured within the 8155 and 8156:

8155/8156
ONE BIT OF PORT A OR PORT B

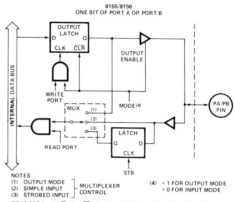

NOTES:
(1) OUTPUT MODE
(2) SIMPLE INPUT   MULTIPLEXER
(3) STROBED INPUT   CONTROL

(4) = 1 FOR OUTPUT MODE
    = 0 FOR INPUT MODE

READ PORT = (IO/$\overline{M}$=1) • ($\overline{RD}$=0) • (CE ACTIVE) • (PORT ADDRESS SELECTED)
WRITE PORT = (IO/$\overline{M}$=1) • ($\overline{WR}$=0) • (CE ACTIVE) • (PORT ADDRESS SELECTED)

Note in the diagram that when the I/O ports are programmed to be output ports, the contents of the output ports can still be read by a READ operation when appropriately addressed.

Note also that the output latch is cleared when the port enters the input mode. The output latch cannot be loaded by writing to the port if the port is in the input mode. The result is that each time a port mode is changed from input to output, the output pins will go low. When the 8155/56 is RESET, the output latches are all cleared and all 3 ports enter the input mode.

When in the ALT 1 or ALT 2 modes, the bits of PORT C are structured like the diagram above in the simple input or output mode, respectively.

Reading from an input port with nothing connected to the pins will provide unpredictable results.

Pin	ALT 1	ALT 2	ALT 3	ALT 4
PC0	Input Port	Output Port	A INTR (Port A Interrupt)	A INTR (Port A Interrupt)
PC1	Input Port	Output Port	A BF (Port A Buffer Full)	A BF (Port A Buffer Full)
PC2	Input Port	Output Port	A $\overline{STB}$ (Port A Strobe)	A $\overline{STB}$ (Port A Strobe)
PC3	Input Port	Output Port	Output Port	B INTR (Port B Interrupt)
PC4	Input Port	Output Port	Output Port	B BF (Port B Buffer Full)
PC5	Input Port	Output Port	Output Port	B $\overline{STB}$ (Port B Strobe)

The set and reset of INTR and BF with respect to $\overline{STB}$, $\overline{WR}$ and $\overline{RD}$ timing is shown in Figure 8.

To summarize, the registers' assignments are:

Address	Pinouts	Functions	No. of Bits
XXXXX000	Internal	Command/Status Register	8
XXXXX001	PA0-7	General Purpose I/O Port	8
XXXXX010	PB0-7	General Purpose I/O Port	8
XXXXX011	PC0-5	General Purpose I/O Port or Control Lines	6

8155/8156

TIMER SECTION

The timer is a 14-bit counter that counts the 'timer input' pulses and provides either a square wave or pulse when terminal count (TC) is reached.

The timer has the I/O address XXXXX100 for the low order byte of the register and the I/O address XXXXX101 for the high order byte of the register.

The timer addresses serve a dual purpose. During WRITE operation, a COUNT LENGTH REGISTER (CLR) with a count length (bits 0-13) and a timer mode (bits 14-15) are loaded. During READ operation the contents of the counter (the present count) and the mode bits are read.

To be sure that the right content of the counter is read, it is preferable to stop counting, read it, and then load it again and continue counting.

To program the timer, the COUNT LENGTH REG is loaded first, one byte at a time, by selecting the timer addresses. Bits 0-13 will specify the length of the next count and bits 14-15 will specify the timer output mode.

There are four modes to choose from:

0. Puts out low during second half of count.
1. Square wave
2. Single pulse upon TC being reached
3. Repetitive single pulse everytime TC is readied and automatic reload of counter upon TC being reached, until instructed to stop by a new command loaded into C/S.

Bits 6-7 of Command/Status Register Contents are used to start and stop the counter. There are four commands to choose from:

Note: See the further description on Command/Status Register.

C/S7	C/S6	
0	0	NOP — Do not affect counter operation.
0	1	STOP — NOP if timer has not started; stop counting if the timer is running.
1	0	STOP AFTER TC — Stop immediately after present TC is reached (NOP if timer has not started)
1	1	START — Load mode and CNT length and start immediately after loading (if timer is not presently running). If timer is running, start the new mode and CNT length immediately after present TC is reached.

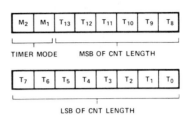

FIGURE 4. TIMER FORMAT

$M2$ $M1$ defines the timer mode as follows:

M2	M1	
0	0	Puts out low during second half of count.
0	1	Square wave, i.e., the period of the square wave equals the count length programmed with automatic reload at terminal count.
1	0	Single pulse upon TC being reached.
1	1	Automatic reload, i.e., single pulse everytime TC is reached.

Note: In case of an asymmetric count, i.e. 9, larger half of the count will be high, the larger count will stay active as shown in Figure 5.

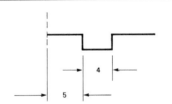

Note: 5 and 4 refer to the number of clock cycles in that time period.

FIGURE 5. ASYMMETRIC COUNT.

The timer in the 8155 is not initialized to any particular mode when hardware RESET occurs, but RESET does stop the counting. Therefore, counting cannot begin following RESET until the desired mode and count length and START command are issued.

8155/8156

8085 MINIMUM SYSTEM CONFIGURATION

Figure 6 shows that a minimum system is possible using only three chips:

- 256 Bytes RAM
- 2K Bytes ROM
- 38 I/O Pins
- 1 Interval Timer
- 4 Interrupt Levels

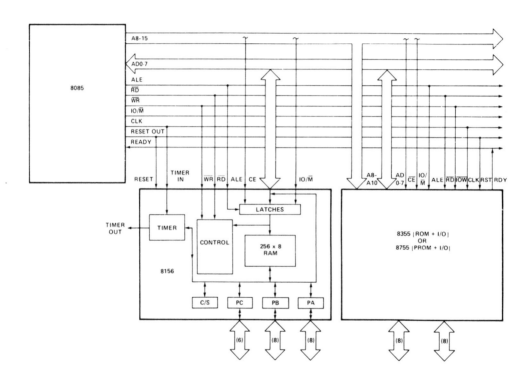

FIGURE 6. 8085 MINIMUM SYSTEM CONFIGURATION.

8155/8156

ABSOLUTE MAXIMUM RATINGS*

Temperature Under Bias .... 0°C to +70°C
Storage Temperature .... -65°C to +150°C
Voltage on Any Pin
  With Respect to Ground .... -0.3V to +7V
Power Dissipation 1.5W

COMMENT: Stresses above those listed under "Absolute Maximum Ratings" may cause permanent damage to the device. This is a stress rating only and functional operation of the device at these or any other conditions above those indicated in the operational sections of this specification is not implied. Exposure to absolute maximum rating conditions for extended periods may affect device reliability.

D.C. CHARACTERISTICS (T_A = 0°C to 70°C; V_{CC} = 5V ± 5%)

SYMBOL	PARAMETER	MIN.	MAX.	UNITS	TEST CONDITIONS
V_{IL}	Input Low Voltage	-0.5	0.8	V	
V_{IH}	Input High Voltage	2.0	V_{CC}+0.5	V	
V_{OL}	Output Low Voltage		0.45	V	I_{OL} = 2mA
V_{OH}	Output High Voltage	2.4		V	I_{OH} = -400μA
I_{IL}	Input Leakage		10	μA	V_{IN} = V_{CC} to 0V
I_{LO}	Output Leakage Current		±10	μA	0.45V ≤ V_{OUT} ≤ V_{CC}
I_{CC}	V_{CC} Supply Current		180	mA	

A.C. CHARACTERISTICS ($T_A = 0°C$ to $70°C$; $V_{CC} = 5V \pm 5\%$)

SYMBOL	PARAMETER	MIN.	MAX.	UNITS	TEST CONDITIONS
t_{AL}	Address to Latch Set Up Time	50		ns	
t_{LA}	Address Hold Time after Latch	80		ns	
t_{LC}	Latch to READ/WRITE Control	100		ns	
t_{RD}	Valid Data Out Delay from READ Control		150	ns	
t_{AD}	Address Stable to Data Out Valid		400	ns	
t_{LL}	Latch Enable Width	100		ns	
t_{RDF}	Data Bus Float After READ	0	100	ns	
t_{CL}	READ/WRITE Control to Latch Enable	20		ns	
t_{CC}	READ/WRITE Control Width	250		ns	
t_{DW}	Data In to WRITE Set Up Time	150		ns	
t_{WD}	Data In Hold Time After WRITE	0		ns	
t_{RV}	Recovery Time Between Controls	300		ns	
t_{WP}	WRITE to Port Output		400	ns	
t_{PR}	Port Input Setup Time	50		ns	
t_{RP}	Port Input Hold Time	50		ns	150 pF Load
t_{SBF}	Strobe to Buffer Full		400	ns	
t_{SS}	Strobe Width	200		ns	
t_{RBE}	READ to Buffer Empty		400	ns	
t_{SI}	Strobe to INTR On		400	ns	
t_{RDI}	READ to INTR Off		400	ns	
t_{PSS}	Port Setup Time to Strobe Strobe	50		ns	
t_{PHS}	Port Hold Time After Strobe	100		ns	
t_{SBE}	Strobe to Buffer Empty		400	ns	
t_{WBF}	WRITE to Buffer Full		400	ns	
t_{WI}	WRITE to INTR Off		400	ns	
t_{TL}	TIMER-IN to $\overline{\text{TIMER-OUT}}$ Low	400		ns	
t_{TH}	TIMER-IN to $\overline{\text{TIMER-OUT}}$ High	400		ns	
t_{RDE}	Data Bus Enable from READ Control	10		ns	

Note: For Timer Input Specification, see Figure 10.

8155/8156

A. READ CYCLE

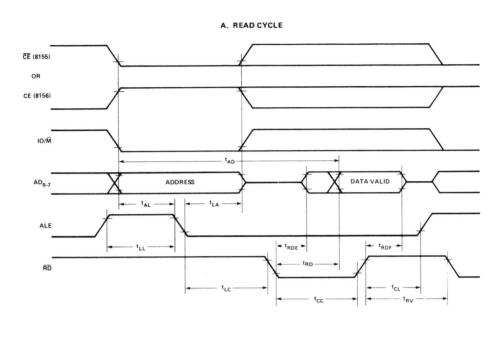

B. WRITE CYCLE

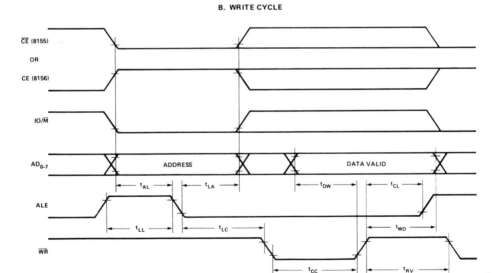

FIGURE 7. 8155/8156 READ/WRITE TIMING DIAGRAMS.

8155/8156

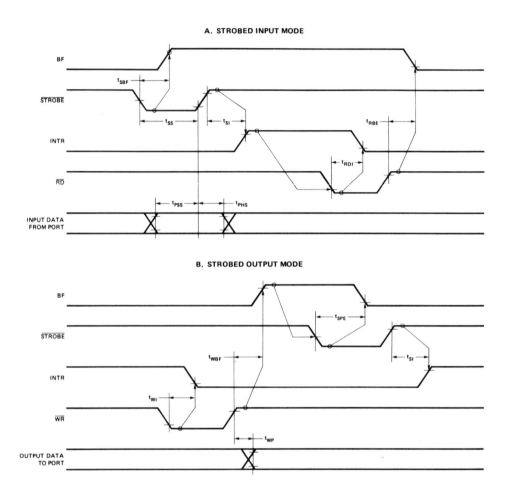

FIGURE 8. STROBED I/O TIMING.

8155/8156

A. BASIC INPUT MODE

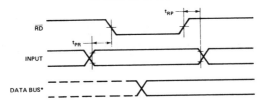

B. BASIC OUTPUT MODE

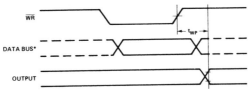

*DATA BUS TIMING IS SHOWN IN FIGURE 7.

FIGURE 9. BASIC I/O TIMING WAVEFORM.

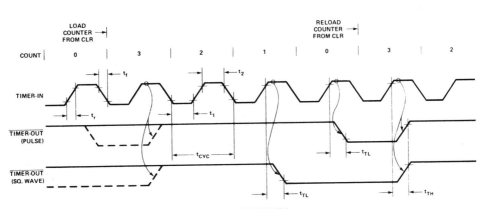

COUNTDOWN FROM 3 TO 0

t_{CYC}	320 ns MIN.
t_{RISE} & t_{FALL}	30 ns MAX.
t_1	80 ns MIN.
t_2	120 ns MIN.
t_{TL}	TIMER-IN TO $\overline{\text{TIMER-OUT}}$ LOW (TO BE DEFINED).
t_{TH}	TIMER-IN TO $\overline{\text{TIMER-OUT}}$ HIGH (TO BE DEFINED).

FIGURE 10. TIMER OUTPUT WAVEFORM.

8259, 8259-5
PROGRAMMABLE INTERRUPT CONTROLLER

- **MCS-85™ Compatible 8259-5**
- **Eight Level Priority Controller**
- **Expandable to 64 Levels**
- **Programmable Interrupt Modes**

- **Individual Request Mask Capability**
- **Single +5V Supply (No Clocks)**
- **28 Pin Dual-In-Line Package**
- **Fully Compatible with Intel CPUs**

The 8259 handles up to eight vectored priority interrupts for the CPU. It is cascadable for up to 64 vectored priority interrupts, without additional circuitry. It will be packaged in a 28-pin plastic DIP, uses nMOS technology and requires a single +5V supply. Circuitry is static, requiring no clock input.

The 8259 is designed to minimize the software and real time overhead in handling multi-level priority interrupts. It has several modes, permitting optimization for a variety of system requirements.

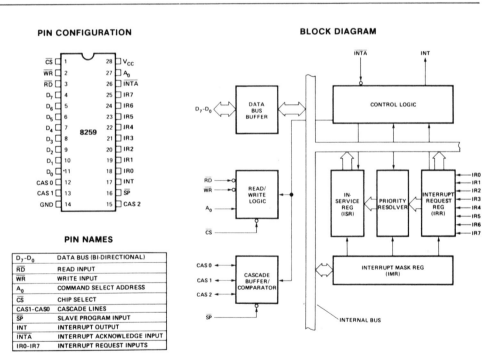

8259, 8259-5

INTERRUPTS IN MICROCOMPUTER SYSTEMS

Microcomputer system design requires that I/O devices such as keyboards, displays, sensors and other components receive servicing in an efficient method so that large amounts of the total system tasks can be assumed by the microcomputer with little or no effect on throughput.

The most common method of servicing such devices is the **Polled** approach. This is where the processor must test each device in sequence and in effect "ask" each one if it needs servicing. It is easy to see that a large portion of the main program is looping through this continuence polling cycle and that such a method would have a serious, detrimental effect on system throughput thus limiting the tasks that could be assumed by the microcomputer and reducing the cost effectiveness of using such devices.

A more desireable method would be one that would allow the microprocessor to be executing its main program and only stop to service peripheral devices when it is told to do so by the device itself. In effect, the method would provide an external asynchronous input that would inform the processor that it should complete whatever instruction that is currently being executed and fetch a new routine that will service the requesting device. Once this servicing is complete however the processor would resume exactly where it left off.

This method is called **Interrupt**. It is easy to see that system throughput would drastically increase, and thus more tasks could be assumed by the microcomputer to further enhance its cost effectiveness.

The Programmable Interrupt Controller (PIC) functions as an overall manager in an Interrupt-Driven system environment. It accepts requests from the peripheral equipment, determines which of the incoming requests is of the highest importance (priority), ascertains whether the incoming request has a higher priority value than the level currently being serviced and issues an Interrupt to the CPU based on this determination.

Each peripheral device or structure usually has a special program or "routine" that is associated with its specific functional or operational requirements; this is referred to as a "service routine". The PIC, after issuing an Interrupt to the CPU, must somehow input information into the CPU that can "point" the Program Counter to the service routine associated with the requesting device. The PIC does this by providing the CPU with a 3-byte CALL instruction.

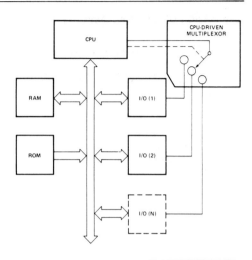

POLLED METHOD

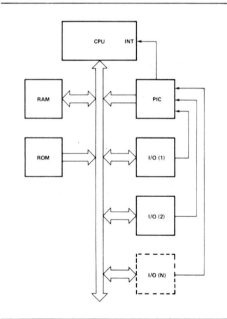

INTERRUPT METHOD

8259 BASIC FUNCTIONAL DESCRIPTION

General

The 8259 is a device specifically designed for use in real time, interrupt driven, microcomputer systems. It manages eight levels or requests and has built-in features for expandability to other 8259s (up to 64 levels). It is programmed by the system's software as an I/O peripheral. A selection of priority modes is available to the programmer so that the manner in which the requests are processed by the 8259 can be configured to match his system requirements. The priority modes can be changed or reconfigured dynamically at any time during the main program. This means that the complete interrupt structure can be defined as required, based on the total system environment.

Interrupt Request Register (IRR) and In-Service Register (ISR)

The interrupts at the IR input lines are handled by two registers in cascade, the Interrupt Request Register (IRR) and the In-Service Register (ISR). The IRR is used to store all the interrupt levels which are requesting service; and the ISR is used to store all the interrupt levels which are being serviced.

Priority Resolver

This logic block determines the priorities of the bits set in the IRR. The highest priority is selected and strobed into the corresponding bit of the ISR during $\overline{INTA}$ pulse.

INT (Interrupt)

This output goes directly to the CPU interrupt input. The V_{OH} level on this line is designed to be fully compatible with the 8080 input level.

$\overline{INTA}$ (Interrupt Acknowledge)

Three $\overline{INTA}$ pulses will cause the 8259 to release a 3-byte CALL instruction onto the Data Bus.

Interrupt Mask Register (IMR)

The IMR stores the bits of the interrupt lines to be masked. The IMR operates on the ISR. Masking of a higher priority input will not affect the interrupt request lines of lower priority.

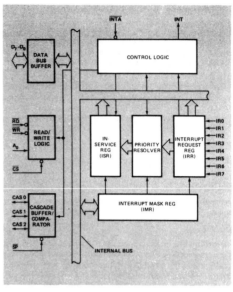

8259 BLOCK DIAGRAM

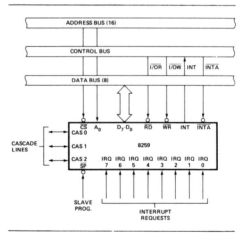

8259 INTERFACE TO STANDARD SYSTEM BUS

8259, 8259-5

Data Bus Buffer

This 3-state, bi-directional, 8-bit buffer is used to interface the 8259 to the system Data Bus. Control words and status information are transferred through the Data Bus Buffer.

Read/Write Control Logic

The function of this block is to accept OUTput commands from the CPU. It contains the Initialization Command Word (ICW) registers and Operation Command Word (OCW) registers which store the various control formats for device operation. This function block also allows the status of the 8259 to be transferred onto the Data Bus.

$\overline{CS}$ (Chip Select)

A "low" on this input enables the 8259. No reading or writing of the chip will occur unless the device is selected.

$\overline{WR}$ (Write)

A "low" on this input enables the CPU to write control words (ICWs and OCWs) to the 8259.

$\overline{RD}$ (Read)

A "low" on this input enables the 8259 to send the status of the Interrupt Request Register (IRR), In Service Register (ISR), the Interrupt Mask Register (IMR) or the BCD of the Interrupt level on to the Data Bus.

A0

This input signal is used in conjunction with $\overline{WR}$ and $\overline{RD}$ signals to write commands into the various command registers as well as reading the various status registers of the chip. This line can be tied directly to one of the address lines.

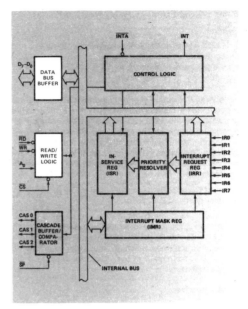

8259 BLOCK DIAGRAM

8259 BASIC OPERATION

A_0	D_4	D_3	$\overline{RD}$	$\overline{WR}$	$\overline{CS}$	INPUT OPERATION (READ)
0			0	1	0	IRR, ISR or Interrupting Level ⇒ DATA BUS (Note 1)
1			0	1	0	IMR ⇒ DATA BUS
						OUTPUT OPERATION (WRITE)
0	0	0	1	0	0	DATA BUS ⇒ OCW2
0	0	1	1	0	0	DATA BUS ⇒ OCW3
0	1	X	1	0	0	DATA BUS ⇒ ICW1
1	X	X	1	0	0	DATA BUS ⇒ OCW1, ICW2, ICW3 (Note 2)
						DISABLE FUNCTION
X	X	X	1	1	0	DATA BUS ⇒ 3-STATE
X	X	X	X	X	1	DATA BUS ⇒ 3-STATE

Note 1: Selection of IRR, ISR or Interrupting Level is based on the content of OCW3 written before the READ operation.

Note 2: On-chip sequencer logic queues these commands into proper sequence.

$\overline{SP}$ (Slave Program)

More than one 8259 can be used in the system to expand the priority interrupt scheme up to 64 levels. In such case, one 8259 acts as the master, and the others act as slaves. A "high" on the $\overline{SP}$ pin designates the 8259 as the master, a "low" designates it as a slave.

The Cascade Buffer/Comparator

This function block stores and compares the IDs of all 8259 used in the system. The associated three I/O pins (CAS0-2) are outputs when the 8259 is used as a master ($\overline{SP}$ = 1), and are inputs when the 8259 is used as a slave ($\overline{SP}$ = 0). As a master, the 8259 sends the ID of the interrupting slave device onto the CAS0-2 lines. The slave thus selected will send its preprogrammed subroutine addressed onto the Data Bus during next two consecutive $\overline{INTA}$ pulses. (See section "Cascading the 8259".)

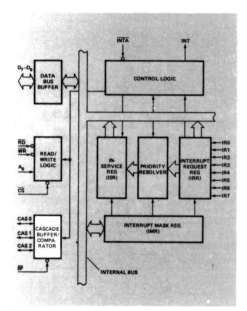

8259 BLOCK DIAGRAM

8259 DETAILED OPERATIONAL SUMMARY

General

The powerful features of the 8259 in a microcomputer system are its programmability and its utilization of the CALL instruction to jump into any address in the memory map. The normal sequence of events that the 8259 interacts with the CPU is as follows:

1. One or more of the INTERRUPT REQUEST lines (IR7-0) are raised high, setting the corresponding IRR bit(s).

2. The 8259 accepts these requests, resolves the priorities, and sends an INT to the CPU.

3. The CPU acknowledges the INT and responds with an $\overline{INTA}$ pulse.

4. Upon receiving an $\overline{INTA}$ from the CPU group, the highest priority ISR bit is set, and the corresponding IRR bit is reset. The 8259 will also release a CALL instruction code (11001101) onto the 8-bit Data Bus through its D7-0 pins.

5. This CALL instruction will initiate two more $\overline{INTA}$ pulses to be sent to the 8259 from the CPU group.

6. These two $\overline{INTA}$ pulses allow the 8259 to release its preprogrammed subroutine address onto the Data Bus. The lower 8-bit address is released at the first $\overline{INTA}$ pulse and the higher 8-bit address is released at the second $\overline{INTA}$ pulse.

7. This completes the 3-byte CALL instruction released by the 8259. ISR bit is not reset until the end of the subroutine when an EOI (End of interrupt) command is issued to the 8259.

Programming The 8259

The 8259 accepts two types of command words generated by the CPU:

1. Initialization Command Words (ICWs):
   Before normal operation can begin, each 8259 in the system must be brought to a starting point — by a sequence of 2 or 3 bytes timed by $\overline{WR}$ pulses. This sequence is described in Figure 1.

2. Operation Command Words (OCWs):
   These are the command words which command the 8259 to operate in various interrupt modes. These modes are:
   a. Fully nested mode
   b. Rotating priority mode
   c. Special mask mode
   d. Polled mode

The OCWs can be written into the 8259 at anytime after initialization.

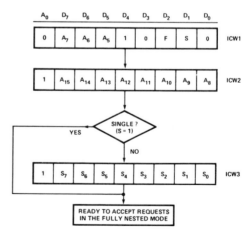

FIGURE 1. INITIALIZATION SEQUENCE

8259, 8259-5

Initialization Command Words 1 and 2: (ICW1 and ICW2)

Whenever a command is issued with A0 = 0 and D4 = 1, this is interpreted as Initialization Command Word 1 (ICW1), and initiates the initialization sequence. During this sequence, the following occur automatically:

a. The edge sense circuit is reset, which means that following initialization, an interrupt request (IR) input must make a low to high transition to generate an interrupt.

b. The interrupt Mask Register is cleared.

c. IR 7 input is assigned priority 7.

d. Special Mask Mode Flip-flop and status Read Flip-flop are reset.

The 8 requesting devices have 8 addresses equally spaced in memory. The addresses can be programmed at intervals of 4 or 8 bytes; the 8 routines thus occupying a page of 32 or 64 bytes respectively in memory.

The address format is:

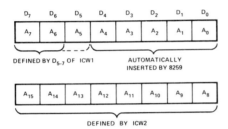

A0-4 are automatically inserted by the 8259, while A15-6 are programmed by ICW1 and ICW2. When interval = 8, A5 is fixed by the 8259. If interval = 4, A5 is programmed in ICW1. Thus, the interrupt service routines can be located anywhere in the memory space. The 8 byte interval will maintain compatibility with current 8080 RESTART instruction software, while the 4 byte interval is best for compact jump table.

The address format inserted by the 8259 is described in Table 1.

The bits F and S are defined by ICW1 as follows:

F: Call address interval. F = 1, then interval = 4; F = 0, then interval = 8.

S: Single. S = 1 means that this is the only 8259 in the system. It avoids the necesity of programming ICW3.

		INTERVAL = 4							INTERVAL = 8						
					LOWER MEMORY	ROUTINE	ADDRESS									
		D7	D6	D5	D4	D3	D2	D1	D0	D7	D6	D5	D4	D3	D2	D1	D0
IR	7	A7	A6	A5	1	1	1	0	0	A7	A6	1	1	1	0	0	0
IR	6	A7	A6	A5	1	1	0	0	0	A7	A6	1	1	0	0	0	0
IR	5	A7	A6	A5	1	0	1	0	0	A7	A6	1	0	1	0	0	0
IR	4	A7	A6	A5	1	0	0	0	0	A7	A6	1	0	0	0	0	0
IR	3	A7	A6	A5	0	1	1	0	0	A7	A6	0	1	1	0	0	0
IR	2	A7	A6	A5	0	1	0	0	0	A7	A6	0	1	0	0	0	0
IR	1	A7	A6	A5	0	0	1	0	0	A7	A6	0	0	1	0	0	0
IR	0	A7	A6	A5	0	0	0	0	0	A7	A6	0	0	0	0	0	0

TABLE 1.

Example of Interrupt Acknowledge Sequence

Assume the 8259 is programmed with F = 1 (CALL address interval = 4), and IR5 is the interrupting level. The 3 byte sequence released by the 8259 timed by the $\overline{INTA}$ pulses is as follows:

	D7	D6	D5	D4	D3	D2	D1	D0	
1st INTA	1	1	0	0	1	1	0	1	CALL CODE
2nd INTA	A7	A6	A5	1	0	1	0	0	LOWER ROUTINE ADDRESS
3rd $\overline{INTA}$	A15	A14	A13	A12	A11	A10	A9	A8	HIGHER ROUTINE ADDRESS

Initialization Command Word 3 (ICW3)

This will load the 8-bit slave register. The functions of this register are as follows:

a. If the 8259 is the master, a "1" is set for each slave in the system. The master then will release byte 1 of the CALL sequence and will enable the corresponding slave to release bytes 2 and 3, through the cascade lines.

b. If the 8259 is a slave, bits 2 - 0 identify the slave. The slave compares its CAS0-2 inputs (sent by the master) with these bits. If they are equal, bytes 2 and 3 of the CALL sequence are released.

If bit S is set in ICW1, there is no need to program ICW3.

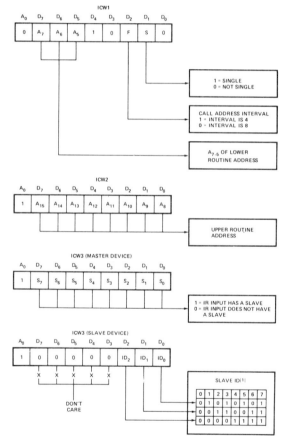

NOTE 1: SLAVE ID IS EQUAL TO THE CORRESPONDING MASTER IR INPUT.

INITIALIZATION COMMAND WORD FORMAT

Operation Command Words (OCWs)

After the Initialization Command Words (ICWs) are programmed into the 8259, the chip is ready to accept interrupt requests at its input lines. However, during the 8259 operation, a selection of algorithms can command the 8259 to operate in various modes through the Operation Command Words (OCWs). These various modes and their associated OCWs are described below.

Interrupt Masks

Each Interrupt Request input can be masked individually by the Interrupt Masked Register (IMR) programmed through OCW1.

The IMR operates on the In-Service Register. Note that if an interrupt is already acknowledged by the 8259 (an $\overline{\text{INTA}}$ pulse has occurred), then the Interrupting level, although masked, will inhibit the lower priorities. To enable these lower priority interrupts, one can do one of two things: (1) Write an End of Interrupt (EOI) command (OCW2) to reset the IST bit or (2) Set the special mask mode using OCW3 (as will be explained later in the special mask mode.)

Fully Nested Mode

The 8259 will operate in the fully nested mode after the execution of the initialization sequence without any OCW being written. In this mode, the interrupt requests are ordered in priorities from 0 through 7. When an interrupt is acknowledged, the highest priority request is determined and its address vector placed on the bus. In addition, a bit of the Interrupt service register (IS 7-0) is set. This bit remains set until the CPU issues an End of Interrupt (EOI) command immediately before returning from the service routine. While the IS bit is set, all further interrupts of lower priority are inhibited, while higher levels will be able to generate an interrupt (which will only be acknowledged if the CPU has enabled its own interrupt input through software).

After the Initialization sequence, IR0 has the highest priority and IR7 the lowest. Priorities can be changed, as will be explained in the rotating priority mode.

Rotating Priority Commands

There are two variations of rotating priority: auto rotate and specific rotate.

1. Auto Rotate — Executing the Rotate-at-EOI (Auto) command, resets the highest priority ISR bit and assigns that input the lowest priority. Thus, a device requesting an interrupt will have to wait, in the worst case, until 7 other devices are serviced at most once each, i.e., if the priority and "in-service" status is:

BEFORE ROTATE	IS7	IS6	IS5	IS4	IS3	IS2	IS1	IS0
"IS" STATUS	0	1	0	1	0	0	0	0

	LOWEST PRIORITY				HIGHEST PRIORITY			
PRIORITY STATUS	7	6	5	4	3	2	1	0

AFTER ROTATE	IS7	IS6	IS5	IS4	IS3	IS2	IS1	IS0
"IS" STATUS	0	1	0	0	0	0	0	0

	LOWEST PRIORITY				HIGHEST PRIORITY			
PRIORITY STATUS	4	3	2	1	0	7	6	5

In this example, the In-Service FF corresponding to line 4 (the highest priority FF set) was reset and line 4 became the lowest priority, while all the other priorities rotated correspondingly.

The Rotate command is issued in OCW2, where: R = 1, EOI = 1, SEOI = 0.

2. Specific Rotate — The programmer can change priorities by programming the bottom priority, and by doing this, to fix the highest priority: i.e., if IR5 is programmed as the bottom priority device, the IR6 will have the highest one. This command can be used with or without resetting the selected ISR bit.

The Rotate command is issued in OCW2 where: R = 1, SEOI = 1. L2, L1, L0 are the BCD priority level codes of the bottom priority device. if EOI = 1 also, the ISR bit selected by L2-L0 is reset.

Observe that this mode is independent of the End of Interrupt Command and priority changes can be executed during EOI command or independently from the EOI command.

End of Interrupt (EOI) and Specific End of Interrupt (SEOI)

An End of Interrupt command word must be issued to the 8259 before returning from a service routine, to reset the appropriate IS bit.

There are two forms of EOI command: Specific and non-Specific. When the 8259 is operated in modes which preserve the fully nested structure, it can determine which IS bit to reset on EOI. When a non-Specific EOI command is issued the 8259 will automatically reset the highest IS bit of those that are set, since in the nested mode, the highest IS level was necessarily the last level acknowledged and will necessarily be the next routine level returned from.

However, when a mode is used which may disturb the fully nested structure, such as in the rotating priority case, the 8259 may no longer be able to determine the last level acknowledged. In this case, a specific EOI (SEOI) must be issued which includes the IS level to be reset as part of the command. The End of the Interrupt is issued whenever EOI = "1" in OCW2. For specific EOI, SEOI = "1", and EOI = 1. L2, L1, L0 is then the BCD level to be reset. As explained in the Rotate Mode earlier, this can also be the bottom priority code. Note that although the Rotate command can be issued during an EOI = 1, it is not necessarily tied to it.

8259, 8259-5

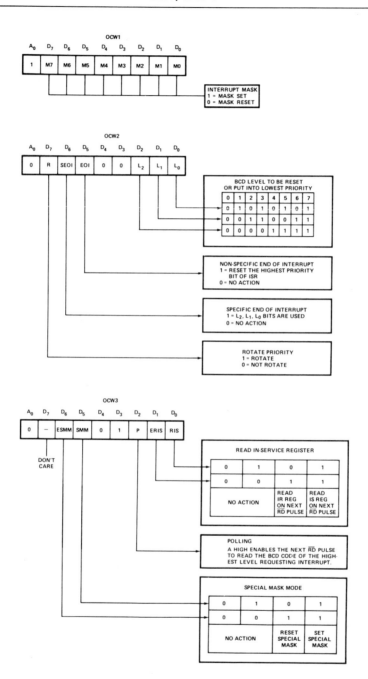

OPERATION COMMAND WORD FORMAT

8259, 8259-5

Special Mask Mode (SMM)

This mode is useful when some bit(s) are set (masked) by the Interrupt Mask Register (IMR) through OCW1. If, for some reason, we are currently in an interrupt service routine which is masked (this could happen when the subroutine intentionally mask itself off), it is still possible to enable the lower priority lines by setting the Special Mask mode. In this mode the lower priority lines are enabled until the SMM is reset. The higher priorities are not affected.

The special mask mode FF is set by OCW3 where ESMM = 1, SMM = 1, and reset where: ESSM = 1 and SMM = 0.

Polled Mode

In this mode, the CPU must disable its interrupt input. Service to device is achieved by programmer initiative by a Poll command.

The poll command is issued by setting P = "1" in OCW3 during a $\overline{WR}$ pulse.

The 8259 treats the next $\overline{RD}$ pulse as an interrupt acknowledge, sets the appropriate IS Flip-flop, if there is a request, and reads the priority level.

For polling operation, an OCW3 must be written before every read.

The word enabled onto the data bus during $\overline{RD}$ is:

D7	D6	D5	D4	D3	D2	D1	D0
I	—	—	—	—	W2	W1	W0

W0 — 2: BCD code of the highest priority level requesting service.

I: Equal to a "1" if there is an interrupt.

This mode is useful if there is a routine common to several levels — so that the $\overline{INTA}$ sequence is not needed (and this saves ROM space). Another application is to use the poll mode to expand the number of priority levels to more than 64.

SUMMARY OF OPERATION COMMAND WORD PROGRAMMING

	A0	D4	D3				
OCW1	1				M7-M0		IMR (Interrupt Mask Register). $\overline{WR}$ will load it while status can be read with $\overline{RD}$.
OCW2	0	0	0	R	SEOI	EOI	
				0	0	0	No Action.
				0	0	1	Non-specific End of Interrupt.
				0	1	0	No Action.
				0	1	1	Specific End of Interrupt. L2, L1, L0 is the BCD level to be reset.
				1	0	0	No Action.
				1	0	1	Rotate priority at EOI. (Auto Mode)
				1	1	0	Rotate priority, L2, L1, L0 becomes bottom priority without Ending of Interrupt.
				1	1	1	Rotate priority at EOI (Specific Mode), L2, L1, L0 becomes bottom priority, and its corresponding IS FF is reset.
OCW3	0	0	1	ESMM	SMM		
				0	0		Special Mask not Affected.
				0	1		
				1	0		Reset Special Mask.
				1	1		Set Special Mask.
				ERIS	RIS		
				0	0		No Action.
				0	1		
				1	0		Read IR Register Status.
				1	1		Read IS Register Status.

Note: The CPU interrupt input must be disabled during:
1. Initialization sequence for all the 8259 in the system.
2. Any control command execution.

8259, 8259-5

Reading 8259 Status

The input status of several internal registers can be read to update the user information on the system. The following registers can be read by issuing a suitable OCW3 and reading with $\overline{RD}$.

Interrupt Requests Register (IRR): 8-bit register which contains the levels requesting an interrupt to be acknowledged. The highest request level is reset from the IRR when an interrupt is acknowledged. (Not affected by IMR).

In Service Register (ISR): 8-bit register which contains the priority levels that are being serviced. The ISR is updated when an End of Interrupt command is issued.

Interrupt Mask Register: 8-bit register which contains the interrupt request lines which are masked.

The IRR can be read when prior to the $\overline{RD}$ pulse, an $\overline{WR}$ pulse is issued with OCW3, and ERIS = 1, RIS = 0.

The ISR can be read in a similar mode, when ERIS = 1, RIS = 1.

There is no need to write an OCW3 before every status read operation as long as the status read corresponds with the previous one, i.e. the 8259 "remembers" whether the IRR or ISR has been previously selected by the OCW3.

For reading the IMR, a $\overline{WR}$ pulse is not necessary to preceed the $\overline{RD}$. The output data bus will contain the IMR whenever $\overline{RD}$ is active and A0 = 1.

Polling overrides status read when P = 1, ERIS = 1 in OCW3.

Cascading

The 8259 can be easily interconnected in a system of one master with up to eight slaves to handle up to 64 priority levels.

A typical system is shown in Figure 2. The master controls, through the 3 line cascade bus, which one of the slaves will release the corresponding address.

As shown in Figure 2, the slaves interrupt outputs are connected to the master interrupt request inputs. When a slave request line is activated and afterwards acknowledged, the master will release the 8080 CALL code during byte 1 of $\overline{INTA}$ and will enable the corresponding slave to release the device routine address during bytes 2 and 3 of $\overline{INTA}$.

The cascade bus lines are normally low and will contain the slave address code from the trailing edge of the first $\overline{INTA}$ pulse to the trailing edge of the third pulse. It is obvious that each 8259 in the system must follow a separate initialization sequence and can be programmed to work in a different mode. An EOI command must be issued twice: once for the master and once for the corresponding slave. An address decoder is required to activate the Chip Select ($\overline{CS}$) input of each 8259. The slave program pin ($\overline{SP}$) must be at a "low" level for a slave (and then the cascade lines are inputs) and at a "high" level for a master (and then the cascade lines are outpus).

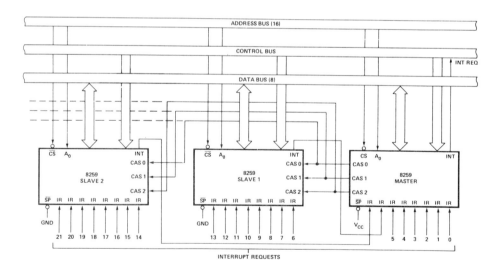

FIGURE 2. CASCADING THE 8259

8259, 8259-5

8259 INSTRUCTION SET

INST. NO.		A0	D7	D6	D5	D4	D3	D2	D1	D0	OPERATION DESCRIPTION
1	ICW1 A	0	A7	A6	A5	1	0	1	1	0	Byte 1 initialization, format = 4, single.
2	ICW1 B	0	A7	A6	A5	1	0	1	0	0	Byte 1 initialization, format = 4, not single.
3	ICW1 C	0	A7	A6	A5	1	0	0	1	0	Byte 1 initialization, format = 8, single.
4	ICW1 D	0	A7	A6	A5	1	0	0	0	0	Byte 1 initialization, format = 8, not single.
5	ICW2	1	A15	A14	A13	A12	A11	A10	A9	A8	Byte 2 initialization (Address No. 2)
6	ICW3 M	1	S7	S6	S5	S4	S3	S2	S1	S0	Byte 3 initialization — master.
7	ICW3 S	1	0	0	0	0	0	S2	S1	S0	Byte 3 initialization — slave.
8	OCW1	1	M7	M6	M5	M4	M3	M2	M1	M0	Load mask reg, read mask reg.
9	OCW2 E	0	0	0	1	0	0	0	0	0	Non specific EOI.
10	OCW2 SE	0	0	1	1	0	0	L2	L1	L0	Specific EOI. L2, L1, L0 code of IS FF to be reset.
11	OCW2 RE	0	1	0	1	0	0	0	0	0	Rotate at EOI (Auto Mode).
12	OCW2 RSE	0	1	1	1	0	0	L2	L1	L0	Rotate at EOI (Specific Mode). L2, L1, L0, code of line to be reset and selected as bottom priority.
13	OCW2 RS	0	1	1	0	0	0	L2	L1	L0	L2, L1, L0 code of bottom priority line.
14	OCW3 P	0	—	0	0	0	1	1	0	0	Poll mode.
15	OCW3 RIS	0	—	0	0	0	1	0	1	1	Read IS register.
16	OCW3 RR	0	—	0	0	0	1	0	1	0	Read requests register.
17	OCW3 SM	0	—	1	1	0	1	0	0	0	Set special mask mode.
18	OCW3 RSM	0	—	1	0	0	1	0	0	0	Reset special mask mode.

Notes:

1. In the master mode $\overline{SP}$ pin = 1, in slave mode $\overline{SP}$ = 0.

2. (—) = do not care.

8259, 8259-5

ABSOLUTE MAXIMUM RATINGS*

Ambient Temperature Under Bias .... 0° C to 70° C
Storage Temperature .... −65° C to +150° C
Voltage On Any Pin
  With Respect to Ground .... −0.5 V to +7 V
Power Dissipation .... 1 Watt

*COMMENT:
Stresses above those listed under "Absolute Maximum Ratings" may cause permanent damage to the device. This is a stress rating only and functional operation of the device at these or any other conditions above those indicated in the operational sections of this specification is not implied.

D.C. CHARACTERISTICS (T_A = 0°C to 70°C; V_{CC} = 5V ±5%)

SYMBOL	PARAMETER	MIN.	MAX.	UNITS	TEST CONDITIONS
V_{IL}	Input Low Voltage	−.5	.8	V	
V_{IH}	Input High Voltage	2.0	V_{CC}+.5V	V	
V_{OL}	Output Low Voltage		.45	V	I_{OL} = 2 mA
V_{OH}	Output High Voltage	2.4		V	I_{OH} = −400 μA
V_{OH-INT}	Interrupt Output High Voltage	2.4		V	I_{OH} = −400 μA
		3.5		V	I_{OH} = −50 μA
$I_{IL(IR_{0-7})}$	Input Leakage Current for IR_{0-7}		−300	μA	V_{IN} = 0V
			10	μA	V_{IN} = V_{CC}
I_{IL}	Input Leakage Current for Other Inputs		10	μA	V_{IN} = V_{CC} to 0V
I_{OFL}	Output Float Leakage		±10	μA	V_{OUT} = 0.45V to V_{CC}
I_{CC}	V_{CC} Supply Current		100	mA	

CAPACITANCE T_A = 25°C; V_{CC} = GND = 0V

SYMBOL	PARAMETER	MIN.	TYP.	MAX.	UNIT	TEST CONDITIONS
C_{IN}	Input Capacitance			10	pF	fc = 1 MHz
$C_{I/O}$	I/O Capacitance			20	pF	Unmeasured pins returned to V_{SS}

8259, 8259-5

A.C. CHARACTERISTICS (T_A = 0°C to 70°C; V_{CC} = +5V ±5%, GND = 0V)
BUS PARAMETERS
READ

SYMBOL	PARAMETER	8259		8259-5		UNIT
		MIN.	MAX.	MIN.	MAX.	
t_{AR}	$\overline{CS}/A_0$ Stable Before $\overline{RD}$ or $\overline{INTA}$	50		50		ns
t_{RA}	$\overline{CS}/A_0$ Stable After $\overline{RD}$ or $\overline{INTA}$	5		30		ns
t_{RR}	$\overline{RD}$ Pulse Width	420		300		ns
t_{RD}	Data Valid From $\overline{RD}/\overline{INTA}$ [1]		300		200	ns
t_{DF}	Data Float After $\overline{RD}/\overline{INTA}$	20	200	20	100	ns

WRITE

SYMBOL	PARAMETER	8259		8259-5		UNIT
		MIN.	MAX.	MIN.	MAX.	
t_{AW}	A_0 Stable Before $\overline{WR}$	50		50		ns
t_{WA}	A_0 Stable After $\overline{WR}$	20		30		ns
t_{WW}	$\overline{WR}$ Pulse Width	400		300		ns
t_{DW}	Data Valid to $\overline{WR}$ (T.E.)	300		250		ns
t_{WD}	Data Valid After $\overline{WR}$	40		30		ns

OTHER TIMINGS

SYMBOL	PARAMETER	8259		8259-5		UNIT
		MIN.	MAX.	MIN.	MAX.	
t_{IW}	Width of Interrupt Request Pulse	100		100		ns
t_{INT}	INT ↑ After IR ↑	400		350		ns
t_{IC}	Cascade Line Stable After $\overline{INTA}$ ↑	400		400		ns

Note 1:   8259: C_L = 100pF, 8259-5: C_L = 150pF.

INPUT WAVEFORMS FOR A.C. TESTS

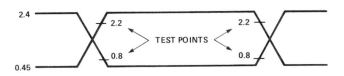

8259, 8259-5

WAVEFORMS

READ TIMING

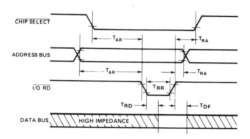

WRITE TIMING

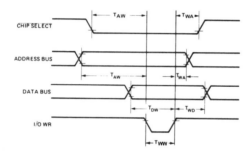

OTHER TIMING

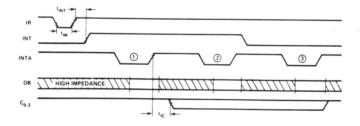

Note: Interrupt Request must remain "HIGH" (at least) until leading edge of first INTA.

8259, 8259-5

READ STATUS/POLL MODE

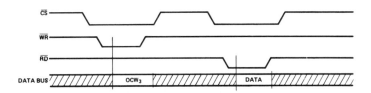

Appendix 6 The Intel 8080/8085 instruction set

INSTRUCTION SET

A computer, no matter how sophisticated, can only do what it is "told" to do. One "tells" the computer what to do via a series of coded instructions referred to as a **Program**. The realm of the programmer is referred to as **Software**, in contrast to the **Hardware** that comprises the actual computer equipment. A computer's software refers to all of the programs that have been written for that computer.

When a computer is designed, the engineers provide the Central Processing Unit (CPU) with the ability to perform a particular set of operations. The CPU is designed such that a specific operation is performed when the CPU control logic decodes a particular instruction. Consequently, the operations that can be performed by a CPU define the computer's **Instruction Set**.

Each computer instruction allows the programmer to initiate the performance of a specific operation. All computers implement certain arithmetic operations in their instruction set, such as an instruction to add the contents of two registers. Often logical operations (e.g., OR the contents of two registers) and register operate instructions (e.g., increment a register) are included in the instruction set. A computer's instruction set will also have instructions that move data between registers, between a register and memory, and between a register and an I/O device. Most instruction sets also provide **Conditional Instructions**. A conditional instruction specifies an operation to be performed only if certain conditions have been met; for example, jump to a particular instruction if the result of the last operation was zero. Conditional instructions provide a program with a decision-making capability.

By logically organizing a sequence of instructions into a coherent program, the programmer can "tell" the computer to perform a very specific and useful function.

The computer, however, can only execute programs whose instructions are in a binary coded form (i.e., a series of 1's and 0's), that is called **Machine Code**. Because it would be extremely cumbersome to program in machine code, programming languages have been developed. There are programs available which convert the programming language instructions into machine code that can be interpreted by the processor.

One type of programming language is **Assembly Language**. A unique assembly language mnemonic is assigned to each of the computer's instructions. The programmer can write a program (called the **Source Program**) using these mnemonics and certain operands; the source program is then converted into machine instructions (called the **Object Code**). Each assembly language instruction is converted into one machine code instruction (1 or more bytes) by an **Assembler** program. Assembly languages are usually machine dependent (i.e., they are usually able to run on only one type of computer).

THE 8080 INSTRUCTION SET

The 8080 instruction set includes five different types of instructions:

- **Data Transfer Group**—move data between registers or between memory and registers

- **Arithmetic Group** — add, subtract, increment or decrement data in registers or in memory

- **Logical Group** — AND, OR, EXCLUSIVE-OR, compare, rotate or complement data in registers or in memory

- **Branch Group** — conditional and unconditional jump instructions, subroutine call instructions and return instructions

- **Stack, I/O and Machine Control Group** — includes I/O instructions, as well as instructions for maintaining the stack and internal control flags.

Instruction and Data Formats:

Memory for the 8080 is organized into 8-bit quantities, called Bytes. Each byte has a unique 16-bit binary address corresponding to its sequential position in memory.

The 8080 can directly address up to 65,536 bytes of memory, which may consist of both read-only memory (ROM) elements and random-access memory (RAM) elements (read/write memory).

Data in the 8080 is stored in the form of 8-bit binary integers:

DATA WORD

D$_7$	D$_6$	D$_5$	D$_4$	D$_3$	D$_2$	D$_1$	D$_0$

MSB   LSB

When a register or data word contains a binary number, it is necessary to establish the order in which the bits of the number are written. In the Intel 8080, BIT 0 is referred to as the **Least Significant Bit (LSB)**, and BIT 7 (of an 8 bit number) is referred to as the **Most Significant Bit (MSB)**.

The 8080 program instructions may be one, two or three bytes in length. Multiple byte instructions must be stored in successive memory locations; the address of the first byte is always used as the address of the instructions. The exact instruction format will depend on the particular operation to be executed.

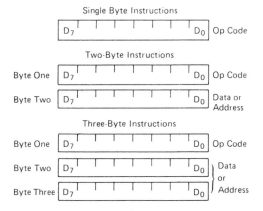

Single Byte Instructions

| D$_7$ | | | | | | | D$_0$ | Op Code |

Two-Byte Instructions

Byte One | D$_7$ | | | | | | | D$_0$ | Op Code
Byte Two | D$_7$ | | | | | | | D$_0$ | Data or Address

Three-Byte Instructions

Byte One | D$_7$ | | | | | | | D$_0$ | Op Code
Byte Two | D$_7$ | | | | | | | D$_0$ | Data
Byte Three | D$_7$ | | | | | | | D$_0$ | or Address

Addressing Modes:

Often the data that is to be operated on is stored in memory. When multi-byte numeric data is used, the data, like instructions, is stored in successive memory locations, with the least significant byte first, followed by increasingly significant bytes. The 8080 has four different modes for addressing data stored in memory or in registers:

- Direct — Bytes 2 and 3 of the instruction contain the exact memory address of the data item (the low-order bits of the address are in byte 2, the high-order bits in byte 3).
- Register — The instruction specifies the register or register-pair in which the data is located.
- Register Indirect — The instruction specifies a register-pair which contains the memory

address where the data is located (the high-order bits of the address are in the first register of the pair, the low-order bits in the second).

- Immediate — The instruction contains the data itself. This is either an 8-bit quantity or a 16-bit quantity (least significant byte first, most significant byte second).

Unless directed by an interrupt or branch instruction, the execution of instructions proceeds through consecutively increasing memory locations. A branch instruction can specify the address of the next instruction to be executed in one of two ways:

- Direct — The branch instruction contains the address of the next instruction to be executed. (Except for the 'RST' instruction, byte 2 contains the low-order address and byte 3 the high-order address.)
- Register indirect — The branch instruction indicates a register-pair which contains the address of the next instruction to be executed. (The high-order bits of the address are in the first register of the pair, the low-order bits in the second.)

The RST instruction is a special one-byte call instruction (usually used during interrupt sequences). RST includes a three-bit field; program control is transferred to the instruction whose address is eight times the contents of this three-bit field.

Condition Flags:

There are five condition flags associated with the execution of instructions on the 8080. They are Zero, Sign, Parity, Carry, and Auxiliary Carry, and are each represented by a 1-bit register in the CPU. A flag is "set" by forcing the bit to 1; "reset" by forcing the bit to 0.

Unless indicated otherwise, when an instruction affects a flag, it affects it in the following manner:

Zero: If the result of an instruction has the value 0, this flag is set; otherwise it is reset.

Sign: If the most significant bit of the result of the operation has the value 1, this flag is set; otherwise it is reset.

Parity: If the modulo 2 sum of the bits of the result of the operation is 0, (i.e., if the result has even parity), this flag is set; otherwise it is reset (i.e., if the result has odd parity).

Carry: If the instruction resulted in a carry (from addition), or a borrow (from subtraction or a comparison) out of the high-order bit, this flag is set; otherwise it is reset.

Auxiliary Carry: If the instruction caused a carry out of bit 3 and into bit 4 of the resulting value, the auxiliary carry is set; otherwise it is reset. This flag is affected by single precision additions, subtractions, increments, decrements, comparisons, and logical operations, but is principally used with additions and increments preceding a DAA (Decimal Adjust Accumulator) instruction.

Symbols and Abbreviations:

The following symbols and abbreviations are used in the subsequent description of the 8080 instructions:

SYMBOLS	MEANING
accumulator	Register A
addr	16-bit address quantity
data	8-bit data quantity
data 16	16-bit data quantity
byte 2	The second byte of the instruction
byte 3	The third byte of the instruction
port	8-bit address of an I/O device
r,r1,r2	One of the registers A,B,C,D,E,H,L
DDD,SSS	The bit pattern designating one of the registers A,B,C,D,E,H,L (DDD=destination, SSS= source):

DDD or SSS	REGISTER NAME
111	A
000	B
001	C
010	D
011	E
100	H
101	L

rp	One of the register pairs:

B represents the B,C pair with B as the high-order register and C as the low-order register;

D represents the D,E pair with D as the high-order register and E as the low-order register;

H represents the H,L pair with H as the high-order register and L as the low-order register;

SP represents the 16-bit stack pointer register.

RP	The bit pattern designating one of the register pairs B,D,H,SP:

RP	REGISTER PAIR
00	B-C
01	D-E
10	H-L
11	SP

rh	The first (high-order) register of a designated register pair.
rl	The second (low-order) register of a designated register pair.
PC	16-bit program counter register (PCH and PCL are used to refer to the high-order and low-order 8 bits respectively).
SP	16-bit stack pointer register (SPH and SPL are used to refer to the high-order and low-order 8 bits respectively).
r_m	Bit m of the register r (bits are number 7 through 0 from left to right).
Z,S,P,CY,AC	The condition flags: Zero, Sign, Parity, Carry, and Auxiliary Carry, respectively.
( )	The contents of the memory location or registers enclosed in the parentheses.
←	"Is transferred to"
∧	Logical AND
⩛	Exclusive OR
∨	Inclusive OR
+	Addition
−	Two's complement subtraction
*	Multiplication
↔	"Is exchanged with"
‾	The one's complement (e.g., $(\overline{A})$)
n	The restart number 0 through 7
NNN	The binary representation 000 through 111 for restart number 0 through 7 respectively.

Description Format:

The following pages provide a detailed description of the instruction set of the 8080. Each instruction is described in the following manner:

1. The MAC 80 assembler format, consisting of the instruction mnemonic and operand fields, is printed in **BOLDFACE** on the left side of the first line.

2. The name of the instruction is enclosed in parenthesis on the right side of the first line.

3. The next line(s) contain a symbolic description of the operation of the instruction.

4. This is followed by a narative description of the operation of the instruction.

5. The following line(s) contain the binary fields and patterns that comprise the machine instruction.

6. The last four lines contain incidental information about the execution of the instruction. The number of machine cycles and states required to execute the instruction are listed first. If the instruction has two possible execution times, as in a Conditional Jump, both times will be listed, separated by a slash. Next, any significant data addressing modes (see Page 4-2) are listed. The last line lists any of the five Flags that are affected by the execution of the instruction.

Data Transfer Group:

This group of instructions transfers data to and from registers and memory. **Condition flags are not affected** by any instruction in this group.

MOV r1, r2   (Move Register)

(r1) ◄— (r2)

The content of register r2 is moved to register r1.

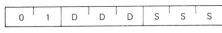

```
Cycles:      1
States:      5
Addressing:  register
Flags:       none
```

MOV r, M   (Move from memory)

(r) ◄— ((H) (L))

The content of the memory location, whose address is in registers H and L, is moved to register r.

```
Cycles:      2
States:      7
Addressing:  reg. indirect
Flags:       none
```

MOV M, r   (Move to memory)

((H) (L)) ◄— (r)

The content of register r is moved to the memory location whose address is in registers H and L.

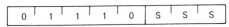

```
Cycles:      2
States:      7
Addressing:  reg. indirect
Flags:       none
```

MVI r, data   (Move Immediate)

(r) ◄— (byte 2)

The content of byte 2 of the instruction is moved to register r.

```
Cycles:      2
States:      7
Addressing:  immediate
Flags:       none
```

MVI M, data   (Move to memory immediate)

((H) (L)) ◄— (byte 2)

The content of byte 2 of the instruction is moved to the memory location whose address is in registers H and L.

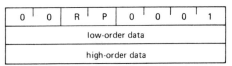

```
Cycles:      3
States:      10
Addressing:  immed./reg. indirect
Flags:       none
```

LXI rp, data 16   (Load register pair immediate)

(rh) ◄— (byte 3),

(rl) ◄— (byte 2)

Byte 3 of the instruction is moved into the high-order register (rh) of the register pair rp. Byte 2 of the instruction is moved into the low-order register (rl) of the register pair rp.

0	0	R	P	0	0	0	1
low-order data							
high-order data							

```
Cycles:      3
States:      10
Addressing:  immediate
Flags:       none
```

LDA addr   (Load Accumulator direct)

(A) ◄— ((byte 3)(byte 2))

The content of the memory location, whose address is specified in byte 2 and byte 3 of the instruction, is moved to register A.

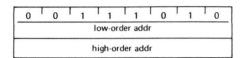

Cycles: 4
States: 13
Addressing: direct
Flags: none

STA addr   (Store Accumulator direct)

((byte 3)(byte 2)) ◄— (A)

The content of the accumulator is moved to the memory location whose address is specified in byte 2 and byte 3 of the instruction.

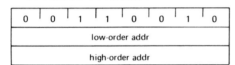

Cycles: 4
States: 13
Addressing: direct
Flags: none

LHLD addr   (Load H and L direct)

(L) ◄— ((byte 3)(byte 2))

(H) ◄— ((byte 3)(byte 2) + 1)

The content of the memory location, whose address is specified in byte 2 and byte 3 of the instruction, is moved to register L. The content of the memory location at the succeeding address is moved to register H.

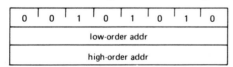

Cycles: 5
States: 16
Addressing: direct
Flags: none

SHLD addr   (Store H and L direct)

((byte 3)(byte 2)) ◄— (L)

((byte 3)(byte 2) + 1) ◄— (H)

The content of register L is moved to the memory location whose address is specified in byte 2 and byte 3. The content of register H is moved to the succeeding memory location.

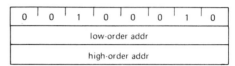

Cycles: 5
States: 16
Addressing: direct
Flags: none

LDAX rp   (Load accumulator indirect)

(A) ◄— ((rp))

The content of the memory location, whose address is in the register pair rp, is moved to register A. Note: only register pairs rp=B (registers B and C) or rp=D (registers D and E) may be specified.

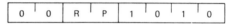

Cycles: 2
States: 7
Addressing: reg. indirect
Flags: none

STAX rp   (Store accumulator indirect)

((rp)) ◄— (A)

The content of register A is moved to the memory location whose address is in the register pair rp. Note: only register pairs rp=B (registers B and C) or rp=D (registers D and E) may be specified.

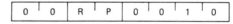

Cycles: 2
States: 7
Addressing: reg. indirect
Flags: none

XCHG   (Exchange H and L with D and E)

(H) ◄—► (D)

(L) ◄—► (E)

The contents of registers H and L are exchanged with the contents of registers D and E.

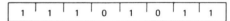

Cycles: 1
States: 4
Addressing: register
Flags: none

Arithmetic Group:

This group of instructions performs arithmetic operations on data in registers and memory.

Unless indicated otherwise, all instructions in this group affect the Zero, Sign, Parity, Carry, and Auxiliary Carry flags according to the standard rules.

All subtraction operations are performed via two's complement arithmetic and set the carry flag to one to indicate a borrow and clear it to indicate no borrow.

ADD r (Add Register)

(A) ◄— (A) + (r)

The content of register r is added to the content of the accumulator. The result is placed in the accumulator.

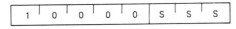

1	0	0	0	0	S	S	S

Cycles: 1
States: 4
Addressing: register
Flags: Z,S,P,CY,AC

ADD M (Add memory)

(A) ◄— (A) + ((H) (L))

The content of the memory location whose address is contained in the H and L registers is added to the content of the accumulator. The result is placed in the accumulator.

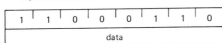

1	0	0	0	0	1	1	0

Cycles: 2
States: 7
Addressing: reg. indirect
Flags: Z,S,P,CY,AC

ADI data (Add immediate)

(A) ◄— (A) + (byte 2)

The content of the second byte of the instruction is added to the content of the accumulator. The result is placed in the accumulator.

1	1	0	0	0	1	1	0
data							

Cycles: 2
States: 7
Addressing: immediate
Flags: Z,S,P,CY,AC

ADC r (Add Register with carry)

(A) ◄— (A) + (r) + (CY)

The content of register r and the content of the carry bit are added to the content of the accumulator. The result is placed in the accumulator.

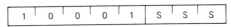

1	0	0	0	1	S	S	S

Cycles: 1
States: 4
Addressing: register
Flags: Z,S,P,CY,AC

ADC M (Add memory with carry)

(A) ◄— (A) + ((H) (L)) + (CY)

The content of the memory location whose address is contained in the H and L registers and the content of the CY flag are added to the accumulator. The result is placed in the accumulator.

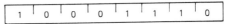

1	0	0	0	1	1	1	0

Cycles: 2
States: 7
Addressing: reg. indirect
Flags: Z,S,P,CY,AC

ACI data (Add immediate with carry)

(A) ◄— (A) + (byte 2) + (CY)

The content of the second byte of the instruction and the content of the CY flag are added to the contents of the accumulator. The result is placed in the accumulator.

1	1	0	0	1	1	1	0
data							

Cycles: 2
States: 7
Addressing: immediate
Flags: Z,S,P,CY,AC

SUB r (Subtract Register)

(A) ◄— (A) − (r)

The content of register r is subtracted from the content of the accumulator. The result is placed in the accumulator.

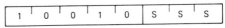

1	0	0	1	0	S	S	S

Cycles: 1
States: 4
Addressing: register
Flags: Z,S,P,CY,AC

SUB M   (Subtract memory)

(A) ◄— (A) − ((H) (L))

The content of the memory location whose address is contained in the H and L registers is subtracted from the content of the accumulator. The result is placed in the accumulator.

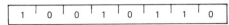

```
| 1 | 0 | 0 | 1 | 0 | 1 | 1 | 0 |
```

Cycles: 2
States: 7
Addressing: reg. indirect
Flags: Z,S,P,CY,AC

SUI data   (Subtract immediate)

(A) ◄— (A) − (byte 2)

The content of the second byte of the instruction is subtracted from the content of the accumulator. The result is placed in the accumulator.

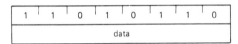

```
| 1 | 1 | 0 | 1 | 0 | 1 | 1 | 0 |
|          data          |
```

Cycles: 2
States: 7
Addressing: immediate
Flags: Z,S,P,CY,AC

SBB r   (Subtract Register with borrow)

(A) ◄— (A) − (r) − (CY)

The content of register r and the content of the CY flag are both subtracted from the accumulator. The result is placed in the accumulator.

```
| 1 | 0 | 0 | 1 | 1 | S | S | S |
```

Cycles: 1
States: 4
Addressing: register
Flags: Z,S,P,CY,AC

SBB M   (Subtract memory with borrow)

(A) ◄— (A) − ((H) (L)) − (CY)

The content of the memory location whose address is contained in the H and L registers and the content of the CY flag are both subtracted from the accumulator. The result is placed in the accumulator.

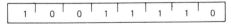

```
| 1 | 0 | 0 | 1 | 1 | 1 | 1 | 0 |
```

Cycles: 2
States: 7
Addressing: reg. indirect
Flags: Z,S,P,CY,AC

SBI data   (Subtract immediate with borrow)

(A) ◄— (A) − (byte 2) − (CY)

The contents of the second byte of the instruction and the contents of the CY flag are both subtracted from the accumulator. The result is placed in the accumulator.

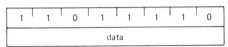

```
| 1 | 1 | 0 | 1 | 1 | 1 | 1 | 0 |
|          data          |
```

Cycles: 2
States: 7
Addressing: immediate
Flags: Z,S,P,CY,AC

INR r   (Increment Register)

(r) ◄— (r) + 1

The content of register r is incremented by one. Note: All condition flags **except CY** are affected.

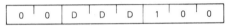

```
| 0 | 0 | D | D | D | 1 | 0 | 0 |
```

Cycles: 1
States: 5
Addressing: register
Flags: Z,S,P,AC

INR M   (Increment memory)

((H) (L)) ◄— ((H) (L)) + 1

The content of the memory location whose address is contained in the H and L registers is incremented by one. Note: All condition flags **except CY** are affected.

```
| 0 | 0 | 1 | 1 | 0 | 1 | 0 | 0 |
```

Cycles: 3
States: 10
Addressing: reg. indirect
Flags: Z,S,P,AC

DCR r   (Decrement Register)

(r) ◄— (r) − 1

The content of register r is decremented by one. Note: All condition flags **except CY** are affected.

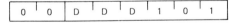

```
| 0 | 0 | D | D | D | 1 | 0 | 1 |
```

Cycles: 1
States: 5
Addressing: register
Flags: Z,S,P,AC

DCR M   (Decrement memory)

((H) (L)) ◄─── ((H) (L)) − 1

The content of the memory location whose address is contained in the H and L registers is decremented by one. Note: All condition flags **except CY** are affected.

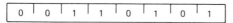

0	0	1	1	0	1	0	1

Cycles: 3
States: 10
Addressing: reg. indirect
Flags: Z,S,P,AC

INX rp   (Increment register pair)

(rh) (rl) ◄─── (rh) (rl) + 1

The content of the register pair rp is incremented by one. Note: **No condition flags are affected.**

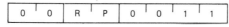

0	0	R	P	0	0	1	1

Cycles: 1
States: 5
Addressing: register
Flags: none

DCX rp   (Decrement register pair)

(rh) (rl) ◄─── (rh) (rl) − 1

The content of the register pair rp is decremented by one. Note: **No condition flags are affected.**

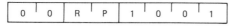

0	0	R	P	1	0	1	1

Cycles: 1
States: 5
Addressing: register
Flags: none

DAD rp   (Add register pair to H and L)

(H) (L) ◄─── (H) (L) + (rh) (rl)

The content of the register pair rp is added to the content of the register pair H and L. The result is placed in the register pair H and L. Note: **Only the CY flag is affected.** It is set if there is a carry out of the double precision add; otherwise it is reset.

0	0	R	P	1	0	0	1

Cycles: 3
States: 10
Addressing: register
Flags: CY

DAA   (Decimal Adjust Accumulator)

The eight-bit number in the accumulator is adjusted to form two four-bit Binary-Coded-Decimal digits by the following process:

1. If the value of the least significant 4 bits of the accumulator is greater than 9 **or** if the AC flag is set, 6 is added to the accumulator.

2. If the value of the most significant 4 bits of the accumulator is now greater than 9, **or** if the CY flag is set, 6 is added to the most significant 4 bits of the accumulator.

NOTE: All flags are affected.

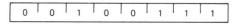

0	0	1	0	0	1	1	1

Cycles: 1
States: 4
Flags: Z,S,P,CY,AC

Logical Group:

This group of instructions performs logical (Boolean) operations on data in registers and memory and on condition flags.

Unless indicated otherwise, all instructions in this group affect the Zero, Sign, Parity, Auxiliary Carry, and Carry flags according to the standard rules.

ANA r   (AND Register)

(A) ◄─── (A) ∧ (r)

The content of register r is logically anded with the content of the accumulator. The result is placed in the accumulator. **The CY flag is cleared.**

1	0	1	0	0	S	S	S

Cycles: 1
States: 4
Addressing: register
Flags: Z,S,P,CY,AC

ANA M   (AND memory)

(A) ◄─── (A) ∧ ((H) (L))

The contents of the memory location whose address is contained in the H and L registers is logically anded with the content of the accumulator. The result is placed in the accumulator. **The CY flag is cleared.**

1	0	1	0	0	1	1	0

Cycles: 2
States: 7
Addressing: reg. indirect
Flags: Z,S,P,CY,AC

ANI data   (AND immediate)

(A) ◄── (A) ∧ (byte 2)

The content of the second byte of the instruction is logically anded with the contents of the accumulator. The result is placed in the accumulator. **The CY and AC flags are cleared.**

1	1	1	0	0	1	1	0
data							

Cycles: 2
States: 7
Addressing: immediate
Flags: Z,S,P,CY,AC

XRA r   (Exclusive OR Register)

(A) ◄── (A) ⊻ (r)

The content of register r is exclusive-or'd with the content of the accumulator. The result is placed in the accumulator. **The CY and AC flags are cleared.**

1	0	1	0	1	S	S	S

Cycles: 1
States: 4
Addressing: register
Flags: Z,S,P,CY,AC

XRA M   (Exclusive OR Memory)

(A) ◄── (A) ⊻ ((H) (L))

The content of the memory location whose address is contained in the H and L registers is exclusive-OR'd with the content of the accumulator. The result is placed in the accumulator. **The CY and AC flags are cleared.**

1	0	1	0	1	1	1	0

Cycles: 2
States: 7
Addressing: reg. indirect
Flags: Z,S,P,CY,AC

XRI data   (Exclusive OR immediate)

(A) ◄── (A) ⊻ (byte 2)

The content of the second byte of the instruction is exclusive-OR'd with the content of the accumulator. The result is placed in the accumulator. **The CY and AC flags are cleared.**

1	1	1	0	1	1	1	0
data							

Cycles: 2
States: 7
Addressing: immediate
Flags: Z,S,P,CY,AC

ORA r   (OR Register)

(A) ◄── (A) V (r)

The content of register r is inclusive-OR'd with the content of the accumulator. The result is placed in the accumulator. **The CY and AC flags are cleared.**

1	0	1	1	0	S	S	S

Cycles: 1
States: 4
Addressing: register
Flags: Z,S,P,CY,AC

ORA M   (OR memory)

(A) ◄── (A) V ((H) (L))

The content of the memory location whose address is contained in the H and L registers is inclusive-OR'd with the content of the accumulator. The result is placed in the accumulator. **The CY and AC flags are cleared.**

1	0	1	1	0	1	1	0

Cycles: 2
States: 7
Addressing: reg. indirect
Flags: Z,S,P,CY,AC

ORI data   (OR Immediate)

(A) ◄── (A) V (byte 2)

The content of the second byte of the instruction is inclusive-OR'd with the content of the accumulator. The result is placed in the accumulator. **The CY and AC flags are cleared.**

1	1	1	1	0	1	1	0
data							

Cycles: 2
States: 7
Addressing: immediate
Flags: Z,S,P,CY,AC

CMP r   (Compare Register)

(A) − (r)

The content of register r is subtracted from the accumulator. The accumulator remains unchanged. The condition flags are set as a result of the subtraction. **The Z flag is set to 1 if (A) = (r). The CY flag is set to 1 if (A) < (r).**

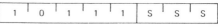

1	0	1	1	1	S	S	S

Cycles: 1
States: 4
Addressing: register
Flags: Z,S,P,CY,AC

CMP M (Compare memory)

$(A) - ((H) (L))$

The content of the memory location whose address is contained in the H and L registers is subtracted from the accumulator. The accumulator remains unchanged. The condition flags are set as a result of the subtraction. The Z flag is set to 1 if $(A) = ((H) (L))$. The CY flag is set to 1 if $(A) < ((H) (L))$.

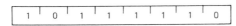

Cycles: 2
States: 7
Addressing: reg. indirect
Flags: Z,S,P,CY,AC

CPI data (Compare immediate)

$(A) - (byte 2)$

The content of the second byte of the instruction is subtracted from the accumulator. The condition flags are set by the result of the subtraction. The Z flag is set to 1 if $(A) = (byte 2)$. The CY flag is set to 1 if $(A) < (byte 2)$.

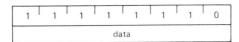

data

Cycles: 2
States: 7
Addressing: immediate
Flags: Z,S,P,CY,AC

RLC (Rotate left)

$(A_{n+1}) \leftarrow (A_n) ; (A_0) \leftarrow (A_7)$
$(CY) \leftarrow (A_7)$

The content of the accumulator is rotated left one position. The low order bit and the CY flag are both set to the value shifted out of the high order bit position. **Only the CY flag is affected.**

Cycles: 1
States: 4
Flags: CY

RRC (Rotate right)

$(A_n) \leftarrow (A_{n+1}) ; (A_7) \leftarrow (A_0)$
$(CY) \leftarrow (A_0)$

The content of the accumulator is rotated right one position. The high order bit and the CY flag are both set to the value shifted out of the low order bit position. **Only the CY flag is affected.**

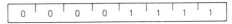

Cycles: 1
States: 4
Flags: CY

RAL (Rotate left through carry)

$(A_{n+1}) \leftarrow (A_n) ; (CY) \leftarrow (A_7)$
$(A_0) \leftarrow (CY)$

The content of the accumulator is rotated left one position through the CY flag. The low order bit is set equal to the CY flag and the CY flag is set to the value shifted out of the high order bit. **Only the CY flag is affected.**

Cycles: 1
States: 4
Flags: CY

RAR (Rotate right through carry)

$(A_n) \leftarrow (A_{n+1}) ; (CY) \leftarrow (A_0)$
$(A_7) \leftarrow (CY)$

The content of the accumulator is rotated right one position through the CY flag. The high order bit is set to the CY flag and the CY flag is set to the value shifted out of the low order bit. **Only the CY flag is affected.**

Cycles: 1
States: 4
Flags: CY

CMA (Complement accumulator)

$(A) \leftarrow (\overline{A})$

The contents of the accumulator are complemented (zero bits become 1, one bits become 0). **No flags are affected.**

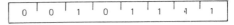

Cycles: 1
States: 4
Flags: none

CMC   (Complement carry)

$(CY) \leftarrow (\overline{CY})$

The CY flag is complemented. **No other flags are affected.**

0	0	1	1	1	1	1	1

Cycles: 1
States: 4
Flags: CY

STC   (Set carry)

$(CY) \leftarrow 1$

The CY flag is set to 1. **No other flags are affected.**

0	0	1	1	0	1	1	1

Cycles: 1
States: 4
Flags: CY

Branch Group:

This group of instructions alter normal sequential program flow.

Condition flags are not affected by any instruction in this group.

The two types of branch instructions are unconditional and conditional. Unconditional transfers simply perform the specified operation on register PC (the program counter). Conditional transfers examine the status of one of the four processor flags to determine if the specified branch is to be executed. The conditions that may be specified are as follows:

CONDITION		CCC
NZ	— not zero (Z = 0)	000
Z	— zero (Z = 1)	001
NC	— no carry (CY = 0)	010
C	— carry (CY = 1)	011
PO	— parity odd (P = 0)	100
PE	— parity even (P = 1)	101
P	— plus (S = 0)	110
M	— minus (S = 1)	111

JMP addr   (Jump)

$(PC) \leftarrow$ (byte 3) (byte 2)

Control is transferred to the instruction whose address is specified in byte 3 and byte 2 of the current instruction.

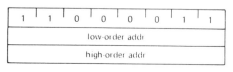

1	1	0	0	0	0	1	1

| low-order addr |
| high-order addr |

Cycles: 3
States: 10
Addressing: immediate
Flags: none

Jcondition addr   (Conditional jump)

If (CCC),

$(PC) \leftarrow$ (byte 3) (byte 2)

If the specified condition is true, control is transferred to the instruction whose address is specified in byte 3 and byte 2 of the current instruction; otherwise, control continues sequentially.

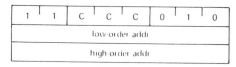

1	1	C	C	C	0	1	0

| low-order addr |
| high-order addr |

Cycles: 3
States: 10
Addressing: immediate
Flags: none

CALL addr   (Call)

$((SP) - 1) \leftarrow (PCH)$
$((SP) - 2) \leftarrow (PCL)$
$(SP) \leftarrow (SP) - 2$
$(PC) \leftarrow$ (byte 3) (byte 2)

The high-order eight bits of the next instruction address are moved to the memory location whose address is one less than the content of register SP. The low-order eight bits of the next instruction address are moved to the memory location whose address is two less than the content of register SP. The content of register SP is decremented by 2. Control is transferred to the instruction whose address is specified in byte 3 and byte 2 of the current instruction.

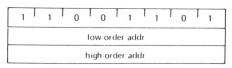

1	1	0	0	1	1	0	1

| low-order addr |
| high-order addr |

Cycles: 5
States: 17
Addressing: immediate/reg. indirect
Flags: none

Ccondition addr   (Condition call)

> If (CCC),
>> ((SP) − 1) ◄── (PCH)
>> ((SP) − 2) ◄── (PCL)
>> (SP) ◄── (SP) − 2
>> (PC) ◄── (byte 3) (byte 2)

If the specified condition is true, the actions specified in the CALL instruction (see above) are performed; otherwise, control continues sequentially.

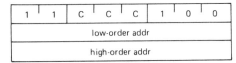

1	1	C	C	C	1	0	0

> low-order addr
>
> high-order addr

Cycles:	3/5
States:	11/17
Addressing:	immediate/reg. indirect
Flags:	none

RET   (Return)

> (PCL) ◄── ((SP));
> (PCH) ◄── ((SP) + 1);
> (SP) ◄── (SP) + 2;

The content of the memory location whose address is specified in register SP is moved to the low-order eight bits of register PC. The content of the memory location whose address is one more than the content of register SP is moved to the high-order eight bits of register PC. The content of register SP is incremented by 2.

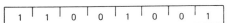

1	1	0	0	1	0	0	1

Cycles:	3
States:	10
Addressing:	reg. indirect
Flags:	none

Rcondition   (Conditional return)

> If (CCC),
>> (PCL) ◄── ((SP))
>> (PCH) ◄── ((SP) + 1)
>> (SP) ◄── (SP) + 2

If the specified condition is true, the actions specified in the RET instruction (see above) are performed; otherwise, control continues sequentially.

1	1	C	C	C	0	0	0

Cycles:	1/3
States:	5/11
Addressing:	reg. indirect
Flags:	none

RST n   (Restart)

> ((SP) − 1) ◄── (PCH)
> ((SP) − 2) ◄── (PCL)
> (SP) ◄── (SP) − 2
> (PC) ◄── 8 * (NNN)

The high-order eight bits of the next instruction address are moved to the memory location whose address is one less than the content of register SP. The low-order eight bits of the next instruction address are moved to the memory location whose address is two less than the content of register SP. The content of register SP is decremented by two. Control is transferred to the instruction whose address is eight times the content of NNN.

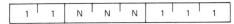

1	1	N	N	N	1	1	1

Cycles:	3
States:	11
Addressing:	reg. indirect
Flags:	none

15	14	13	12	11	10	9	8	7	6	5	4	3	2	1	0
0	0	0	0	0	0	0	0	0	0	N	N	N	0	0	0

Program Counter After Restart

PCHL   (Jump H and L indirect − move H and L to PC)

> (PCH) ◄── (H)
> (PCL) ◄── (L)

The content of register H is moved to the high-order eight bits of register PC. The content of register L is moved to the low-order eight bits of register PC.

1	1	1	0	1	0	0	1

Cycles:	1
States:	5
Addressing:	register
Flags:	none

Stack, I/O, and Machine Control Group:

This group of instructions performs I/O, manipulates the Stack, and alters internal control flags.

Unless otherwise specified, **condition flags are not affected by any instructions in this group.**

FLAG WORD

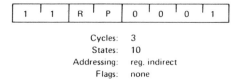

D_7	D_6	D_5	D_4	D_3	D_2	D_1	D_0
S	Z	0	AC	0	P	1	CY

PUSH rp   (Push)

$((SP) - 1) \leftarrow (rh)$
$((SP) - 2) \leftarrow (rl)$
$(SP) \leftarrow (SP) - 2$

The content of the high-order register of register pair rp is moved to the memory location whose address is one less than the content of register SP. The content of the low-order register of register pair rp is moved to the memory location whose address is two less than the content of register SP. The content of register SP is decremented by 2. **Note: Register pair rp = SP may not be specified.**

1	1	R	P	0	1	0	1

Cycles: 3
States: 11
Addressing: reg. indirect
Flags: none

PUSH PSW   (Push processor status word)

$((SP) - 1) \leftarrow (A)$
$((SP) - 2)_0 \leftarrow (CY), ((SP) - 2)_1 \leftarrow 1$
$((SP) - 2)_2 \leftarrow (P), ((SP) - 2)_3 \leftarrow 0$
$((SP) - 2)_4 \leftarrow (AC), ((SP) - 2)_5 \leftarrow 0$
$((SP) - 2)_6 \leftarrow (Z), ((SP) - 2)_7 \leftarrow (S)$
$(SP) \leftarrow (SP) - 2$

The content of register A is moved to the memory location whose address is one less than register SP. The contents of the condition flags are assembled into a processor status word and the word is moved to the memory location whose address is two less than the content of register SP. The content of register SP is decremented by two.

1	1	1	1	1	0	1	0	1

Cycles: 3
States: 11
Addressing: reg. indirect
Flags: none

POP rp   (Pop)

$(rl) \leftarrow ((SP))$
$(rh) \leftarrow ((SP) + 1)$
$(SP) \leftarrow (SP) + 2$

The content of the memory location, whose address is specified by the content of register SP, is moved to the low-order register of register pair rp. The content of the memory location, whose address is one more than the content of register SP, is moved to the high-order register of register pair rp. The content of register SP is incremented by 2. **Note: Register pair rp = SP may not be specified.**

1	1	R	P	0	0	0	1

Cycles: 3
States: 10
Addressing: reg. indirect
Flags: none

POP PSW   (Pop processor status word)

$(CY) \leftarrow ((SP))_0$
$(P) \leftarrow ((SP))_2$
$(AC) \leftarrow ((SP))_4$
$(Z) \leftarrow ((SP))_6$
$(S) \leftarrow ((SP))_7$
$(A) \leftarrow ((SP) + 1)$
$(SP) \leftarrow (SP) + 2$

The content of the memory location whose address is specified by the content of register SP is used to restore the condition flags. The content of the memory location whose address is one more than the content of register SP is moved to register A. The content of register SP is incremented by 2.

1	1	1	1	0	0	0	1

Cycles: 3
States: 10
Addressing: reg. indirect
Flags: Z,S,P,CY,AC

XTHL   (Exchange stack top with H and L)

(L) ←→ ((SP))

(H) ←→ ((SP) + 1)

The content of the L register is exchanged with the content of the memory location whose address is specified by the content of register SP. The content of the H register is exchanged with the content of the memory location whose address is one more than the content of register SP.

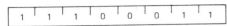

1	1	1	0	0	0	1	1

Cycles: 5
States: 18
Addressing: reg. indirect
Flags: none

SPHL   (Move HL to SP)

(SP) ←— (H) (L)

The contents of registers H and L (16 bits) are moved to register SP.

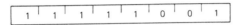

1	1	1	1	1	0	0	1

Cycles: 1
States: 5
Addressing: register
Flags: none

IN port   (Input)

(A) ←— (data)

The data placed on the eight bit bi-directional data bus by the specified port is moved to register A.

1	1	0	1	1	0	1	1
port							

Cycles: 3
States: 10
Addressing: direct
Flags: none

OUT port   (Output)

(data) ←— (A)

The content of register A is placed on the eight bit bi-directional data bus for transmission to the specified port.

1	1	0	1	0	0	1	1
port							

Cycles: 3
States: 10
Addressing: direct
Flags: none

EI   (Enable interrupts)

The interrupt system is enabled **following the execution of the next instruction.**

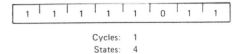

1	1	1	1	1	0	1	1

Cycles: 1
States: 4
Flags: none

DI   (Disable interrupts)

The interrupt system is disabled **immediately following the execution of the DI instruction.**

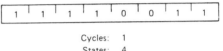

1	1	1	1	0	0	1	1

Cycles: 1
States: 4
Flags: none

HLT   (Halt)

The processor is stopped. The registers and flags are unaffected.

0	1	1	1	0	1	1	0

Cycles: 1
States: 7
Flags: none

NOP   (No op)

No operation is performed. The registers and flags are unaffected.

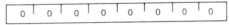

0	0	0	0	0	0	0	0

Cycles: 1
States: 4
Flags: none

8080 INSTRUCTION SET

Summary of Processor Instructions

Mnemonic	Description	D7	D6	D5	D4	D3	D2	D1	D0	Clock[2] Cycles
MOVE, LOAD, AND STORE										
MOVr1,r2	Move register to register	0	1	D	D	D	S	S	S	5
MOV M,r	Move register to memory	0	1	1	1	0	S	S	S	7
MOV r,M	Move memory to register	0	1	D	D	D	1	1	0	7
MVI r	Move immediate register	0	0	D	D	D	1	1	0	7
MVI M	Move immediate memory	0	0	1	1	0	1	1	0	10
LXI B	Load immediate register Pair B & C	0	0	0	0	0	0	0	1	10
LXI D	Load immediate register Pair D & E	0	0	0	1	0	0	0	1	10
LXI H	Load immediate register Pair H & L	0	0	1	0	0	0	0	1	10
STAX B	Store A indirect	0	0	0	0	0	0	1	0	7
STAX D	Store A indirect	0	0	0	1	0	0	1	0	7
LDAX B	Load A indirect	0	0	0	0	1	0	1	0	7
LDAX D	Load A indirect	0	0	0	1	1	0	1	0	7
STA	Store A direct	0	0	1	1	0	0	1	0	13
LDA	Load A direct	0	0	1	1	1	0	1	0	13
SHLD	Store H & L direct	0	0	1	0	0	0	1	0	16
LHLD	Load H & L direct	0	0	1	0	1	0	1	0	16
XCHG	Exchange D & E, H & L Registers	1	1	1	0	1	0	1	1	4
STACK OPS										
PUSH B	Push register Pair B & C on stack	1	1	0	0	0	1	0	1	11
PUSH D	Push register Pair D & E on stack	1	1	0	1	0	1	0	1	11
PUSH H	Push register Pair H & L on stack	1	1	1	0	0	1	0	1	11
PUSH PSW	Push A and Flags on stack	1	1	1	1	0	1	0	1	11
POP B	Pop register Pair B & C off stack	1	1	0	0	0	0	0	1	10
POP D	Pop register Pair D & E off stack	1	1	0	1	0	0	0	1	10
POP H	Pop register Pair H & L off stack	1	1	1	0	0	0	0	1	10
POP PSW	Pop A and Flags off stack	1	1	1	1	0	0	0	1	10
XTHL	Exchange top of stack, H & L	1	1	1	0	0	0	1	1	18
SPHL	H & L to stack pointer	1	1	1	1	1	0	0	1	5
LXI SP	Load immediate stack pointer	0	0	1	1	0	0	0	1	10
INX SP	Increment stack pointer	0	0	1	1	0	0	1	1	5
DCX SP	Decrement stack pointer	0	0	1	1	1	0	1	1	5
JUMP										
JMP	Jump unconditional	1	1	0	0	0	0	1	1	10
JC	Jump on carry	1	1	0	1	1	0	1	0	10
JNC	Jump on no carry	1	1	0	1	0	0	1	0	10
JZ	Jump on zero	1	1	0	0	1	0	1	0	10
JNZ	Jump on no zero	1	1	0	0	0	0	1	0	10
JP	Jump on positive	1	1	1	1	0	0	1	0	10
JM	Jump on minus	1	1	1	1	1	0	1	0	10
JPE	Jump on parity even	1	1	1	0	1	0	1	0	10
JPO	Jump on parity odd	1	1	1	0	0	0	1	0	10
PCHL	H & L to program counter	1	1	1	0	1	0	0	1	5
CALL										
CALL	Call unconditional	1	1	0	0	1	1	0	1	17
CC	Call on carry	1	1	0	1	1	1	0	0	11/17
CNC	Call on no carry	1	1	0	1	0	1	0	0	11/17
CZ	Call on zero	1	1	0	0	1	1	0	0	11/17
CNZ	Call on no zero	1	1	0	0	0	1	0	0	11/17
CP	Call on positive	1	1	1	1	0	1	0	0	11/17
CM	Call on minus	1	1	1	1	1	1	0	0	11/17
CPE	Call on parity even	1	1	1	0	1	1	0	0	11/17
CPO	Call on parity odd	1	1	1	0	0	1	0	0	11/17
RETURN										
RET	Return	1	1	0	0	1	0	0	1	10
RC	Return on carry	1	1	0	1	1	0	0	0	5/11
RNC	Return on no carry	1	1	0	1	0	0	0	0	5/11
RZ	Return on zero	1	1	0	0	1	0	0	0	5/11
RNZ	Return on no zero	1	1	0	0	0	0	0	0	5/11
RP	Return on positive	1	1	1	1	0	0	0	0	5/11
RM	Return on minus	1	1	1	1	1	0	0	0	5/11
RPE	Return on parity even	1	1	1	0	1	0	0	0	5/11
RPO	Return on parity odd	1	1	1	0	0	0	0	0	5/11
RESTART										
RST	Restart	1	1	A	A	A	1	1	1	11
INCREMENT AND DECREMENT										
INR r	Increment register	0	0	D	D	D	1	0	0	5
DCR r	Decrement register	0	0	D	D	D	1	0	1	5
INR M	Increment memory	0	0	1	1	0	1	0	0	10
DCR M	Decrement memory	0	0	1	1	0	1	0	1	10
INX B	Increment B & C registers	0	0	0	0	0	0	1	1	5
INX D	Increment D & E registers	0	0	0	1	0	0	1	1	5
INX H	Increment H & L registers	0	0	1	0	0	0	1	1	5
DCX B	Decrement B & C	0	0	0	0	1	0	1	1	5
DCX D	Decrement D & E	0	0	0	1	1	0	1	1	5
DCX H	Decrement H & L	0	0	1	0	1	0	1	1	5
ADD										
ADD r	Add register to A	1	0	0	0	0	S	S	S	4
ADC r	Add register to A with carry	1	0	0	0	1	S	S	S	4
ADD M	Add memory to A	1	0	0	0	0	1	1	0	7
ADC M	Add memory to A with carry	1	0	0	0	1	1	1	0	7
ADI	Add immediate to A	1	1	0	0	0	1	1	0	7
ACI	Add immediate to A with carry	1	1	0	0	1	1	1	0	7
DAD B	Add B & C to H & L	0	0	0	0	1	0	0	1	10
DAD D	Add D & E to H & L	0	0	0	1	1	0	0	1	10
DAD H	Add H & L to H & L	0	0	1	0	1	0	0	1	10
DAD SP	Add stack pointer to H & L	0	0	1	1	1	0	0	1	10

NOTES: 1. DDD or SSS B 000, C 001, D 010, E 011, H 100, L 101, Memory 110, A 111

2. Two possible cycle times. (6/12) indicate instruction cycles dependent on condition flags

All mnemonics copyright Intel Corporation 1977

8080 INSTRUCTION SET

Summary of Processor Instructions (Cont.)

Mnemonic	Description	D7	D6	D5	D4	D3	D2	D1	D0	Clock[2] Cycles
SUBTRACT										
SUB r	Subtract register from A	1	0	0	1	0	S	S	S	4
SBB r	Subtract register from A with borrow	1	0	0	1	1	S	S	S	4
SUB M	Subtract memory from A	1	0	0	1	0	1	1	0	7
SBB M	Subtract memory from A with borrow	1	0	0	1	1	1	1	0	7
SUI	Subtract immediate from A	1	1	0	1	0	1	1	0	7
SBI	Subtract immediate from A with borrow	1	1	0	1	1	1	1	0	7
LOGICAL										
ANA r	And register with A	1	0	1	0	0	S	S	S	4
XRA r	Exclusive Or register with A	1	0	1	0	1	S	S	S	4
ORA r	Or register with A	1	0	1	1	0	S	S	S	4
CMP r	Compare register with A	1	0	1	1	1	S	S	S	4
ANA M	And memory with A	1	0	1	0	0	1	1	0	7
XRA M	Exclusive Or memory with A	1	0	1	0	1	1	1	0	7
ORA M	Or memory with A	1	0	1	1	0	1	1	0	7
CMP M	Compare memory with A	1	0	1	1	1	1	1	0	7
ANI	And immediate with A	1	1	1	0	0	1	1	0	7
XRI	Exclusive Or immediate with A	1	1	1	0	1	1	1	0	7
ORI	Or immediate with A	1	1	1	1	0	1	1	0	7
CPI	Compare immediate with A	1	1	1	1	1	1	1	0	7
ROTATE										
RLC	Rotate A left	0	0	0	0	0	1	1	1	4
RRC	Rotate A right	0	0	0	0	1	1	1	1	4
RAL	Rotate A left through carry	0	0	0	1	0	1	1	1	4
RAR	Rotate A right through carry	0	0	0	1	1	1	1	1	4
SPECIALS										
CMA	Complement A	0	0	1	0	1	1	1	1	4
STC	Set carry	0	0	1	1	0	1	1	1	4
CMC	Complement carry	0	0	1	1	1	1	1	1	4
DAA	Decimal adjust A	0	0	1	0	0	1	1	1	4
INPUT/OUTPUT										
IN	Input	1	1	0	1	1	0	1	1	10
OUT	Output	1	1	0	1	0	0	1	1	10
CONTROL										
EI	Enable Interrupts	1	1	1	1	1	0	1	1	4
DI	Disable Interrupt	1	1	1	1	0	0	1	1	4
NOP	No-operation	0	0	0	0	0	0	0	0	4
HLT	Halt	0	1	1	1	0	1	1	0	7

NOTES: 1. DDD or SSS: B=000, C=001, D=010, E=011, H=100, L=101, Memory=110, A=111.
2. Two possible cycle times. (6/12) indicate instruction cycles dependent on condition flags.

Answers to Questions

1.1 See Figures 1.2, 1.8, 1.9, 1.10, etc.

1.2 The program counter is used by the processor to keep track of the memory location in which the next instruction or part instruction is to be found.

The control section within the processor is concerned with producing and receiving signals for the control bus and controlling the internal operations within the processor. Such operations include: controlling the transfer of data and instructions via the internal bus, placing the correct address on the address bus, setting the control signals on the ALU and transmitting or receiving data on the data bus. The control section performs all of these operations in a strict time sequence which is defined by the clock signals.

1.3

	8002	8085
Register size	16	8
Maximum clock frequency	8 MHz	5.5 MHz
Number of instructions	110+	80
Number of internal registers	16	8
External clock?	Yes	Yes
Number of pins	40	40

1.4 The Motorola 6805R2 has an on-chip RAM of 64 locations each storing 8 bits, a ROM of 2,048 8-bit locations and an ADC. The available instructions are not the same as for the 6800.

1.5 The instruction is fetched from the memory location specified by the current value of the program counter. This is achieved by the control unit in the processor putting the contents of the program counter onto the address bus and indicating to the memory that a 'read' is required. The memory sends the instruction to the processor via the data bus. Once received by the processor, the instruction is sent to the instruction register and decoded. The control section then ensures that the contents of the accumulator are transferred via the internal bus to the data buffers. The address to which this data is to be sent is 1000H. Depending on the type of instruction, this address may already be in the internal registers or it may have to be fetched as the second part of the instruction. In either case once the address is determined it must be placed in the address buffers to indicate the memory location to which the data has to be sent. The control block would also indicate a 'write' operation via the control bus.

During these operations the control section ensures that the program counter is automatically incremented when appropriate, either to fetch the second part of an instruction or to fetch a new instruction when the previous one is completed.

2.1   The 6800 has fewer register to register instructions than the 8080, but it does allow indexed addressing through the use of its index register. This last feature is not available on the 8080. The 6800 only allows memory mapped input and output whereas the 8080/8085 allows IN/OUT instructions as well as memory mapping.

2.2   *(a)*   3
   (b)   1
   (c)   2
   (d)   1
   (e)   1

3.1   In a line-based editor each line is given a number and all editing commands are made with reference to these line numbers. Cursor-based editors have commands that allow a flashing marker called a cursor to be moved across the VDU screen displaying the text. Corrections or insertions can be made at the cursor's position.

3.2   *File name* is the name or label given to a file which is stored in a backing store such as a floppy disk. The file and the text or data it contains can be retrieved by reference to its name.

Text file is a file which contains binary patterns which represent text rather than data or program instructions.

A cursor is a flashing mark on a VDU screen which indicates the current position where corrections and insertions may be made.

Scrolling is the process of moving the displayed text upwards on the VDU, as one line is removed from the display at the top of the screen space is made available for one more at the bottom.

3.3   A LOCAL directive is used to prevent the multiple use of a macro call resulting in a program which has more than one line of the program with the same label.

3.4 To turn the multiplication program into a macro requires a macro definition at the start of the assembler program of the form:

```
MULT   MACRO
       LOCAL   MULT0
       LOCAL   MULT1
       LOCAL   DONE

         .
         .
         .
       multiplication program
         .
         .
         .
       ENDM
```

The macro is called at the required point in the program with the following line of program:

```
MULT   ;Call of mult' segment
```

4.1 Figure 4.8(b) shows a piece of program which can be entered from more than one route, therefore, it is not an example of a structured program.

4.2 Both macros and subroutines save the programmer the chore of writing commonly used lines of instructions. Both can handle the transfer of data to and from the defined segment.

The major difference is that a macro generates lines of instructions each time it is called, but a subroutine call transfers control to the start of the subroutine segment which only exists in one segment of memory. This means that each call to a macro requires extra memory to store the binary patterns representing the instructions, but repeated calls to a subroutine do not require extra memory because the subroutine segment only exists in one place in memory.

4.3 The B register's contents are stored in FFD7 (hex).

4.4 Data can transfer to and from subroutines using the processor's registers or, if there is a lot of data, by transferring the address of the start of the data using a processor register.

5.1 The main factors to be considered when deciding between a parallel or serial data transmission scheme are:
1   The speed of transmission.
2   The distance the data must travel.

Parallel transfers are usually faster than serial because all the bits of the codeword travel at the same time, whereas in a serial transfer the bits travel one after the other.

Serial transfers are often preferred for long distances, because only two cables are required, whereas a parallel transfer requires one cable for each bit plus a common return cable.

5.2 The function of the control register in the PIO is to set the mode of operation of the handshake signals, to retain the status information and to select between the data direction and data registers.

The data direction register is used to determine whether the individual bits of the A and B ports are to function as inputs or outputs.

The data register is used as a temporary storage location for the input and output data words.

5.3 The main advantage of a memory-mapped I/O scheme is that all the instructions that can be used to operate on memory locations can be used with the data in the input and output ports. For example the contents of the data register of a PIO can be incremented using the increment memory instruction.

5.4 Handshake signals between a peripheral and its interface are used to control the timing of the flow of data. If they were not used data could be transferred at the wrong time and so would be lost.

6.1 The function of a DAC is to generate an analogue output voltage from a binary input codeword.

The function of an ADC is to generate a binary codeword from an analogue input signal.

6.2 Quantisation errors arise in a successive approximation ADC because the digitally generated voltage used in the comparison process can only change in small discrete steps. These steps are called the quantisation levels. At the end of the conversion process there is usually a small difference between the analogue input voltage and the digitally generated voltage, which is the quantisation error.

6.3 An n-bit converter can represent 2^n voltage levels and can resolve 1 part in 2^n. Hence a 10-bit converter has a resolution of 1 part in 2^{10} (or 1,024).

The quantisation interval of an n-bit converter is equal to the full scale output voltage divided by 2^n. Hence a 10-bit converter with a full scale output of ± 10 V has a quantisation interval of $20/2^{10}$, or 19.5 mV.

6.4 A dual slope integration ADC works by comparing the time taken for the input voltage to charge a capacitor and the time taken for a reference voltage to discharge the same capacitor. The process is illustrated for several input voltages in Figure A.

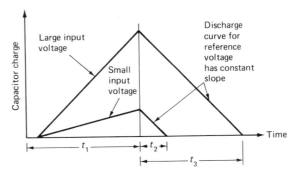

Figure A Timing diagram for dual slope integration ADC

7.1 The main advantage of the vectored interrupt system is speed, because the interface directs the microprocessor to the specific interrupt service routine.

In the case of polled interrupts the microprocessor must first determine which interface requested the interrupt by interrogating all the interfaces. Only after this has been done can the microprocessor execute the specific interrupt service routine.

7.2 The function of an interrupt priority scheme is to ensure that interfaces that need a very rapid response to an interrupt take precedence over those interfaces that do not.

In a multiple-interrupt system it may be necessary for high-speed peripherals to be able to suspend the interrupt service routines of slow peripherals in order to meet time constraints.

The priority scheme can be implemented in software or by special integrated circuits.

7.3 A non-maskable interrupt is an interrupt that cannot be disabled by microprocessor instructions. The prime use of such an interrupt would be for power failure detection or emergency shut down procedures which must take precedence over all other activities.

7.4 An interrupt mask register is used in a multiple-interrupt system to enable the program to select which interrupts are enabled and which are disabled. A typical application might be a priority interrupt scheme which allows each interrupt service routine to establish which other interfaces are to have a higher priority.

8.1   A transducer measurement system consists of a transducer, a signal conditioning unit and an amplification unit as shown in Figure 8.1. The transducer converts the changes in the measured variable into an electrical signal, which is then converted to a voltage by the signal conditioning unit. The amplifier may be needed to match the range of this signal to the input range of the ADC.

8.2   The signal conditioning unit is used to convert the output of a transducer to a voltage and to correct the errors in the calibration or response of the device. The main functions are:
(a)   Linearisation – to correct for the response of the transducer.
(b)   Offsetting – to allow for calibration.
(c)   Filtering – for noise removal and to prevent aliasing.
(d)   Signal conversion – to convert the electrical output signal to a voltage.

8.3   The gain required for this system must be sufficient to ensure that a $2°C$ temperature variation is equal to a quantisation interval of the converter. The quantisation interval is $10/256$ V $= 39$ mV, hence the gain equals
$$59 \text{ mV}/200 \text{ }\mu\text{V} = 195$$

8.4   The function of the buffer block is to limit excessive power dissipation in the digital devices and to protect the digital circuitry from mains voltages. Both functions can be fulfilled by an 'opto-isolator' type of device. Alternatively a transformer could be used to provide the electrical isolation, and transistors used to provide additional power-handling capabilities.

9.1   One possible program listing for the memory test program is shown in Figure B. You can try this version, or your own, on Hektor.

9.2   A suitable flow diagram for the DAC and ADC test is shown in Figure C (page 267). Your own answer may differ in detail, but should perform the same basic functions.

Figure B

```
PRNL:    EQU   02DAH
PRWD:    EQU   0351H
PRMSG:   EQU   030AH
PRSP:    EQU   02E7H
MON:     EQU   57H
MEMCNT:  EQU   00FFH         ;Define number of locations to test
BOTMEM:  EQU   4000H         ;Define first location to test
         ORG   3800H         ;Define starting address of program
PAT1:    DB    55H           ;Define first test pattern
PAT2:    DB    0AAH          ;Define second test pattern
START:   LXI   D,MEMCNT      ;Load memory count in D register pair
         LXI   H,BOTMEM      ;Load first location address into H
                            ;register pair
LOOP:    LDA   PAT1          ;Load first pattern into accumulator
         MOV   M,A           ;Write pattern into memory
         MOV   A,M           ;Read pattern from memory
         CDI   55H           ;Compare with test pattern
         CHZ   ERROR         ;Call error subroutine if result not zero
         LDA   PAT2          ;Load second pattern into accumulator
         MOV   M,A           ;Write pattern into memory
         MOV   A,M           ;Read pattern from memory
         CPI   0AAH          ;Compare with test pattern
         CNZ   ERROR         ;Call error subroutine if result not zero
         INX   H             ;Increment H register pair
         DCX   D             ;Decrement D register pair
         MOV   A,E           ;Test for zero
         ORA   D
         JNZ   LOOP          ;More locations to test, so go back
                            ;to loop
         JMP   MON           ;All tested, so return to monitor
ERROR:   MOV   B,H           ;Save contents of H register pair
         MOV   C,L
         LXI   H,MSG         ;Get memory address of message to be printed
         CALL  PRMES         ;Print the message on the display screen
         CALL  PRSP          ;Print a space
         MOV   H,B           ;Get address of faulty memory location
         MOV   L,C           ;to be printed on screen
         CALL  PRWD          ;Print 16-bit word as four hex characters
         CALL  PRNL          ;Print a new line
         MOV   H,B           ;Restore contents of H register pair
         MOV   L,C
         RET
```

(Continued)

```
Figure B – continued
MSG:      DB     20H        ;Hex codes for ASCII message
          DB     45H        ;ERROR LOCATION
          DB     52H
          DB     4FH
          DB     52H
          DB     20H
          DB     4CH
          DB     4FH
          DB     43H
          DB     41H
          DB     54H
          DB     49H
          DB     4FH
          DB     4EH
          DB     20H
          DB     00H        ;Message terminator
          END    START
```

Figure B   Memory test program

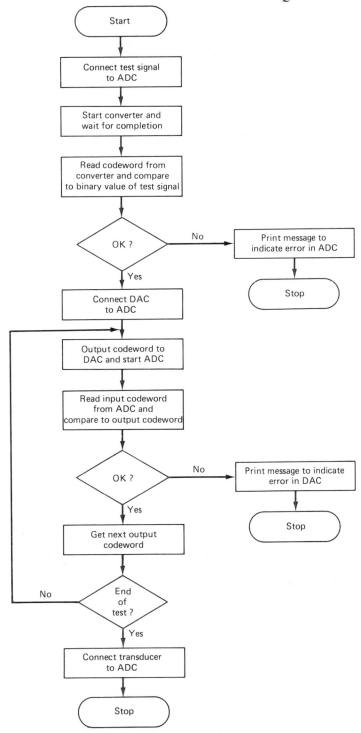

Figure C Flow diagram for DAC and ADC test program

Index